FAST ETHERNET

Dawn of a New Network

Howard W. Johnson
Olympic Technology Group, Inc.

For book and bookstore information

http://www.prenhall.com

Prentice Hall PTR
Upper Saddle River, New Jersey 07458

Library of Congress Cataloging-in-Publication Data

Johnson, Howard W.

     Fast Ethernet : dawn of a new network / by Howard W. Johnson
        p. cm.
     Includes bibliographical references and index.
     ISBN 0-13-352643-7
     1. Ethernet (Local area network system). I. Title.

TK5105.8.E83J65   1996

004.6'8--dc20   95-23393
                                             CIP

Editorial/production supervision*: Joanne Anzalone*
Manufacturing manager: *Alexis R. Heydt*
Acquisitions editor: *Karen Gettman*
Editorial assistant: *Barbara Alfieri*
Cover design: *Gryphon Three Design*
Cover illustration: *Tom Post*
Cover design director: *Jerry Votta*
Art director: *Gail Cocker-Bogusz*

© 1996 by Prentice Hall PTR
Prentice-Hall, Inc.
A Simon & Schuster Company
Upper Saddle River, New Jersey 07458

The publisher offers discounts on this book when ordered in bulk quantities.
For more information, contact:

Corporate Sales Department
PTR Prentice Hall
1 Lake Street
Upper Saddle River, NJ 07458

Phone: 800-382-3419, Fax: 201-236-7141
E-mail: corpsales@prenhall.com

Printed in the United States of America
10 9 8 7 6 5 4 3

ISBN 0-13-352643-7

Prentice-Hall International (UK) Limited, *London*
Prentice-Hall of Australia Pty. Limited, *Sydney*
Prentice-Hall Canada Inc., *Toronto*
Prentice-Hall Hispanoamericana, S.A., *Mexico*
Prentice-Hall of India Private Limited, *New Delhi*
Prentice-Hall of Japan, Inc., *Tokyo*
Simon & Schuster Asia Pte. Ltd., *Singapore*
Editora Prentice-Hall do Brasil, Ltda., *Rio de Janeiro*

Where possible, trademarks have been listed in this book. The companies listed here are the owners of their trademarks: 3270®, IBM®, NetBios® and System Network Architecture® (SNA) are registered trademarks of International Business Machines Corporation; Apple™ and Macintosh™ are trademarks and AppleTalk® and Local-Talk® are registered trademarks of Apple Computer, Inc.; DEC™ is a trademark of Digital Equipment Corporation; 80X86™ and Pentium™ are trademarks of Intel Corporation; Interop® is a registered trademark of Interop Company; NetWare® is a registered trademark of Novell, Inc.; NuBus™ is a trademark of Texas Instruments; SC™ is a trademark of NTT Advanced Technology Corporation; ST® and StarLAN® are registered trademarks of American Telephone & Telegraph Co.; Teflon™ is a trademark of E.I. DuPont de Nemours & Co.; Windows™ is a trademark of Microsoft Corporation.

All other product names mentioned herein are the trademarks of their respective owners.

Figure 3.3 and Table 3.14 are adapted from IEEE Standard 802.3u, Copyright © 1995 by the Institute of Electrical and Electronics Engineers, Inc.; The IEEE takes no responsibility for and will assume no liability for damages resulting from the readers' misinterpretation of said information resulting from the placement and context in this publication. Information is reproduced with the permission of IEEE.

for Sandy and Kate

Contents

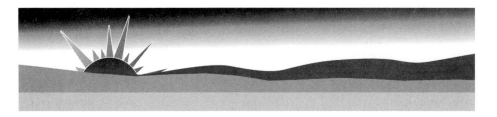

Preface

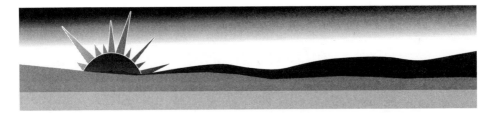

F *ast Ethernet* is the 100-million-bit-per-second successor to the world's most popular local area network, Ethernet. It resembles 10BASE-T, the most widely deployed form of Ethernet, only it runs ten times faster. Fast Ethernet is the newest and most powerful addition to the Ethernet family of local area network standards.

WHAT YOU WILL GET FROM THIS BOOK

- If you buy, install, or maintain Ethernet, this book will equip you with penetrating questions to ask your vendor about Fast Ethernet products—the kind of questions that prevent installation mistakes and save you money.
- If you set company strategy or plan network growth, the details about future developments will show you where Fast Ethernet technology is going.
- If you sell (or sell against) Fast Ethernet, the point-by-point analysis of competing high-speed networks will show you which networks best suit which applications.

ORGANIZATION

The chapters are each self-contained and may be read in any order. Each section ends with a summary of its most important tips and hints.

Chapter 1	Origin of 10 Mb/s Ethernet, why it developed, how Fast Ethernet emerged.
Chapter 2	Overview of the Fast Ethernet product family, its architecture and applications.

Chapter 3   Interpretive guide to the Fast Ethernet standard, with detailed explanations of its options and features.

Chapter 4   Introduction to worldwide building wiring standards, and guidelines for wiring a building so it will work with Fast Ethernet.

Chapter 5   Compendium of future trends in local area networking, including switching, full duplex, multimedia, flow control, new link transmission technologies, and WAN issues.

Chapter 6   Pros and cons of Fast Ethernet versus other networks.

Chapter 7   Technical explanation of collision domain timing and its impact on network configuration.

Chapter 8   Collected references, including a list of good books, a glossary, instructions for ordering standards, and a catalog of supplements to the Ethernet standard.

THANKS TO ALL THE STANDARDS PEOPLE

No treatment of Ethernet would be complete without paying tribute to the many hardworking individuals who created the Ethernet standards. Without open, publicly accessible standards, the networking business would not be where it is today.

PLEASE BE ADVISED

We have done our best to provide an accurate and complete guide to the Fast Ethernet standard. Still, the fine folks at the IEEE standards office would like us to remind you that this book is not an *official* definition of Fast Ethernet or any other standard. To obtain the complete text of the Fast Ethernet standard, or other local area networking standards, please consult the sources included in Chapter 8.

A PERSONAL NOTE OF GRATITUDE

Literally hundreds of individuals were involved in the production of the Fast Ethernet standard. To all of those people involved in the standard, I extend my sincere thanks. To the members of the 802.3 working group, and the IEEE standards production staff, I extend not only my thanks but also my congratulations on a job well done. To the following individuals who served as staff, officers, committee chair-persons and regular technical contributors to the 802.3 process I have only the highest praise. The success of the standard clearly reflects your hard work, determination and sound judgment: Larry Birenbaum, Paul Booth, Rich Bowers, Bill Bunch, Jack St. Clair, Ron Crane, Ian Crayford, David Fischer, Howard Frazier, Tom Gandy, Walter Hurwitz, David Law, John McCool, Colin Mick, Shimon Muller, Lloyd Oliver, Sandeep Patel, Bill Quackenbush, J. R. Rivers, David Schwartz, Paul Sherer, Charan Singh, Peter Tarrant, Tim Teckman, Geoff Thompson, Moshe Veloshin, Paul Woodruff, and Nariman Yousefi.

Regarding this book, I would like to acknowledge the many individuals who participated in its development, especially those that helped educate me about the Ethernet market, its customers, and the many technical issues surrounding the standard itself. In addition, many of these same persons helped review portions of the book for technical accuracy: Charlie Adams, Abe Ali, Larry Birenbaum, David Boggs, Rich Brand, Bob Campbell, Ron Crane, Kristen Dittman, Kingston Duffie, David Flynn, Howard Frazier, Ed Frymore, Walter Hurwitz, Elisabeth Johnson, Jim Long, Ken MacLeod, Colin Mick, Mart Molle, Larry Nicolson, Paul Sherer, Geoff Thompson, Fouad Tobagi, Tim Teckman, and, of course, my assistant Rebecca Sweetman.

AN INVITATION

The author welcomes comments, suggestions, and general inquires about Fast Ethernet, although he may not be able to personally respond to every request:

Howard W. Johnson
Olympic Technology Group, Inc.
16541 Redmond Way, Suite 264
Redmond, WA 98052

Ethernet

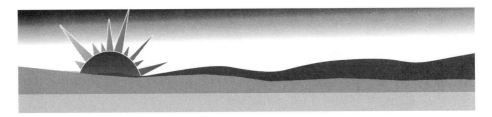

E *thernet* is a *10 Mb/s* local area network standard actively
supported by scores of network equipment manufacturers. As
standardized by the IEEE 802.3 working group, it is the most
popular *local area network* (LAN) in the world. It has been verified,
tested and installed in the field by the tens of millions.

Fast Ethernet is a *100 Mb/s* LAN standard. It is like Ethernet, only
it runs ten times faster. Fast Ethernet is the newest and most powerful
addition to the Ethernet family of local area network standards.

Fast Ethernet is an extension to Ethernet, providing interoperable
service at both 10 and 100 Mb/s. It is not merely a new network. It is a
compatible, high-speed version of the greatest network blockbuster of all
time, Ethernet.

Of the many Ethernet variants, Fast Ethernet most resembles
10BASE-T. The 10BASE-T system is the most widely deployed form of
Ethernet. To emphasize the similarity, the official designation for Fast
Ethernet is *100BASE-T*.

This book explores Fast Ethernet. It highlights the new Fast
Ethernet product architectures, points out where the technology is
going, and explains which products best suit which applications. It is an
all-around guide to the Fast Ethernet standard.

HOW ETHERNET GOT ITS NAME

According to Greek legend, Helios, the sun-god, soared across the sky in
a shimmering chariot of gold. Each dawn his fiery, winged steeds
charged up the long narrow path from his palace in the east to the crest
of the heavens. At noon he turned earthward, galloping back to his
palace of the evening. The brilliant blue backdrop for Helios' daily flight,
the sky itself, the Greeks called *aether* (αιθηρ).

Seventeenth-century astronomers enlarged the meaning of the word aether[1] well beyond the bounds of our earthly atmosphere. The French philosopher Rene Descartes, for one, believed that aether literally filled all of space. It was, in his view, "the solitary tenant of the universe, save that infinitesimal fraction of space occupied by ordinary matter." [2] Descartes' aether, while imperceptible to the senses, conveyed celestial forces through space. These forces caused the whirling behavior of planets and stars. The aether unified the planets and stars into a coherent whole.

Belief in this rather beautiful concept of a mechanical aether peaked with the scientific literature of the 19th century. During that era James Clerk Maxwell, the father of modern electrical engineering, theorized that light itself propagated through the *lumineferous aether* in the same way that sound propagated through the air. His aether permeated all of space, and it conveyed not only physical but electrical forces as well. It tied everything together. This compelling theory was widely believed.

In 1887, Maxwell's theory ran into a serious obstacle. Albert A. Michelson and Edward W. Morley, in a dramatic series of experiments, challenged the very existence of lumineferous aether. If the earth were really hurling at great speed through the aether, as predicted by Maxwell's theory, then the speed of light should be minutely different in various directions—yet their measurements said it was not.[3] Their evidence, if true, would deliver a hammer blow to the physical sciences. It simultaneously cast doubt on the accepted theories of light, gravity and cosmology. The response from the scientific community was incredulous.

A great debate ensued over the existence of aether. Meanwhile, Michelson and Morley's experiments became more precise, and their conclusions more formidable. In the end, after a protracted battle, the proponents of aether were forced to concede the obvious: Michelson and Morley were right. At the International Congress of Physics in 1900, the great physicist Poincaré expressed his dismay, and his sense of loss, in a speech titled "Our aether, does it really exist?" The theory of aether

---

[1] We retain here the English spelling aether, as reported by Sir Edmund Whittaker, *A History of the Theories of Aether and Electricity*, American Institute of Physics, 1987.

[2] Ibid., p. 6.

[3] Tipler, Paul A., *Physics*, Worth Publishers, Inc., New York, NY, 1976.

collapsed shortly afterward. For the next 70 years, all thoughts of aether as a unifying force lay dormant.

Then in 1973, a young engineer named Bob Metcalfe, working at the Xerox Palo Alto Research Center, conceived a brilliant new plan for a computer network. It was to be a network that connected all computers. He envisioned this network as a ubiquitous force, flowing through walls and around corners, an invisible, almost magical, presence that went everywhere and connected everything. It was a kind of aether. Metcalfe called it *Ethernet*.

When the first two Xerox Alto computers were connected with a working Ethernet prototype, they were promptly code named *Michelson* and *Morley*.

EARLY DEVELOPMENT

Fast Ethernet did not spring, fully formed, from the secret laboratory of some industrial megalith. On the contrary, it developed in the best tradition of open, public debate as an extension to the internationally acclaimed Ethernet standard. A proper understanding of Fast Ethernet, its architecture, and its reason for being requires a thorough understanding of its parent standard, Ethernet, and the market forces that shaped its early development.

Before Local Area Networks

From the beginning, the design of computer systems revolved around the idea of minimizing hardware cost. Engineers are good at that. Given a fixed set of requirements, a good engineer strives to design the cheapest possible system. It sounds simple, and is. So, why are there hundreds of different computer companies? Why are there so many different types of networks? Why doesn't everyone use the same architecture?

The key to understanding the computer industry is simple: customers do not agree on the requirements. For every new customer, there is a new set of requirements. *Systems that succeed in the marketplace are adaptable to a broad range of requirements.*

Among the most significant of computer system requirements is the issue of scale, that is, how many people will use the system.

In the early days of computing, each machine served one user. The R1, for example, built at Rice University in the early 1960s, included one keyboard, one card reader, and one bank of colored flashing lights. After a while, manufacturers noticed that their very expensive, single-user machines spent most of the time waiting for the users to do something. This observation led to the development of time-sharing operating systems, which opened up computers to more than one person. Whole departments could begin making use of a computer system.

Once customers started wanting multi-user computers, system designers had to ask themselves a very important question: "For how many users should I optimize this system design? Five? Five hundred? Five thousand?" This question of scale influenced almost every aspect of system design. A system designed for five users might not work for large numbers of people. On the other hand, a system designed to serve a hundred people might require too much overhead to be cost effective in small configurations. Computer companies searched for an architecture that would serve both small and large user communities. Such an architecture would be highly scaleable.

Growth is another key component of the requirement equation. Customers expect computer systems to make them more efficient, and they expect their businesses to grow as a result. The customer that needs a two-person computer system today might need a hundred-person system tomorrow. It is not sufficient to make a system that can be configured at the factory to suit different numbers of users. A system must be upgradable in the field to expand its capabilities (Figure 1.1).

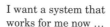
I want a system that works for me now …

…and keeps working as my company grows.

Figure 1.1 Customers Want Modularity

In response to these challenges, manufacturers began designing highly modular systems. A modular system is one that uses additional components to boost performance as the situation warrants. Customers like modularity because they can buy a little now and add more later as needed. *Well-engineered modularity solves both the scale problem and the growth problem.*

One of the more successful early solutions to the modularity problem was the IBM® *System Network Architecture*® (SNA). Announced in 1974 as an accompaniment to the System 370 host information processor, SNA addressed the needs of large data center applications. In that realm it achieved significant economies of scale. In one of its classic configurations, SNA comprised a four-level hierarchy. At the top of the hierarchy stood a mainframe. One or more front end processors were attached to the mainframe. To each front end processor, one or more terminal controllers were attached. To each terminal controller one or more terminals were attached. Users could expand the hierarchy in a number of ways, buying hardware as needed to support the peripherals and terminals needed for their applications.

One thing users could not do was connect a dumb display device directly to the mainframe. The popular 3270® display, for instance, lacked the brains to communicate directly with a host CPU. The hierarchy could not be collapsed. Why not?

IBM designed the 3270 display to support massive applications. Given those requirements, IBM development engineers went about minimizing its production costs. They consolidated redundant hardware functions from the display up into the terminal controller and from the terminal controller into the front end processor. At each level, functions not critical to operation at that level of the hierarchy were removed. This design approach minimized costs for big installations, but, as a by-product, 3270 displays could not hook up directly to the mainframe. They had to go through the I/O hierarchy. So much intelligence had been stripped from them that they could not speak the mainframe's language.

The four-level hierarchy was efficient for large installations, but cost too much for small ones. At the time, this looked like a smart system architecture. Big systems were the way to go.

By the late 1970s, the pendulum was beginning to swing the other way. Engineers at Xerox (and other places) were betting that hardware costs would drop. Cheaper hardware would make it reasonable to incorporate substantial intelligence into the terminals. If it were cheap enough, terminals could become much more autonomous. Perhaps, they dreamed, someday every user's terminal would directly attach to a host computer without dependence on an I/O hierarchy. The intelligence could be distributed.

As it turns out, the engineers at Xerox were right.[4] Over the next decade, hardware costs plummeted. Minicomputers flourished. The seeds of distributed computing were sown.

Tall, deep hierarchies like the IBM I/O subsystem faded from popularity. Modularity, local intelligence, and distributed processing took center stage. Products that capitalized on the trend toward small, highly modular, personal computer systems fared very well.

The Ethernet Architecture

Xerox wanted to sell distributed office computing systems, big systems that would completely eliminate the need for paper in the modern office. Obviously, in any distributed system, the computing modules need to communicate. If Xerox were to succeed at selling distributed intelligence, they would need a communications network.

From the early 1970s, engineers at Xerox pursued an idealistic vision of computer communications. In their ideal world, every computer would come equipped for communications. Just plug them together, and any two machines would instantly join in a sort of Vulcan mind meld of computer bliss. Nothing would impede the communications pathway. That is the vision of Ethernet.

The original Ethernet product blueprints called for a network having no central components. Every computer was attached in the same, simple way to a single piece of wire. The wire snaked through a building, with every computer hooking onto it as it passed by. Because it was just a wire, all computers could hear each other's transmissions. This network architecture, where all computers on the net hook to the same wire, is called a *bus topology*.

The bus topology is not the only way to build a local area network. For example, FDDI uses a ring topology. Many mainframes use an I/O channel that is basically a daisy chain. Infrared communications have

---

[4] However, Xerox as a business failed to capitalize on the trend. See: Douglas K. Smith and Robert C. Alexander, *Fumbling the Future, How Xerox Invented, Then Ignored, the First Personal Computer*, New York, NY: William Morrow and Co., 1988.

interesting line-of-sight properties. None of these other topologies met with the early success of the Ethernet bus topology.

The key advantage of a bus topology is its outstanding modularity. Because all systems on the net are identical, the total system cost is (theoretically) exactly proportional to the number of users. There is no additional overhead. All you need is wire. The wire provides a certain amount of fixed transmission bandwidth, which all users share.

Of course, bus topologies have one big disadvantage: only one device can successfully transmit at a time. Because all transmissions share the same medium (a *shared media* architecture), simultaneous transmissions will obliterate each other. Simultaneous transmissions are unacceptable. Some means must be provided to prevent them.

The solution to the basic problem of simultaneous transmissions was particularly intricate for Ethernet. Because the original developers wanted to build a peer-to-peer network, they sought a fair, unbiased control structure composed of many identical pieces. There was to be no overall controller. No device would posses any special sequencing or traffic handling capabilities. Theirs was to be a network of true peers.

The Ethernet Control System

The Ethernet bus topology might have languished forever in the laboratory had it not been for a clever solution to the multiple-access problem.[5] The protocol that Ethernet uses to solve the multiple access problem is called *Carrier Sense Multiple Access with Collision Detection* (CSMA/CD). This protocol is classified as a *Media Access Control* (MAC) protocol, because it controls who accesses the transmission medium and when.

Without a protocol like CSMA/CD, the bus topology would be unusable. CSMA/CD provides just enough control to ensure that stations do not obliterate each other's transmissions, without introducing unnecessary central control or management tasks. The CSMA/CD protocol is a true peer-to-peer protocol, meaning that it requires no central controller or master station to operate.

The CSMA/CD protocol is an extension of pioneering work on the theory of network communications performed at the University of Hawaii by Norman Abramson in the early 1970s. At that time, the

---

[5] Other networks, including Token-bus, ARC-Net, OmniNet, and the original ALOHA, have developed their own MAC protocols.

University of Hawaii comprised several campuses spread across the Hawaiian Islands. The university administration wanted a computer network that could hook them all together. The communications media selected was radio, a type of shared media. To control this media, the researchers at the University of Hawaii developed a MAC protocol called *ALOHA*.

The CSMA/CD protocol combines three ideas: the original ALOHA concept, a refinement called carrier sensing, and another refinement called collision detection.

ALOHA and the Salt Shaker. ALOHA is the grandfather of many networking protocols. That it emerged in the Hawaiian islands is not surprising, because of the peculiar geographic requirements of the local environment. The University of Hawaii was willing to accept a rather low speed system and was willing to pay almost any price, because *there was no alternative*. The cost of stringing wires between the islands was prohibitive. The absence of reasonable alternatives forced researchers to investigate new and unusual methods of communication that, while they never became commercially viable products, formed the basis of a new industry.

The ALOHA protocol is simple to understand. Imagine that four people are sitting at a dinner table. Place a salt shaker in the middle of the table. The salt shaker will serve as our *shared resource* for this experiment.

Now watch what happens when one person wants the salt. Usually, he or she just grabs it. The food is salted, and the shaker returns (in polite company) to the center of the table. Dinner proceeds.

What happens when two people want the salt at the same time? The specifics depend on the people involved, but most often when two hands reach for the shaker at the same time neither party is successful. Some higher-level protocol, like speech, is invoked to resolve the conflict. In some family situations the protocol may involve shouting or dirty looks. The loser has to try again.

The original ALOHA protocol, called *pure ALOHA*, worked in much the same way. Whenever a station wanted to transmit, it did so. A higher level protocol waited for acknowledgment that the transmission made it through intact. If no acknowledgment arrived, the station repeated its transmission.

The pure ALOHA protocol works well in situations, like with the salt shaker, where the shared resource is not heavily used. In such situations the chances for collision are small.

Sometimes even a very simple protocol gives reasonable results.

In family situations, a more complicated protocol might appear ridiculous. Consider token passing. It is not necessary to pass the salt shaker continuously around the table in order that one and only one person can use the shaker at any given point in time. Central arbitration is equally impracticable. Imagine a father that kept the salt in his pocket, releasing it for use only upon formal request.

Allowing contention simplifies the protocol without degrading the result.

CSMA/CD is based on the ALOHA protocol. Like ALOHA, a CSMA/CD station can transmit at any time, without prior permission. The full CSMA/CD protocol includes two additional measures, *carrier sensing* and *collision detection*, that improve the response of the pure ALOHA protocol substantially during periods of high demand.

Carrier Sensing — A Prudent Measure. If the man next  to you is already using the salt, it is not a good idea to grab it out of his hands. That usually makes the salt go where it isn't wanted.

We can codify this as our first dinner-table rule:

Rule 1: If someone else is already using the salt, don't grab for it.

CSMA/CD incorporates a similar rule: when the transmission medium is in use, do not transmit. This procedure is called *carrier sensing*.

This commonsense approach avoids interfering with data *packets*[6] that are already on the network. This increases the chances of each packet getting through, so the network operates more efficiently for everyone. Most shared-media networks today incorporate some form of carrier sensing.

---

[6] A data packet is a small bundle of data typically transmitted as a continuous stream without interruption. Data packets in Ethernet range from 64 to 1512 octets in length. An octet comprises 8 data bits.

If the salt is sitting unused, two people may still grab for it *at the same instant*. We haven't fixed that problem yet. All that carrier sensing does is make sure that, if the salt is *already* in use, no one else tries to grab it away.

Collision Detection: A Matter of Recovery Time. Earlier we established that it is OK for two people to reach for the salt at the same time, provided they have a way to resolve disputes. When two people grab the salt simultaneously, we call it a *collision*. The process of resolving who gets the salt is called a *collision resolution process*. As a matter of system efficiency, it would be nice if the collision resolution took place as quickly as possible. This leads to a second rule:

Rule 2: If you grab the salt at the same time as someone else,
let go right away.

This rule recognizes that there is no sense wasting time wrestling over the salt. It is better to let go, and try again later.

CSMA/CD is subject to the same effects. Collisions happen between transmitters all the time (that is, two transmitters begin transmitting simultaneously). CSMA/CD includes special circuitry in every transmitter that can detect collisions. When a collision is detected, the transmitter truncates the outgoing packet right away. When a transmitter stops because of a collision, we say it has *backed off* the network.

A very interesting thing happens after a collision. The parties involved must now decide who gets the salt. We will propose next a fair, impartial and rather arbitrary mechanism for deciding. This mechanism has three steps:

Step 1: After a collision, place your hands under the table.

Step 2: Close your eyes and wait a random amount of time

Step 3: Open your eyes. If the salt is available, grab for it.

Step 1 is just being polite. Steps 2 and 3 are the heart of the algorithm. Most of the time, one party or the other opens their eyes first and makes away with the salt. This algorithm does not require explicit coordination among the parties. It does not require central control.

That's why Ethernet enthusiasts like it. On the other hand, it has some disadvantages. For example, the man sitting next to you might grab the salt first. Too bad, you have to wait until he is done. In other cases, the two parties might collide a second time. This is possible, but unlikely to continue very many times before one party or the other wins.

Ethernet controllers work much the same way. After a collision, the controllers execute a *backoff* procedure. The backoff procedure stipulates that each station must wait a random amount of time before trying again for the bus. Details of this algorithm are beyond the scope of this book. Suffice it to say that the backoff algorithm provides fair, even-handed access to the bus and mitigates against the network choking up when many stations try to send data at once.

Ethernet controllers will repeatedly attempt to transmit a packet until they are successful. Higher layers of software are not even aware that collisions are taking place. After each collision, the low-level MAC protocol just executes the backoff procedure, reschedules the transmission, and keeps on working.

A collision in Ethernet is not an error. It just means that the transmitter was not able to transmit at that time and it will try again. An Ethernet MAC will keep trying at least 16 times. If the MAC protocol gives up, higher layers of software have to sort out what didn't get through, and why, and straighten out the mess.

The original ALOHA idea, bolstered by carrier sensing (CS) and collision detection (CD), forms a robust protocol appropriate for local area network applications.

Commercial Development

This is the story of how an industry consortium catalyzed the development of Ethernet and how, in 1976, it saved the name as well.

With the multiple-access problem solved by CSMA/CD, the Ethernet bus topology appeared to have almost ideal modularity properties. The questions remaining about Ethernet were not "Would it work?", but rather "How much would it cost to build?" and "Would other manufacturers adopt it?"

Xerox executives were determined to see Ethernet succeed. The first version of Ethernet was put together in 1973 at Xerox, using many of the ideas laid out by Metcalfe in his doctoral thesis. This first version of Ethernet had a linear bus topology, was implemented in coax, and ran at 2.94 Mb/s.

By 1976, Xerox had formed a new corporate division, SDD, to design and manufacture both their new Star computer and an upgraded version of Ethernet. The Star, like the earlier Xerox Alto computer, would be among the first personal computers to have a local area network connection built into every machine.

Of course, after having formed this new division, with new management, new staff, and a new building, one can hardly blame those in charge for wanting to change the product name as well. The new name would have to be something people could understand, something with marketing appeal, pizzazz. Something that would sound good in the press. Because this was Xerox, it had to be something with an X in it. The new network would be called *X-wire*. Along with the change in name, Xerox decided to upgrade the technology as well (see box entitled *Upgrading the Ethernet Technology*).

Shortly after the formation of SDD, Xerox decided that it would be a good idea to broaden support for the X-wire system. Toward that end, in 1979 Xerox partnered with Digital Equipment Corporation (DEC™) and Intel to jointly promote the new network. The plan was for Xerox to provide the basic Ethernet technology, DEC to assist with transceiver design, and Intel to provide the controller chips that made it all work.

Upgrading the Ethernet Technology

The three young engineers hired to design X-wire were Ron Crane, Bob Garner, and Roy Ogus. They were given, as was common in Silicon Valley in those days, a great deal of latitude in deciding how to best design the product. Shortly after starting the project, they made their first major decision. They decided to increase the network operating speed. Selecting the network speed would affect almost every aspect of system performance. As is natural in engineering projects, many conflicting forces influenced this decision.

From the marketing perspective, too low a speed could be disastrous. Their network would be successful only as long as people perceived it to be *fast*. In the computer marketplace, with processing speeds doubling every few years, whatever speed they chose might soon become obsolete. The higher the speed, the longer the product would survive in the market.

The other side of the speed decision had to do with circuit technology. The higher the speed, the more difficult the system would be to build. Also, at extreme speeds, fundamental limitations began to appear that limited the number and placement of station interfaces along the length of the cable.

After weighing their options, the team increased the operating speed from 2.94 to 10.0 Mb/s, the speed at which Ethernet runs today.

It was a good plan. Working together, these three companies had enough technical resources to put together a first-class system specification. They could also solve the *bandwagon problem*. In the network systems business, a critical mass of manufacturers must first commit to a design and then induce other companies to jump on the bandwagon. Without a core group of support, a new network concept cannot get off the ground. Xerox, DEC, and Intel represented enough of a critical mass in the industry to drive the marketplace.

As far as DEC and Intel were concerned, everything was in place, except for one obstacle: the name. DEC and Intel would not tolerate a network name that started with X. As a gesture of goodwill, Xerox came full circle and closed the issue of names. Xerox agreed to revert to the earlier name: *Ethernet*. The world will never know whether a network could have succeeded with a name like X-wire.

STANDARDS

This section outlines the organizations involved in the standards process, shows how they work together, and explains how Fast Ethernet fits into the picture.

Seven major standards-making bodies produce most of the standards used in the computer networking market. See contact information for these organizations in Chapter 8.

IEEE	Institute of Electrical and Electronic Engineers. Published Ethernet, Token Ring, Token Bus, and many other LAN standards.
ANSI	American National Standards Institute. Accepts IEEE standards and forwards them to ISO. Also publishes its own standards, such as FDDI, HIPPI, SCSI, and Fiber Channel.
IEC	International Electrotechnical Commission. In the field of information technology, the IEC and ISO jointly publish standards.
ISO	International Standards Organization. Ultimate international approval source for all types of standards.

IETF[7]	Internet Engineering Task Force. Publishes standards for Internet operation, including TCP/IP and SNMP.
ITU (formerly CCITT)	International Telecommunications Union (formerly the International Consultative Committee for Telephone and Telegraph). An advisory committee established under the United Nations. The Telecommunications Sector, called UTU-T, publishes standards for ISDN and wide area applications of ATM.
ATM Forum[8]	Asynchronous Transfer Mode Forum. An industry group working on specifications for LAN applications of ATM.

In many ways, networking users in the United States respect all standards bodies equally. Who publishes a standard matters less to them than who supports it. The big questions are "How many vendors support a standard, when will products ship, and how much will they cost?" This attitude differs in other countries.

In the United States, official government recognition of a standard is not as important as in some other countries, because much of the U.S. network industry is privatized. Private companies have the option of adhering to whatever standards they wish. In countries where the majority of the data-processing market is under government control, standards recognized by that government (likely ISO standards) carry more weight. Some countries go as far as mandating ISO standards.

Ethernet is a combined ISO/IEC/ANSI/IEEE standard.

Who Published the Ethernet Standard

IEEE Std 802.3 is an IEEE document, even though it has been released in slightly different forms by three different organizations (see Table 1.1). Most people refer to **IEEE Std 802.3** as the *Ethernet standard*.

Inside the IEEE there are many standards-writing organizations, including the *LAN/MAN Standards Committee*,[9] a sub-branch of the

---

[7] The IETF is not an accredited standards development organization, but it writes standards anyway.

[8] This group claims to write specifications, not standards, but the nuances of this subtle difference escape this author.

[9] Sometimes called *Project 802*.

Table 1.1 Ethernet Specifications

Specification	Source	Notes	
Ethernet (blue book)	DEC-Intel-Xerox	V 1.0	1980
		V 2.0	1982
802.3	IEEE	First approved[a]	1983
		Most recent supplement[b]	1995
8802-3	ISO/IEC	First international draft (DIS)	1985
		Approved international version[c]	1993

[a] This version superseded by **ISO/IEC 8802-3.**
[b] Includes Fast Ethernet.
[c] Next version due in 1995.

IEEE Computer Society. This committee writes standards for many types of computer networks. There are twelve working groups inside the LAN/MAN Standards Committee, including Ethernet (802.3), Token Bus (802.4), Token Ring (802.5) and many others.

The first release of the Ethernet standard, known to industry insiders as the cherished *blue book*, was published by the DEC-Intel-Xerox (DIX) alliance.[10] It predates the IEEE versions. The blue book version has been superseded by 802.3, although some companies still support blue book compatible products (see box entitled *Difference Between DIX Ethernet and 802.3 Ethernet*). The DIX alliance produced two versions of the blue book.

The second major release, actually part of an ongoing series of updates and supplements, was the 802.3 version originally published in 1983. The IEEE is the parent body responsible for maintenance and upgrading of the 802.3 specification.

The official IEEE name of the Ethernet standard is **IEEE Std 802.3**. The IEEE committee does not recognize the name Ethernet, but everybody else in the industry does, so we will continue here to refer to the 802.3 standard as Ethernet (standards bodies can be very particular when it comes to names). In 1984, ANSI elevated the Ethernet standard

---

[10] The first draft of this early standard was written by John Shoch at Xerox.

to joint ANSI/IEEE status, and the document became **ANSI/IEEE Std 802.3**.

The final version, which lagged the IEEE versions by several years, is the ISO version, known as **ISO/IEC 8802-3, ANSI/IEEE Std 802.3**. It is a joint ISO/IEC/ANSI/IEEE publication. The ISO version converted all the units to metric, deleted parochial references to other U.S. standards, and generally used international terminology. It was also formatted to fit international standard A4 size paper. This version established Ethernet as a true international standard. In some countries ISO-recognized standards carry more weight than IEEE standards, so it is a good thing that the IEEE pushed the 802.3 standard series all the way through to ISO approval.

How the IEEE Works with Other Standards Bodies

As a standard is being developed, there is a lot of talk in the press about its progress. At times it may sound as if a standard has been approved and ratified. A few days later, articles may appear about another round of balloting on the same standard. What gives?

A few words about the organization of the IEEE, and the life cycle process of a standard can help to clear up the confusion. The IEEE is an organization of engineers, founded in its present form in 1963 as a merger of the older American Institute of Electrical Engineers (AIEE) and the Institute of Radio Engineers (IRE). Its technical members participate in a broad range of activities. The IEEE publishes technical journals, conducts conferences, prepares educational materials and approves standards. The IEEE is recognized by the American National Standards Institute (ANSI) as a *standards development organization*. As such, it may submit standards through the ANSI for eventually adoption by the International Standards Organization (ISO). Figure 1.2 depicts the relations between the IEEE, ANSI, and ISO.

Within the IEEE there are many subgroups that create standards. The subgroup responsible for computer networking standards is called the LAN/MAN Standards Committee, and within that group the committee responsible for Ethernet is the 802.3 working group (Figure 1.3).

The life cycle of an IEEE 802.3 standard is this: after adoption by the IEEE, it next obtains joint ANSI/IEEE status, and then, finally, approval by ISO/IEC. There are generally no substantive technical changes imposed on a standard as it passes through the ANSI or ISO

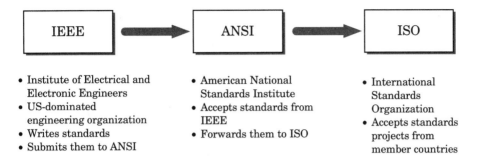

Figure 1.2 Relation of IEEE to ISO

levels. Most of the work happens in lower-level committees. The process may take years.[11]

When the base standard needs to change, the IEEE issues a supplement. A supplement may contain additional new *clauses*,[12] or it may consist solely of changes and corrections to the base standard. Each supplement follows along the standard's life-cycle track, passing through ANSI and eventually heading toward full ISO approval.

At inception, each supplement receives a letter designation. Fast

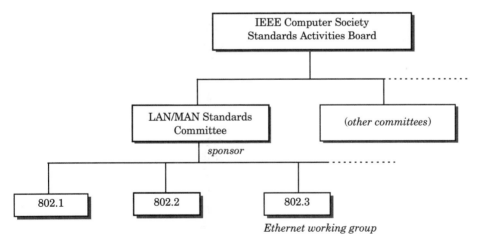

Figure 1.3 Relation of 802.3 Working Group to IEEE

---

[11] For more information about ISO/IEC standards, see *Open Systems Handbook: A Guide to Building Open Systems*, IEEE Standards Press, New York, NY, 1994.

[12] Chapters, or subsections, of an IEEE document are called clauses.

Ethernet has been assigned letter **u**. The Fast Ethernet standard is therefore called **IEEE Std 802.3u**.[13]

During the development of an IEEE 802.3 standard, the terms *working group ballot* and *sponsor ballot* come into play. These terms refer to specific levels of approval internal to the IEEE.

The *working group ballot* is the first level of formal IEEE approval. It is initiated by the 802.3 working group. The 802.3 working group produces a draft, and places it in circulation for review. The circulation period lasts at least 30 days. The review is called a working group ballot. It allows 802.3 members to vote on whether they wish to approve the standard. At this stage many members submit "helpful suggestions" for improvements or modifications to the standard. These comments must

---

How Ethernet Came to the IEEE

In early 1980, members of the DEC-Intel-Xerox alliance (DIX) decided to see if they could get the newly formed IEEE 802 Computer Society standards group to endorse their ideas. During the first 802 meeting in February 1980, the DIX team members were instructed to sit on their hands and say nothing. The meeting opened with a long talk by the 802 executive leadership describing the ideal standards development process. It should be orderly. It should be fair. It should be open. The last thing that 802 wanted to happen was for some vendor to throw down a completed specification and say, "Here it is." But, of course, that is precisely what the DIX alliance wanted to do.

In hindsight, the DIX alliance could not have found a more irritating way to announce their system architecture. To the consternation of the 802 committee, in April 1980 they announced that, yes, they had formed an alliance to work on networking standards. The alliance then also announced that the IEEE would not be permitted to see it–not until it was finished. The projected completion date was set for September 1980.[14]

With such a rocky start, it is not surprising that the IEEE, while eventually accepting large portions of the Ethernet specification, chose to modify certain critical portions. These modifications rendered some earlier product releases technically non-compliant with the final 802 standard. This is the genesis of the difference between "Ethernet blue book" products and "802.3" products.

---

[13] See information about other 802.3 supplements in Chapter 8.

[14] Thanks to Ron Crane, of LAN Media Corporation, for contributing this story.

Difference Between DIX Ethernet and 802.3 Ethernet

In the course of the IEEE process, the DIX Ethernet proposal was modified. Nowadays, companies expect that to happen. After all, when a roomful of engineers picks over a system design for several months, they develop a strong desire to change something. So, of course, the 802.3 committee did.

The original design included a field in the packet header called the *type* field. The type field was intended as a method for low-level hardware to recognize and respond to the needs of various protocol types (perhaps implementing priorities or triggering different routing strategies). After a great deal of discussion, the 802.3 committee changed the type field into a *length* field, which indicates the length of a packet. The length of each packet could, of course, already be determined by looking at the number of bytes in it. Nevertheless, IEEE members voted for the change.[15] They reasoned that additional redundant measures would help ensure accuracy of transmission. This new length field supersedes the older type field.

The length field shenanigans had the side effect of making all the existing DEC-Intel-Xerox equipment technically noncompliant, which was surely an objective of many members of the IEEE committee. Such is the standards world.

The difference between so-called true blue-book Ethernet (with type field) and 802.3 Ethernet (with length field) still persists. The two types can coexist, but do not inter-operate.[16]

---

all be addressed, and the 802.3 committee must achieve significant consensus on all the technical issues. Achieving consensus may mean circulating the draft for several rounds of review. Once the comments from the working group ballot are resolved, the revised draft passes up to the sponsor level.

The *sponsor ballot* is initiated by the LAN/MAN Standards Committee. This committee is sometimes called Project 802, so a sponsor ballot is the same thing as an *802 ballot* (it used to be called a *TCCC*, or *T-triple-C ballot*). Like the working group ballot, the sponsor ballot is another consensus-building exercise. It begins with the revised draft submitted by the 802.3 committee, which again circulates for comments. This time the draft circulates to a wider audience.[17] Anyone

---

[15] Other minor changes were made at the same time.

[16] Most adapter hardware supports both packet types, but there may be software incompatibilities depending on the protocols used.

[17] But only members of the IEEE Computer Society or other IEEE societies get to vote.

in the world can request a copy of an 802 sponsor ballot. The circulation period lasts for at least 30 days.

Once the comments from the sponsor ballot are resolved, the document proceeds to the IEEE Standards Board. If, in the judgment of the Standards Board, it has met all the requirements for openness, consensus, and voting rules, the standard undergoes final approval, editing, and publication. The IEEE Standards Board then forwards the standard to ANSI.

If actively encouraged by the 802.3 membership, the LAN/MAN Standards Committee will pass the standard onto the last step, which is ISO approval. After conclusion of the sponsor ballot, it often takes more than a year for a standard to gain ISO approval.

During the development of a standard, manufacturers typically begin designing products, but do not release them to the public. Product releases usually await approval of at least the working group ballot, for fear the standard might change, rendering products in the field obsolete. After the working group ballot, prospects for changes in the standard diminish. After the sponsor ballot the standard is essentially complete. The IEEE standards board does not impose technical changes.

Where Fast Ethernet Fits in the Picture

Fast Ethernet is an IEEE standard. It was written by members of IEEE working group number 802.3. The technical name for Fast Ethernet is *100BASE-T*.

The 802.3 working group has enjoyed a long history of success. It generated all the existing standards for Ethernet, including 10BASE-T, the dominant 10 Mb/s network in use today. The 802.3 working group intends that 100BASE-T be used as the natural upgrade path for existing Ethernet users.

Fast Ethernet is a supplement to the existing 802.3 suite of standards, not a new standard on its own. Its designation number is 802.3**u**. This supplement includes new Clauses 21 through 30, covering all aspects of Fast Ethernet operation.

EVOLUTION

Today, Ethernet is a mature product. Around it manufacturers have developed a wide range of options, alternate interfaces, and related standards. The IEEE 802.3 Ethernet standard presently supports 12 different transceiver types on hundreds of platforms. Each transceiver incorporates the analog circuitry necessary to communicate over a given type of cabling. It may be located either external to a host computer (external transceiver) or embedded onto an adapter.

This wide diversity of transceiver types gives Ethernet great staying power in the marketplace. Table 1.2 summarizes the transceivers defined for Ethernet up to and including Fast Ethernet. Each transceiver type works with a different style of cable.

Most of the transceiver types defined in Table 1.2 bear strong relationships to each other. For example, Cheapernet is a variant of the original 10BASE5 standard. It inherited its topology, MAC, and signaling from the previous standard, but changed the wiring. In the

Table 1.2 Ethernet Transceiver Types

Transceiver Type	Speed, Mb/s	Segment Length, m	Type of Cable Csed
1BASE5	1	250	Two-pair UTP (StarLAN®)
10BASE5	10	500	Thick yellow coax (original-recipe Ethernet)
10BASE2	10	185	RG58 A/U coax (Cheapernet)
10BROAD-36	10	1800	Broadband coax
10BASE-T	10	100	Two-pair category 3, 4 or 5 UTP (dominant 10 Mb/s network in use today)
FOIRL	10	1000	Dual multimode fiber link used between repeaters (superseded by 10BASE-FL)
10BASE-FP	10	500 (radius)	Dual multimode fiber transmission system used with passive star coupler
10BASE-FB	10	2000	Dual multimode fiber backbone with embedded AUI
10BASE-FL	10	2000	Dual multimode fiber link (compatible with FOIRL)
100BASE-T4	100	100	Four-pair category 3, 4, or 5 UTP
100BASE-TX	100	100	Two-pair category 5 UTP or STP
100BASE-FX	100	2000	Dual multimode fiber link

Fast Ethernet (100BASE-T4, 100BASE-TX, 100BASE-FX)

same way, Fast Ethernet is a descendant of 10BASE-T. Figure 1.4 depicts the antecedent relations among the most popular types.

These transceiver types have grown up over a long period of time in reaction to the changing requirements of the computer system market place. Let's now look at the market forces that molded the evolution of Ethernet and lead to the development of Fast Ethernet.

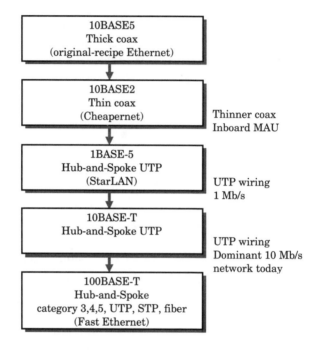

Figure 1.4 Lineage of Fast Ethernet

Thick Coax (Original Recipe)

Thick coax was the first of the 802.3 transceiver standards. It is distinguished by the following properties:

- 500 m segment length (1640 feet)
- 10 Mb/s signaling rate
- Signal-regenerating repeaters used to get maximum network diameter
- Thick yellow coax

This standard was completed in 1983, long before there were any standards for generic building wiring (see Chapter 4). At the time, the mere act of transmitting data from point A to point B was a technological challenge in itself. Additional constraints about the ease of installation, cost of service, and so forth, seemed superfluous. Users cared little about what type of wire was used or how it would be installed. After all, during most of the 1970s, the cost of computer hardware far exceeded the cost of wiring or installation. Minimizing the cost of wiring was not the issue. The issue was maximizing performance.

Given these constraints, the framers of Ethernet chose for their physical medium a very high quality coaxial cable of sufficient physical size to permit long-distance transmission of their signals without degradation. This coaxial cable had many admirable properties, including low attenuation, *excellent* noise immunity, and superior mechanical strength. A single coax cable, terminated at each end, supported a network segment of up to 500 m. With repeaters, segments could be chained together to attain greater lengths. The resulting system could achieve an overall installed system diameter of 3 km.[18]

The original standard called for the cable to snake through a building, passing near every station (Figure 1.5). At each station, a MAU device hooked physically onto the main cable. The MAU was connected to the client by a 50-m AUI cable. Because the AUI cable could be only 50 m long, the main coax cable had to pass within 50 m of each station.

The snaking approach seemed reasonable to the framers of Ethernet. It fit in with their somewhat misguided assumption that customers would wire a whole building at one time, installing Xerox personal computers everywhere simultaneously. It also seemed reasonable to the first few million customers, who had few other choices.

Over time, users began to realize that the wiring of such a system represented a significant part of the total installed system cost. Snaking the wire was troublesome, especially when someone changed offices. If the wire did not go over to the new office location, the whole snake had to move. The coax was bulky and difficult to pull through conduits. The N-type connectors were expensive and difficult to attach.

There were administrative hassles as well. Installation of thick coax throughout a building required the cooperation of the building

---

[18] Four repeaters, three 10BASE5 segments of 500 m each, two FOIRL segments of 500 m each, and a total of 10 AUI cables at 50 m each.

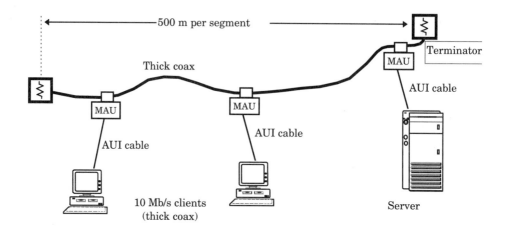

Figure 1.5 Thick Coax Installation

facilities people, and probably upper management. It wasn't the sort of thing a departmental manager could authorize. On the whole, installing a thick coax system was, by today's standards, a real pain.

This is not to say that there were not advantages to the thick coax approach. Use of such a large coax reduced signal losses, so the system could operate over large distances. The shielding (double braid plus double foil), while it made connector installation more difficult, really did a good job of attenuating external electrical noise. Mechanically, the cable was tough. It could be pulled through long vertical shafts. Each of

---

Why Ethernet Uses 50-Ω Coax

There are many myths explaining why the original Ethernet bus architecture used 50-Ω coax instead of the more popular 75-Ω coax used in the broadcast industry. At a recent standards meeting, Ron Crane, designer of some of the first Ethernet transceivers at Xerox (and many others since then), commented on the choice of cable impedance:

"50-Ω coax is less sensitive to reflections caused by transceiver taps than 75-Ω coax. As signals pass each transceiver, little reflections bounce off the transceiver and head back toward their source, just like ripples in a pond bouncing off a small rock or stick in the water. These reflections can add up, degrading the received signal. Collectively, the reflections limit the maximum number of stations permitted on a coaxial segment. With 50-Ω coax, the reflection at each station is less than with 75-Ω coax. Therefore, you can support more stations. That's why we picked 50 Ω."

these factors can be quite useful.

But, for users that did not need the large system diameter, did not have electromagnetic interference problems, and did not have a long vertical shaft, the bulky thick coax was overkill. These customers needed some relief.

Cheapernet

As early as 1983, customers began realizing that the thick coax was not the right answer for every application. Thick coax was great if you needed the 3-km distance, but many people did not. Those who didn't need the distance resented dealing with the bulk and weight of the official Ethernet-style coax.

About the same time, personal computers were hitting the marketplace in a big way. Personal computers changed the nature of the LAN business, because they were purchased at the *departmental level*, not by corporate headquarters. A department manager could easily make the decision to install a handful of personal computers without higher-level approval. They didn't cost much, and they didn't have to connect to the corporate mainframe. This was a perfect entry strategy for personal computers in large corporations.

The Ethernet system lacked an equivalent entry strategy. Thick coax was an all-pervasive system, best suited for one-time installation in a new building. It was not incremental. In response to these concerns, in 1985 the IEEE approved Cheapernet.

The distinguishing properties of Cheapernet are:

- 185 m segment length (607 feet)
- 10 Mb/s signaling rate
- Signal-regenerating repeaters used to get maximum network diameter
- Transceiver integrated onto adapter
- Thin coax (RG 58 A/U)

This variant of Ethernet accomplished two strategic objectives:

1. Easier to install
2. Reduced hardware cost

Installation cost dropped as a direct result of the thinner, easier to install coax (RG 58 A/U). The attenuation properties of this coax were not as good as the original thick coax, so the signals would not propagate as far, but it was a lot easier to install. That was fine with departmental managers, who were beginning to buy PCs in large quantities and needed an easy way to hook them together.

The BNC-style connectors used with RG 58 A/U cable were at the time already widely deployed in the radio, TV, and audio industries. This made them easier to obtain, and more widely understood, than the N-type connectors used with thick coax.

The coax itself was thinner and lighter weight than Ethernet thick-style coax. The size and weight advantages helped reduce costs in several ways. It was lighter, so technicians could carry longer rolls of cable. That saved time, because fewer splices were necessary. It was smaller and took up less inventory storage space. In large buildings, where vertical conduit space is often precious, the smaller cross section of thin coax saved space. The use of thinner coax, while sacrificing network diameter, substantially improved the economics of installation.

Hardware costs fell too, because the outboard transceiver now fit on an adapter board. The original Ethernet architecture called for a standard interface (AUI) at every computer (Figure 1.5). The AUI attached through a cable to an outboard transceiver (MAU), which contained circuitry specific to the particular AUI cable being used. The use of a standard interface, additional cable, and outboard circuitry added substantially to the cost of an Ethernet connection. The Cheapernet system circumvented these costs by allowing manufacturers to place the transceiver circuitry directly on the adapter card, eliminating the AUI and its associated cable. This structure paved the way toward more highly integrated and therefore cheaper products.

With the transceiver integrated into every client station, the system did not wire together like original Ethernet. The new, thinner, coax cable had to be physically brought to every station. It was no longer good enough to pass within 50 m of every station. The cable had to physically plug into the stations.

On the back of each station, a BNC Tee connector was used to daisy chain stations together (Figure 1.6). As a consequence of the additional signal reflections cause by the BNC Tee connectors, the system could not support as many stations as the original thick coax system.

Even with all its disadvantages, the Cheapernet system was very effective. It was effective because it directly countered two of the

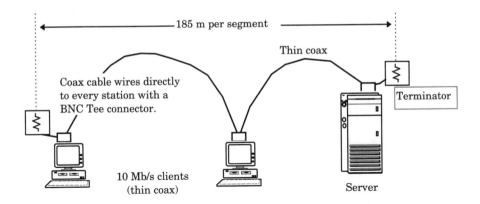

Figure 1.6 Cheapernet Installation

primary objections to thick coax Ethernet: that the thick coax was a pain to use and that the external transceiver boxes were too expensive.

The introduction of 10BASE-2 marked the first time that the 802.3 committee considered the cost of installation as a significant design constraint. That event marked a major paradigm shift. Since 10BASE-2, new designs have always considered both hardware and installation costs.

StarLAN and Hierarchical Wiring

In the mid 1980s, the data community finally recognized that the telephone company was (and still is) doing a darn good job of wiring buildings. For one thing, there was a telephone on every desk. If anybody knew how to install cable cheaply, it was the phone company. Not surprisingly, their methods were very different from data installation practices. What differed were four things.

First, phone wiring is generic. Once installed, people use their telephone wiring to perform many different tasks. In contrast, the data world at that time needed a different type of cable for every data standard. Data devices did not enjoy the benefits of generic wiring standards.

Second, phone wiring is easy to do. The tools, procedures, and accessories for dealing with telephone wire have been highly refined over the years. For example, a telephone technician can terminate 25 pairs of telephone cabling in less than 4 minutes. All they do is pull back the overall cable jacket, hold the colored wires in place, and slam the individual wires down onto connecting posts with a *punch-down tool*. Boom, boom, boom, 10 seconds per pair. They don't even stop to strip the individual wires. The insulation wipes off like magic on cleverly designed connecting posts. How do data connectors compare? It takes longer than 10 seconds just to get one coax connector, and all its parts, out of the bag.

Third, telephone-style wiring, comprising four or more *unshielded twisted pairs* in a common jacket (UTP), is ubiquitous. Systems that use phone wires can often completely skip the wiring installation phase. They just use wires already in the wall. This saves an enormous amount of money.

Finally, telephone wiring is hierarchical. Hierarchical wiring saves money at the time of installation and also later as workers move and reconfigure.

In a generic wiring hierarchy, independent wires lead from each office to nearby common connection points. In modern buildings, architects place the common connection points, called *telephone closets* or *wiring closets*, within 100 m of each office. From each telephone closet, 25-pair or 100-pair cables carry telephone signals to the main telephone switch room. The cost savings realized by this hierarchical approach, compared to pulling separate wires from each office all the way to the switch room, are dramatic.

The hierarchical wiring scheme developed naturally for telephone wiring, because of the tremendous cost savings. The LAN industry became interested in hierarchical wiring for a different reason. The LAN people liked the 100 m distance guarantee. Prior to 1984, common wisdom in the LAN business said that data transmission systems had to operate up to at least 500 m, which is difficult to achieve on telephone-style cables. The hierarchical wiring approach suggested the use of shorter, higher-speed data connections from each office to the wiring closet. Amplifiers and repeaters in the wiring closets could then hook the closets together. This combination of short, high-speed links and active electronics in the wiring closet transformed the LAN business.

Data users would never have received the benefits of telephone wiring were it not for important regulatory developments in the telephone industry. During the early development of Ethernet, prior to 1980, telephone wire was off limits to data communications users. Telephone wiring and the closets that housed it were controlled by the

phone company. Remember that most businesses of that era had
Centrex or other Bell System telephone services. With those services,
the phone company maintained the wiring, even inside the customer's
building. They wouldn't let data people near their wires.

With the breakup of the Bell System and deregulation of telephone
services, wiring policies changed. By 1984, individual ownership of
wiring was commonplace. Customers could contemplate putting data
services on their phone wires.

In 1984, AT&T and Intel approached the 802.3 committee with a
proposal for running Ethernet over telephone wire. The proposal was
adopted by the IEEE in 1987 with the nickname StarLAN.

The distinguishing properties of StarLAN are:

- 250 m segment length (820 feet)
- 1 Mb/s signaling rate
- Signal regenerating repeaters used to get maximum network
  diameter
- Transceiver integrated onto adapter
- Two pairs of unshielded twisted-pair cable (UTP)
- Hub-and-spoke topology

StarLAN was the first 802.3 LAN to use telephone-style cabling, but it
did not enjoy that privileged status for long. StarLAN was quickly
overshadowed by the 10BASE-T, a 10 Mb/s standard that used the same
architecture and the same wiring. Because it was faster,[19] users quickly
gravitated toward 10BASE-T.

10BASE-T Gets the Formula Right

In 1990, the IEEE 802.3 working group approved a second Ethernet
transceiver type that operated over ordinary, unshielded telephone-style
cable.[20] The new standard was called 10BASE-T. It was like StarLAN,
but ran at a full 10 Mb/s rate. Of the many variants of Ethernet defined
to date, 10BASE-T has proven to be the most popular.

The distinguishing properties of 10BASE-T Ethernet are:

---

[19] More important, it was the *same speed* as 10 Mb/s thick coax Ethernet.
Speed-translating bridges (very expensive at the time) were required to connect
StarLAN to existing thick or thin Ethernet segments. With 10BASE-T, simple,
inexpensive repeaters would suffice.

[20] Prestandard 10BASE-T products were available as early as 1987.

- 100 m segment length (328 feet)
- 10 Mb/s signaling rate
- Signal-regenerating repeaters used to get maximum network diameter
- Transceiver integrated onto adapter
- Two pairs of unshielded twisted-pair cable (UTP)
- Hub-and-spoke topology

At the time of introduction, some users expressed concern about the 100 m maximum segment length. The distance limitations of UTP had in the past prevented manufacturers from releasing UTP products. Coaxial cable, because it could carry signals farther, seemed superior.

On the other hand, 10BASE-T could be installed *using existing cables*, without pulling new wires. As a result, the cost of installing Ethernet dropped through the floor. This turned out to be precisely what customers wanted: a cheap, fast LAN. Sales went through the roof. 10BASE-T became an overnight success.

The maximum segment length issue turned out not to be very significant. Telephone industry practice already provided a telephone closet within 100 m of each office. The 802.3 committee capitalized on this existing physical structure by placing signal-regenerating repeaters, called *hubs*, in the closets. Wires from each office connected to the hub. Each hub amplified and restored incoming signals so that everyone could hear each other clearly.[21] The savings in installation more than offset the cost of the hubs.

The network architecture that results from using a central hub, with wires radiating from it, is called a *hub-and-spoke architecture* (Figure 1.7).

With a single repeater, the maximum separation between 10BASE-T stations is 200 m. Users overcome this distance limitation by linking together several hubs. Hubs can be linked using either 10BASE-T style links (limited to 100 m) or by other Ethernet transceiver types with longer distance capabilities. Fiber optic inter-repeater links, for example, can span 1 km or more.

Hubs were the "big idea" behind 10BASE-T. The authors of 10BASE-T realized that with hubs, no data link need be longer than 100 m. If the links could be that short, the system could use the ubiquitous UTP cabling. The use of existing cabling would pay off

---

[21] The same architecture was used by StarLAN.

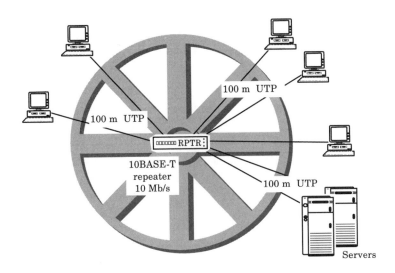

100 m UTP

100 m UTP

RPTR

10BASE-T
repeater
10 Mb/s

100 m UTP

Servers

Figure 1.7 10BASE-T Hub-and-Spoke Architecture

handsomely in terms of reduced installation cost. This crucial combination of ideas, short links, active hubs, and UTP cabling, is now a part of every major LAN standard.[22]

In retrospect, we recognize 10BASE-T as a natural evolutionary step for Ethernet. As with Cheapernet, trading off system performance (maximum segment length) for ease of installation once again proved to be a good idea.

Once a hub-and-spoke network is installed, it can flexibly respond to changes. This is a tremendous advantage. In a typical office, 16% of the workers move or change offices every year. People working in buildings with flexible partition walls move a lot more often than that. If new wires had to be run to the main computer room every time an office changed, the rewiring cost would be outrageous. Yet that is exactly how data installations were wired for years. This author has personally seen bundles of data wiring thicker than a man's waist, all disconnected, running into a computer room. The data people didn't even know where it all went. When someone moved, they just cut the old cables and ran new ones.

---

[22] Ethernet, Token Ring, FDDI, ATM and Fast Ethernet.

The best response to the move and change problem is to deploy hierarchical wiring. With hierarchical wiring, the main cables between wiring closets never move. Permanent wires also run from the wiring closets to each office, whether they are occupied or not. New devices and services are connected to the ends of existing cables in the wall without requiring new cables. All move and change work is confined to the user's desk and the wiring closet. This approach saves a lot of money, time, and wear and tear on a building.

Over the years, users have learned that LAN topologies like the bus and ring topologies cannot keep up with the move and change rate. Reconfiguring backbone cables every time someone wants to move is not practical. By now, all major LAN standards have contrived some way to use hub-and-spoke wiring.[23] Even if packets logically move in rings through the terminal devices, they still go physically in and out of hubs in wiring closets to provide ease of servicing. Hub-and-spoke wiring is the way to go.

Centralized Management

The development of 10BASE-T greatly reduced the cost of network installation and maintenance. It was not, however, the end of the road for service cost reduction. Other gains remained to be made through the technique of *hub management*.

A network hub is a central physical point to which all user devices connect. Network hubs have naturally evolved as the focal point for system debugging and testing efforts. Over time, network manufacturers have realized that they can improve their product offerings by providing features in the hub that reduce long-term service costs. These features are called, in the Ethernet industry, *management* features.

The trend toward centralized management was pioneered by companies in the field of wide area networking. Network Equipment Technologies (NET), Stratacom, and other wide-area network (WAN) vendors have long been making central points of control for far-flung data networks. In the WAN business, you cannot afford to send technicians flying around the world just to reset a port, or shut of a chattering device, or reroute traffic on a heavily congested line. The need for remote control of a wide area network is obvious. By the late

---

[23] Ethernet, Token Ring, FDDI, ATM and Fast Ethernet.

1980s, the same logic was operating in the LAN arena: As a network grows, the network manager can't run around from building to building fixing things. Central control becomes imperative.

The basic management features offered by hub vendors include the ability to monitor traffic, late collisions, and other measures of network health. They also include the ability to shut off, or disable, ports that seem to be going haywire. These basic tools allow managers to keep local problems from spreading and affecting the whole network. This is an important objective. On any given day, it is unlikely that all the devices in a big network will be working simultaneously. You can't let a little failure in one spot bring down the whole net.

In 1992, the IEEE approved standard management features for monitoring and controlling network hubs. Hubs with management features are now available to support all types of Ethernet transceivers.

Bandwidth: The Need for More

The main thrust of Ethernet development throughout the 1980s was directed toward lowering installation and service costs. Starting with the original-recipe thick coax system, the quest for lower costs led to the era of Cheapernet and finally to the adoption 10BASE-T and structured wiring principles. Hub management techniques are, again, an outgrowth of the continuing struggle to contain long-term service costs.

Together, these advances have successfully spurred the growth of an enormous networking market. These advances were obtained by applying a few basic principles:

1. Consolidate hardware where possible (consolidate transceiver into the DTE or repeater).
2. Consolidate wiring into a central hub (10BASE-T).
3. Make installation easier.
4. Put more intelligence into the hub (management).

By the early 1990s, Ethernet was an inexpensive, easy to install system, loaded with helpful installation and service features. Users concluded (by the tens of millions) that the system provided satisfactory benefits, and was available at a reasonable price.

But in any industry, idyllic market conditions rarely last long. Especially in the field of high technology, new developments can easily transcend older equipment. The Ethernet market is no exception. A new factor has appeared on the horizon, one that has the potential to subvert the entire Ethernet hardware base. This factor is *bandwidth*. Bandwidth is a difficult concept to define, because it involves so many factors:

- Raw data transfer speed
- Number of transactions per second
- Average file size
- Network topology
- Traffic patterns

Bandwidth is a many faceted concept. Consequently, each person perceives it differently. Manufacturers argue about how to define it. Users worry if they have enough of it. Test labs get paid to measure it. Academics write papers about it.

Regardless of how bandwidth is defined, most people agree that, over time, applications will demand more of it. Just look at the trend in desktop computing. Over the last decade, the power and performance of desktop computers have grown tremendously. The speed of typical desktop computers has increased over a hundred-fold in little more than a decade (Figure 1.8).

Not only are computers getting faster, applications are getting more data intensive and more communications oriented. Driving this trend is customer demand for data-hogging applications like CAD, CAE, databases, publishing, groupware, video mail, and multimedia. The quantity of data involved is growing rapidly as is the speed with which users expect it to move. Both factors fuel the demand for more bandwidth.

The way modern applications display data amplifies the network

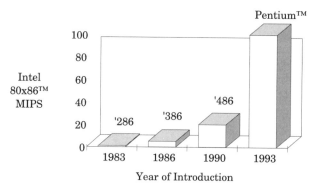

Figure 1.8 Desktop CPU Performance

requirements yet again. The desktop computer industry has evolved from the simple character oriented displays of the early 1980s to today's full-color graphical interfaces. Graphical interfaces require many more bytes to specify the position, color, font, and other attributes of every character on the screen. As a result, file sizes for typical word-processed documents have grown from 2,000 to 20,000 to as much as 200,000 bytes in recent years. All these bytes have to move across the network. The additional requirements of network-capable laser printers, scanners, video servers, and other image-based devices add even more to the network load (Figure 1.9).

Even with all this growth, for many years Ethernet enjoyed a surplus of bandwidth. All through the 1980s, the 10 Mb/s bandwidth of Ethernet easily exceeded the speed of all but the fastest desktop computers. This excess capacity worked to Ethernet's advantage. It masked many inefficiencies in protocol processing, driver throughput, and other areas. As long as the network remained the fastest part of a computer system, nobody worried about it.

By 1992, the demand for network bandwidth had skyrocketed. The situation was reaching a critical stage. Large 10 Mb/s Ethernet systems were overloaded. Whole enterprise networks were strangling on their own data. Users were partitioning their systems with bridges, routers, and switches to conserve bandwidth. The 10 Mb/s shared-media LAN was running out of capacity.

Furthermore, neither FDDI nor ATM had fulfilled their promise to

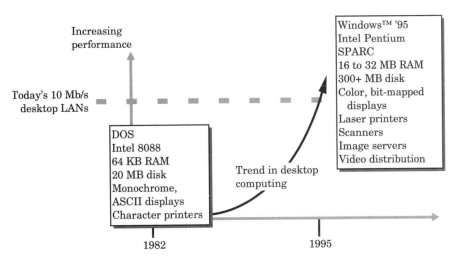

Figure 1.9 Desktop Applications Outgrow 10 Mb/s LANs

bring ubiquitous high-speed networking to every desktop. Users could not look to either of those technologies for a quick solution.

It became widely apparent that Ethernet users needed some relief. In response to this bandwidth crisis the IEEE 802.3 working group commissioned a *Higher Speed Study Group* to consider all ways to speed up Ethernet.

ORIGIN OF *FAST* ETHERNET

The summer of 1992 crackled with excitement as vendors all over the world made plans for a faster Ethernet. The nexus for their ideas, and the designated arena for their anticipated battles was, naturally, the IEEE.

In November of that year, the IEEE 802.3 Higher Speed Study Group began official deliberations concerning the future of Ethernet. The topic of the day was bandwidth. The prevailing wisdom said that users facing bandwidth strangulation had three alternatives:

1. Partition their system with bridges, routers or switches.
2. Design faster, or better, data links.
3. Forgo the benefits of new applications and faster computers.

Of these three alternatives, the Higher-Speed Study Group ultimately decided to address only item 2 (see box entitled *The Other Alternatives*). The result of their work is the Fast Ethernet specification we have today.

During their deliberations, the study group considered many different approaches to the bandwidth problem. Figure 1.10 relates the final Fast Ethernet solution to some of the other approaches. It divides these approaches into the *partitioning* approaches and the *faster–better* approaches. Fast Ethernet is interoperable with, and complementary to, many of these other techniques.

The Other Alternatives

The Higher Speed Study Group, by its charter, was precluded from considering the first alternative. It was commissioned to write physical standards for LAN interoperation, not the software protocols required to standardize switching and partitioning approaches.

The third alternative is unrealistic. Nobody wants to stick with slow, dumb applications.

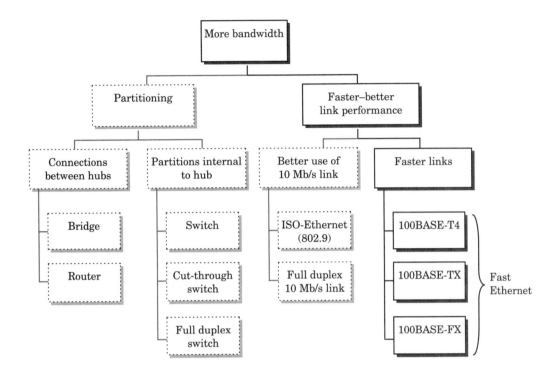

Figure 1.10 Genealogy of Performance Approaches

The basic partitioning approaches include switches, bridges, and routers. All these devices operate on a common principle: they replace a network of repeaters with a collection of more sophisticated hub devices. The new hubs, by better managing the flow of packets in the network, dramatically increase system performance. Fast Ethernet works well with switching, bridging, and routing, but it cannot take credit for their development. It just uses them. See Chapter 2, *Advanced Capabilities*.

The faster–better link alternatives attack the performance of individual links, rather than the architecture of the central hubs. Proponents of these alternatives divide naturally into two camps, the better link camp and the faster link camp.

The better link approaches presume a better, although not necessarily faster, link. These approaches are ISO-Ethernet[24] and full-duplex Ethernet.

ISO-Ethernet (802.9) adds a synchronous side channel to the existing 10BASE-T signaling structure for the purpose of communicating information with fixed-bandwidth, low-delay requirements (like compressed video). The synchronous side channel proposed by 802.9 carries 6 Mb/s.

The full-duplex approach combines switch technology with improvements in the link operation. The full-duplex switch can support simultaneous transmission in both directions between hub and client. It makes use of existing 10BASE-T adapters if they support full-duplex traffic. Especially useful for server connections, the full-duplex technique virtually doubles server performance. The utility of full duplex for client stations is less apparent. Full duplex and ISO-Ethernet are both discussed in greater detail in Chapter 5.

Fast Ethernet falls into the faster link camp. It actually increases the raw link performance by a factor of 10, bringing it to a breathtaking 100 Mb/s. The benefits of increased speed are obvious. Fast Ethernet retains the same hub-and-spoke architecture *and the same types of wiring* as 10BASE-T. The importance of these features in simplifying the migration path is difficult to overstate. An overview of Fast Ethernet and the migration from 10 to 100 Mb/s appears in Chapter 2. A detailed analysis of the Fast Ethernet specification follows in Chapter 3.

One of the more interesting twists in the development of Fast Ethernet has been its convergence with switching. Once viewed as competitors, many vendors now advocate using both technologies. The coalescing of switching and Fast Ethernet surprised a lot of people, but today it is one of the hottest growing segments of the Fast Ethernet market.

Chapter 5 describes how Fast Ethernet, switching, and other techniques work together. These powerful combinations have the potential to increase total system performance by many *orders of magnitude*. The resulting surplus of bandwidth will sustain users of Fast Ethernet for decades.

In comparison with other standards of similar complexity, the Fast Ethernet specification developed rather quickly. By June of 1995, the

---

[24] Here the prefix ISO stands for *isochronous*, not the International Standards Organization.

802.3 working group concluded its business on 100BASE-T, and the IEEE standards board approved the result. On June 14, 1995, Fast Ethernet officially became an IEEE standard.

Why Raise the Link Transmission Rate?

Aren't there other ways to increase performance? This question concerned many network users at a "Birds of a Feather" roundtable session held at Interop® Fall 1993. As discussed in that session, raising the data rate was only one of many ways to increase performance. Some believed bridges, routers, and switches were the answer. Others favored tuning their network drivers. Full-duplex switching had its advocates. The audience couldn't seem to decide whether a link-level speedup was necessary.

Tim Teckman of Intel rose to address the issue. Tim turned the audience's thoughts toward what really counts: bandwidth. Tim started out by saying that he had recently been talking to his friends in Detroit about engine performance. Each of them had an idea about what to do. It was a new carburetor, or a new injection system, or a new exhaust pipe. Everybody had a different idea. But amidst all the controversy, on one point they all agreed:

There's no substitute for cubic inches.

In other words, when it comes to horsepower, raw size matters more than anything else.

Tim went on to explain that networking was much the same way. In the final analysis, bandwidth matters more than anything else. When we want more performance, we want more bandwidth. In the end, the audience agreed. So did 802.3.

Points to Remember

- Fast Ethernet is a 100 Mb/s version of 10BASE-T Ethernet, the dominant 10 Mb/s network in use today.
- Fast Ethernet developed in response to overpowering market requirements for systems that use unshielded twisted-pair wiring and skyrocketing demand for network bandwidth.
- Unshielded twisted-pair wiring (UTP) is generic, easy to use, ubiquitous, hierarchical, and cheap.
- Fast Ethernet, like original Ethernet, is an IEEE standard.

- Fast Ethernet was generated by 802.3, the same committee that developed Ethernet.
- Like Ethernet, it will become an ANSI standard and then an international ISO standard.

2

Fast Ethernet

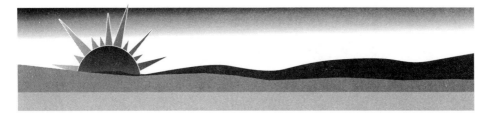

*F*ast Ethernet is a new IEEE local area network standard. It was completed in 1995 by the IEEE 802.3 working group, the same committee that generated the original Ethernet specifications. It is the natural upgrade path for existing Ethernet users. The official name for the Fast Ethernet standard is *100BASE-T*. As Table 2.1 shows, it provides a tenfold increase in performance for less than twice the price.

Table 2.1 Comparison of Ethernet and Fast Ethernet (100BASE-T)

Feature	Ethernet	Fast Ethernet 100BASE-T
Speed[a]	10 Mb/s	100 Mb/s
Cost	$X	Less than $2X
IEEE Standard	802.3	802.3
Media Access Protocol	CSMA/CD	CSMA/CD
Topology	Bus or star	Star
Cable support	Coax, UTP, fiber	UTP, STP, fiber
Collision domain diameter	3000 meters (9842 feet)	412 meters (1352 feet)
Unshielded twisted pair (UTP) link distance	100 meters (328 feet)	100 meters (328 feet)
Media Independent Interface	Yes (AUI)	Yes (MII)
Full-duplex capable?	Yes	Yes
Broad support from many vendors	Yes	Yes

[a] When used in conjuction with switching technology, Fast Ethernet performance skyrockets *another* order of magnitude.

OVERVIEW

Fast Ethernet uses the same *Collision Sense Multiple Access with Collision Detection* (CSMA/CD) *Media Access Control protocol* (MAC) that is at the core of 10 Mb/s Ethernet. All the MAC timing parameters are sped up by a factor of 10, but the remainder of the MAC algorithm remains unchanged.

Fast Ethernet uses the same types of hub-and-spoke topologies used by 10BASE-T Ethernet, the dominant form of 10 Mb/s networking in use today. It uses the same types of wiring and the same software protocols. It is supported by a large number of the same vendors.[1] In short, 100BASE-T provides a nondisruptive, smooth evolution from current 10BASE-T Ethernet to high-speed 100 Mb/s performance.

CSMA/CD

The Fast Ethernet MAC specification uses a speeded-up *bit time* (the time duration of each bit transmitted), but leaves the remainder of the Ethernet CSMA/CD MAC unchanged. The packet format, packet length, error control, and management information in 100BASE-T are practically identical to those in Ethernet.[2] Packets just go faster. To higher layers of software, 100BASE-T appears indistinguishable from regular Ethernet (except for its faster response).

The 100BASE-T CSMA/CD MAC uses the same 96-bit *interpacket gap* (IPG) rule used at 10 Mb/s. The interpacket gap rule places a 96-bit space at the end of each packet. This gap helps make the collision process work evenhandedly. At 100 Mb/s, ten times faster than regular Ethernet, the interpacket gap *time* between packets shrinks by a factor of ten. It is the same number of bits; the bits are just smaller. In regular Ethernet, the IPG is 9.6 μs, in Fast Ethernet the IPG is 0.96 μs.

---

[1] In 1993, a group of vendors supporting Fast Ethernet banded together to form the *Fast Ethernet Alliance*. This alliance was responsible for promoting the Fast Ethernet standard, organizing joint product demonstrations, and general public relations work. Its members contributed heavily to the IEEE standards process. By 1995, its ranks had swelled to 85 companies, most of whom were producing 10BASE-T products. Once the standard was approved the alliance was no longer necessary, and it disbanded.

[2] Two new error control functions have been added; see *MII: New Features*, in Chapter 3.

Fast Ethernet also uses the same number of bits for every other part of the packet protocol, like the preamble, addressing overhead, and CRC. These parts shrink as well. In essence, everything shrinks together. Even the cabling delays shrink. Fast Ethernet permits total cable delays only one-tenth the duration of cable delays allowed in regular Ethernet. Don't worry, the cables are still long enough to hook up most installations (see *Cables Supported* later in this chapter).

If each packet shrinks by a factor of 10 (because it is going 10 times faster), and all other elements of the overhead and protocol delay also shrink by a factor of 10, then overall performance will scale up by exactly 10 times. This scaling principle is central to the Fast Ethernet concept:

> *For the same percentage traffic load, Fast Ethernet transfers*
> *10 times as many packets and 10 times as much information*
> *as regular 10 Mb/s Ethernet.*

The Fast Ethernet architects resisted the temptation to garnish the MAC with any new or "better" features that might conflict with existing applications. All the popular protocols like NetBios®, IPX, and TCP/IP work as well on Fast Ethernet as on the original, only faster.

Network managers benefit substantially from the unchanged MAC. With minimal incremental training they can understand and deploy Fast Ethernet. The value of previous training in Ethernet installation, debugging, and service procedures is preserved.

Basic Topology

10BASE-T was the first widely popular hub-and-spoke architecture for local area networking (Figure 1.4). This architecture is recognized today as one of the seminal advances in the field of networking. Hub-and-spoke wiring simplifies the installation, maintenance, and rework of a data cabling system. Fast Ethernet uses that same hub-and-spoke approach.

As illustrated in Figure 2.1, the hub-and-spoke architecture uses two types of network components: *adapters* and *hubs*. A hub, in Fast Ethernet, is a central device through which data packets flow. The hub typically has an individual star-wired connection to each of its client devices. Each client device may be a personal computer (PC), workstation, server, or another hub. The point-to-point connections from hub to client are called links. An adapter is required at each end of

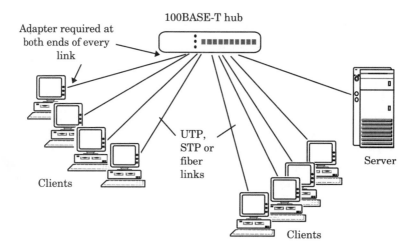

Figure 2.1 Fast Ethernet Basic Topology

every link. An adapter is a circuit that couples computer data onto a physical section of cabling.

An adapter is often called an adapter card, or network interface card (NIC), even though it is not always implemented as a separate card. For example, in some PCs, the adapter may be built directly onto the computer motherboard.

A Fast Ethernet adapter may couple data directly onto any of the approved cable types (see *Cables Supported,* this chapter), or it may use an external transceiver to do so. To use an external transceiver, the adapter must be equipped with a Fast Ethernet MII connector (see *Use of External Transceiver* later in this chapter).

Cables Supported

Fast Ethernet supports structured wiring composed of category 3, 4, and 5 *unshielded twisted pair* (UTP), 150-Ω *shielded twisted pair* (STP), and fiber. These media specifications cover almost all cable types currently in use. Equally important, all supported media types can be mixed together and connected through a repeater or switch, just as with the earlier Ethernet media types.

To support these various wiring types, Fast Ethernet provides three transceiver types. A transceiver is that portion of an adapter containing the analog circuitry necessary to transmit and receive data on a physical cable.[3] The technical term for a transceiver is *Physical Layer Device* (PHY). As shown in Table 2.2, each transceiver type supports a different set of cable applications. Table 2.2 lists two twisted-pair-type transceivers and one fiber transceiver. These three Fast Ethernet transceiver technologies are complementary.

100BASE-T does not support the coax cables that were used in some earlier versions of Ethernet. Network managers have for the most part moved away from coax cable due to the improved reliability and manageability of structured UTP wiring.[4]

Detailed cabling requirements for each transceiver type are listed in Chapter 3. More information about generic cabling for Fast Ethernet appears in Chapter 4.

The utility of the 100BASE-FX fiber link is obvious. Fiber can go long distances, tying together large enterprise-level networks (see *100BASE-FX: Distances* in Chapter 3). The reason for having two

Table 2.2 Cable Support by Transceiver Type

Transceiver Type	Cable Type	Number of Pairs (Number of Fibers)	Notes
100BASE-T4	Category 3 UTP[a]	4	Workhorse design for category 3 cable, 100-m link span
	Category 4 UTP	4	
	Category 5 UTP	4	
100BASE-TX	Category 5 UTP	2	Only needs two pairs, 100-m link span
	150-Ω STP[b]	2	
100BASE-FX	62.5/125 µm multimode fiber	2	Same optics as FDDI, 2-km link span[c]

[a] Unshielded twisted pair (UTP), for example, phone wire.
[b] Shielded twisted pair (STP), for example, IBM type-I cable.
[c] Assumes use of full duplex. Without full duplex, the maximum fiber link span is 412 m (see *100BASE-FX: Distances* in Chapter 3).

---

[3] An adapter may be fitted with an external transceiver (external PHY), or it may incorporate an embedded transceiver (like most 10BASE-T products).

[4] In addition, the design of vampire-style coaxial taps becomes increasingly difficult at higher frequencies. This factor renders the coaxial bus structure unsuitable for Fast Ethernet.

different twisted-pair links is equally important, but more subtle. It involves the characteristics of category 3, 4, and 5 UTP (see Chapter 4, *Horizontal Cabling*).

Category 3 cable, which dominates the older installed base, cannot transmit signals with as high a data rate as the newer category 5 cable. To combat this effect, 100BASE-T4 uses all four pairs in parallel. This parallel transmission strategy lowers the signaling rate on each pair, so 100BASE-T4 can work on category 3 cable. 100BASE-TX uses only two pairs. It transmits on one pair, and receives on the other. Because it transmits a full 100 Mb/s signal on each pair, 100BASE-TX requires category 5 cable.

The advantage of 100BASE-T4 is that it works on category 3, 4, or 5 cable. The advantage of 100BASE-TX is that it needs only two pairs. See Chapter 3 for more information about transceivers and Chapter 4, *Planning an Installation* about selecting the right transceiver type.

Other new transceiver types are on the way. See *Link Transmission Technology* in Chapter 5.

Fast Ethernet supports link distances of at least 100 m on all media types. This distance is a basic requirement of the hub-and-spoke architecture, as codified by the building wiring standards **EIA/TIA 568-A** and **ISO/IEC 11801** (see Chapter 4).

Use of External Transceiver

A Fast Ethernet adapter may couple data directly onto one (or more) of the approved cable types (see *Cables Supported,* this chapter). A typical direct-coupled adapter has a computer I/O bus interface on one side, and a data connector (like an RJ-45) on the other. No external components are required. A direct-coupled design is compact and efficient. It is a good choice if you know what cable plant the adapter is expected to support. This is the architecture most often used with 10BASE-T.

In cases where the intended cable plant is unknown, a better choice might be a combination of adapter and external transceiver. An adapter equipped for external transceiver operation provides a fixed interface to the local computer on one side, and a standard connector, called the *Media Independent Interface* (MII), on the other. A variety of external transceivers may then be connected to the MII. The external transceivers may be selected to communicate with any of the approved Fast Ethernet cabling types (Figure 2.2).

In principle, the MII resembles the *Media Attachment Unit Interface* (AUI), used in regular Ethernet to connect a 10 Mb/s external transceiver to its adapter. Both interfaces provide a standard connector to which users may later attach a variety of external transceivers. This feature is particularly valuable to manufacturers that plan to integrate the adapter hardware onto a large motherboard. They can design-in the standard MII interface without knowing which external transceiver will later be attached.

The MII performs the same function in Fast Ethernet as the AUI does in regular 10 Mb/s Ethernet. Both act to isolate the upper protocol layers (MAC, packet buffers, and adapter I/O interface) from the transceiver functions (transmit amplifier, wave-shaping, and receive discriminator). The exact positioning of the MII in the protocol stack differs slightly from the AUI (Figure 2.3). In Fast Ethernet, the MII fits between the Reconciliation sublayer and the PCS. The part below the MII, the part that connects to the physical cabling, is usually called a transceiver. The official Fast Ethernet term for transceiver is *Physical Layer Device* (PHY).

Why was the MII interconnection point redefined? Why didn't Fast Ethernet put it in the same place as the AUI? The answer to these questions has to do with data coding, as explained next.

The MII function was moved to its new location because the old AUI functionality did not fit the needs of Fast Ethernet transceivers.

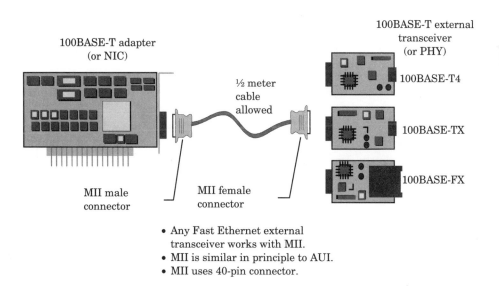

- Any Fast Ethernet external transceiver works with MII.
- MII is similar in principle to AUI.
- MII uses 40-pin connector.

Figure 2.2 Media Independent Interface (MII)

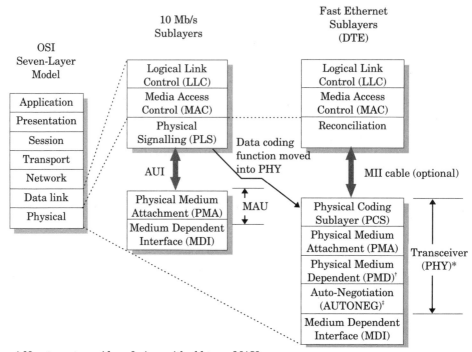

Figure 2.3 Fast Ethernet and 10 Mb/s Ethernet Protocol Sublayers

The primary function that is missing in the AUI setup is a provision for customized data coding in the PMA sublayer.

Early in the 100BASE-T project the 802.3 committee determined that no single data-coding scheme would be ideal for all media.[5] Therefore, the coding function should reside in the replaceable transceiver module, not in the generic DTE circuitry. Previous incarnations of the Ethernet specification placed the coding function (Manchester coding) in the PLS, above the AUI. The Fast Ethernet standard rearranges the sublayers to provide a coding sublayer (PCS)

---

[5] Details about coding appear in the *T4, TX,* and *FX* sections of Chapter 3.

downstream of the MII. As a result, each transceiver can use the data coding best suited for its intended application.

New Protocol Sublayers

New protocol sublayers in the Fast Ethernet standard include the Reconciliation sublayer, the PMD, and Auto-Negotiation (Figure 2.3).

As is common in the standards world, Figure 2.3 contains some acronyms that need explaining:

AUI	*Attachment Unit Interface.* 10 Mb/s standard transceiver interface.
AUTONEG	*Auto-Negotiation.* Optional support for determination of link options and optimal settings.
DTE	*Data Terminal Equipment.* The client, PC, workstation, server, or other device served by a hub.
MDI	*Medium Dependant Interface.* The cabling connector.
MII	*Media Independent Interface.* 100 Mb/s standard transceiver interface.
PCS	*Physical Coding Sublayer.* Responsible for data coding.
PHY	*Physical Layer Device.* Official term for *transceiver.* The PHY contains the analog circuitry necessary to communicate with the physical medium.
	The PHY is a combination of the PCS, PMA, PMD, and AUTONEG sublayers. The PHY may be located either external to a host computer (external transceiver) or embedded onto an adapter.
PMA	*Physical Media Attachment* sublayer. In T4, it is responsible for analog functions like transmit amplification, wave-shaping and received data discrimination. In TX and FX, it provides an interface to the FDDI-style PMD sublayer, which contains the same analog functions.
PMD	*Physical Media Dependent* sublayer. In TX and FX, it is responsible for analog functions like transmit amplification, wave-shaping and received data discrimination. This sublayer is borrowed from FDDI.

The Reconciliation sublayer is what we standards experts call a "weenie" sublayer. It translates the terminology used in the MAC into the terminology appropriate for the MII sublayer. That's it. To the MAC, it is a transparent, functionless sublayer. Signals just pass through it.

There are no options, configuration choices, or user-accessible features in the Reconciliation sublayer.

The PMD is a sublayer used in the TX and FX standards (but not in T4). This sublayer references the ANSI TP-PMD and fiber-PMD standards, respectively. These are the same low-level physical sublayers used by FDDI. The TX and FX standards use these FDDI sublayers intact and unmodified (except for pinouts). The use of these previously defined physical layer transmission standards is beneficial because many vendors can reuse their existing FDDI chips and circuits. Re-use of existing chips lowers finished system costs and reduces the time to market.

The optional Auto-Negotiation (AUTONEG) sublayer provides extensive support for determination of link options and optimal settings. With Auto-Negotiation enabled, an adapter may determine for itself what physical signal capabilities exist at the far end of the link and select the best mode as needed. This is highly useful when dealing with adapters that have more than one network capability (for example, 10BASE-T/100BASE-TX combo cards).

Advanced Capabilities

Fast Ethernet transceivers support switching and in many cases full-duplex services. The capabilities of the various transceivers are listed in Table 2.3.

Table 2.3 Advanced Capabilities

Transceiver Type	Support for Switching	Support for Full Duplex
100BASE-T4	Yes	No
100BASE-TX	Yes	Yes
100BASE-FX	Yes	Yes
10BASE-T	Yes	Yes

Switching is a hub feature that costs extra, but boosts system performance. A hub with switching functionality is called a *switch*. Switching belongs to a general family of techniques that are not unique to Fast Ethernet, although Fast Ethernet works very well with all of them. Other members of the family include *bridges* and *routers*. For all practical purposes, switches and bridges accomplish identical functions. These terms are differentiated solely for marketing reasons. Usually, the term *switch* refers to a multi-port bridge, particularly a 10BASE-T or Fast Ethernet multi-port bridge, whereas the term *bridge* may be reserved for products with as few as two ports, or with the ability to translate between LAN standards (like Ethernet to Token Ring). Both switches and bridges manage the flow of packets to improve network efficiency. A router performs a similar task, but also accomplishes additional functions related to isolation of multi-cast traffic between LAN domains and management of long-distance transmission facilities (see Chapter 5, *Wide Area Networking*).

Switching is often used to boost the performance of a local area network. In a typical application a switching hub replaces a repeater, or network of repeaters. The switching hub, by virtue of its better ability to manage the flow of packets, dramatically increases overall system performance (see how in *Switch Architecture*, later in this chapter).

A switch can handle links of different speeds, making it naturally suited as a transition product between regular Ethernet at 10 Mb/s and Fast Ethernet at 100 Mb/s. In the example of Figure 2.4, a switch provides one high speed, 100 Mb/s connection to a local server, and three ordinary 10 Mb/s connections to its other client devices.

As part of its traffic management capability, the switch permits all its clients to talk simultaneously. This stands in stark contrast to a repeater, which permits only one successful transmission at a time. The switch in Figure 2.4 allows multiple conversations and then, bandwidth permitting, concentrates all the server-bound traffic onto the 100 Mb/s server connection.

Full duplex is an optional link feature that works with switching. This feature, when enabled, permits the simultaneous flow of data in both directions across a link. Full-duplex works only between two full-duplex switches or between a full-duplex switch and a full-duplex DTE.

In full-duplex mode, a DTE is free to transmit or receive at any time (Figure 2.4). This mode bypasses parts of the Ethernet MAC, which does not normally permit simultaneous transmission and reception. As a consequence, collisions on full-duplex lines are nonexistent. The same packet format, bit signaling, and timing are used, but not the MAC CSMA/CD protocol.

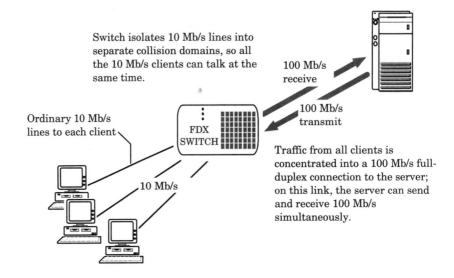

Switch isolates 10 Mb/s lines into separate collision domains, so all the 10 Mb/s clients can talk at the same time.

Ordinary 10 Mb/s lines to each client

100 Mb/s receive

100 Mb/s transmit

FDX SWITCH

10 Mb/s

Traffic from all clients is concentrated into a 100 Mb/s full-duplex connection to the server; on this link, the server can send and receive 100 Mb/s simultaneously.

Figure 2.4 Full-Duplex Operation

Full-duplex mode can only be used with switching. With a repeater, full duplex makes no sense. In the repeater architecture, when one device talks, all other devices listen. Simultaneous transmission and reception is logically impossible. Repeaters do not support full-duplex, switches do.

When connected to a server, the full-duplex technique virtually doubles *theoretical* server performance by allowing the server to send and receive at the same time. Improvements attained under actual conditions depend heavily on local traffic patterns (see Chapter 5, *Full-Duplex Ethernet*) and rarely approach 100%. Nevertheless, full duplex never hurts, so many customers use it.

Flow control features associated with full duplex are discussed in greater detail in Chapter 5, *Flow Control*. For information about automatic detection of full duplex as provided by Auto-Negotiation, see Chapter 3, *Auto-Negotiation*. Use of full duplex extends the useful range of fiber links to 2 km or more (see *100BASE-FAX: Distances* in Chapter 3).

Points to Remember

- Fast Ethernet is also called 100BASE-T.
- Fast Ethernet is like 10BASE-T Ethernet, only 10 times faster.
- Fast Ethernet uses the same CSMA/CD Media Access Control (MAC) that is at the core of 10 Mb/s Ethernet.
- Fast Ethernet uses the same types of hub-and-spoke topologies used by 10BASE-T.
- Fast Ethernet works with category 3, 4, and 5 unshielded twisted pair (UTP), type 1 shielded twisted pair (STP), and fiber.
- The MII performs the same function in Fast Ethernet as the AUI in regular 10 Mb/s Ethernet.
- Switching is an integral part of Fast Ethernet.
- Some Fast Ethernet adapters support full-duplex services.

PRODUCTS

Fast Ethernet products fall into two generic categories: *adapters* and *hubs* (see the previous section, *Basic Topology*). Adapter architectures are pretty simple. They have a bus interface on one side. It conveys data to a host computer, or into a repeater or hub. The other side connects to the medium of choice, be it twisted pair, fiber, an MII, or something else. The interesting part of an adapter is not its architecture, but the media to which it can connect.[6]

Hub products are more varied. They come in two basic architectures: *shared* and *switched* (for repeaters and switches respectively). Both architectures use star wiring to each client. Both accomplish the transfer of packets among a group of Ethernet users. Both operate at the lowest levels of the protocol stack. From the perspective of an individual client, they are indistinguishable.

From the perspective of cost and performance, shared and switched architecture hubs differ markedly. Shared architecture hubs (also called repeaters) are inexpensive, but permit only one client to successfully transmit at a time. Switched architecture hubs (called switches) cost more, but manage the flow of packets to improve network efficiency. For

---

[6] At the 1995 Spring Interop in Las Vegas, one vendor, to show the robustness of their T4 transceiver, actually ran data over *barbed wire*.

example, a switch may permit multiple simultaneous conversations between independent devices, a repeater does not.

Both shared and switched architectures are available at either 10 or 100 Mb/s. That makes four possible combinations. Table 2.4 lists these four basic hub architectures.

The first column lists the name used in this book to refer to each architecture. Be aware that various publications and vendors use different names for the same architectures.

The second column lists the product speed. Some of the products support ports operating at two speeds (10 and 100 Mb/s), in which case we report the most prevalent speed.

The final columns report whether the product is a switch or a repeater, the resulting aggregate bandwidth, and other special notes.

Table 2.4 Types of Ethernet Hubs

Product Type	Link Speed (Mb/s)	Architecture	Total System Bandwidth (Mb/s)[a]	Special Features
10 Mb/s repeater	10	Shared	10	Connects to any 10 Mb/s port on a Fast Ethernet hub.
100 Mb/s repeater	100	Shared	100	May include ports bridged to 10 Mb/s for connectivity with existing 10 Mb/s network.
10 Mb/s switch	10	Switch	N x 10	May include ports bridged to 100 Mb/s for server connections or connections to 100 Mb/s network.
100 Mb/s switch	100	Switch	N x 100	May include ports bridged to 10 Mb/s for connectivity with existing 10 Mb/s network.

[a] N is the number of hub ports. These figures assume use of full-duplex switching. Without full duplex, switching bandwidths are N/2 x 100 and N/2 x 10, respectively.

Adapter Architecture

As explained in *Use of External Transceiver*, adapters are available in two generic styles: direct-coupled, or with an external transceiver.

An external-transceiver style adapter is illustrated in Figure 2.2. It connects to an external transceiver (also called an external PHY) through an MII connector. The primary advantage of the external transceiver is its flexibility, as an MII port can accommodate any external transceiver.

The direct-coupled style adapter houses all the necessary transceiver circuits (also called PHY circuits) directly on the adapter. No other parts are required. The primary advantage of the direct-coupled adapter is its low cost, as the MII connector, MII cable, and external transceiver housing are all eliminated. This is the architecture most often used with 10BASE-T products.

A third possibility, called the *dual transceiver configuration*, is discussed under *MII: Management Features* in Chapter 3. It combines an internal transceiver *and* an MII interface on the same adapter.

In all three cases, the same options exist for media support. For the purpose of this section, we need not differentiate between the MII options. In this book, we will refer to the combination of adapter and optional external transceiver as simply an *adapter*.

Adapters are available for many different computer bus architectures, including ISA, EISA, PCI, Sun S-Bus and Macintosh™ NuBus™. Fast Ethernet is not limited to any particular bus architecture. Fast Ethernet adapters may also be integrated onto a computer motherboard.

Some users worry that Fast Ethernet will be *too* fast for their computers. That is no need for concern. The computer itself does not have to support continuous 100 Mb/s transactions in order to participate in a Fast Ethernet network. This same concern surfaced regarding original Ethernet in the early 1980s when many computers could not keep pace at 10 Mb/s. Nevertheless, they still worked fine on Ethernet. They worked because adapters store and buffer packets from the network and then release them at internal speeds convenient to the computer. This fixes the speed-matching problem. In addition, transport layer protocols prevent the server from overrunning its clients, and vice versa. Anyway, the point is rapidly becoming moot. Many '486 or Pentium-class computers can handle continuous 100 Mb/s transmission without difficulty.

Fast Ethernet adapters, interestingly, are available as either plain 100 Mb/s adapters or as *dual-speed* 10/100 adapters (Table 2.5). This feature is different from the *dual-transceiver configuration* discussed in Chapter 3, *MII: Management Features*. Dual-speed adapters support Fast Ethernet (T4 or TX) as well as 10BASE-T. A computer equipped with a dual-speed adapter will work at 10 Mb/s with any 10BASE-T hub. When connected to a Fast Ethernet hub, it will immediately start working at 100 Mb/s.[7] Nothing about the adapter or its host computer must change! This feature is perfect for upgrade scenarios.

Dual-speed operation applies to hubs, too. Some vendors have taken advantage of this to provide, for example, a switching product where any port can operate at either 10 or 100 Mb/s (see *Switch Architecture* later in this chapter).

Adapters support various options for determining when to operate in 10BASE-T mode versus higher-speed modes. The best of these options is full support for Auto-Negotiation (100BASE-T Clause 28, see also

Table 2.5 Types of Fast Ethernet Adapters

100 Mb/s Adapters	Dual-Speed 10/100 Mb/s Adapters
100BASE-T4 Four-pair category 3 UTP	100BASE-T4 *and* 10BASE-T
100BASE-TX Two-pair category 5 UTP, STP	100BASE-TX *and* 10BASE-T
100BASE-FX Two-strand 62.5/125 μm multimode fiber	Most Fast Ethernet fiber adapters operate at only one speed.[a]

[a] 100BASE-FX uses 1300 nm optics. 100BASE-F uses 850 nm optics. Construction of a single device compliant with both modes, while theoretically possible, is not likely to happen.

---

[7] We assume here the adapter vendor has chosen to support Auto-Negotiation or some other equivalent means of automatically switching between modes. Some adapters may not switch automatically.

Chapter 3, *Auto-Negotiation*). The Auto-Negotiation option provides extensive support for determination of link options and optimal settings. With Auto-Negotiation enabled, the adapter card determines for itself what capabilities exist at the far end of the link and selects the best mode as needed.

Users should take maximum advantage of dual-speed products. From the outset, all new, fast PCs should be configured with dual-speed 10/100 adapters. Until the need for 100 Mb/s performance arises, connect these PCs to regular 10BASE-T hubs, running at 10 Mb/s. As 100 Mb/s hubs penetrate the network, these preconfigured PCs stand ready to operate in full 100 Mb/s mode.

When the time comes to upgrade part of the network to 100 Mb/s, all the network manager has to do is cross-connect the appropriate dual-speed adapters to a 100 Mb/s hub. This change takes place entirely within the wiring closet. No modifications of the desktop hardware or software are necessary. That saves running around to perhaps hundreds of offices, and the downtime that would result as each desktop computer underwent change. With dual-speed adapters, the extra cost of the adapters themselves is more than offset by the savings in maintenance and downtime when the network shifts to 100 Mb/s operation.

The existence of 10/100 capable adapter cards splits the work of upgrading into two separate, manageable tasks (Figure 2.5):

1. Upgrading the adapters to dual-speed capability.
2. Upgrading the hubs to 100 Mb/s.

Splitting the work in two allows upgrades to proceed in an orderly fashion. The network population need never be jolted with a massive enterprise-wide shift in desktop hardware. Users can upgrade one by one, as needed. Users without high-bandwidth requirements may even stay permanently connected to 10 Mb/s resources.

Anyone who has experienced a sudden, massive desktop upgrade process knows what a disaster it can be. Fast Ethernet neatly sidesteps that pitfall.

Repeater Architecture (Shared Architecture)

A repeater is a relatively simple, bit-oriented device. Simple, but effective. Figure 2.6 shows how a repeater works. The Fast Ethernet repeater architecture is identical to a 10 Mb/s 10BASE-T repeater architecture, only it runs 10 times faster.

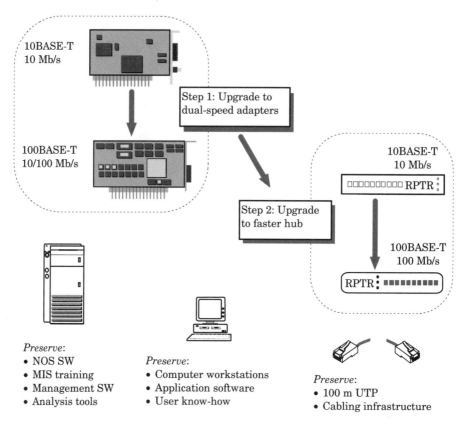

Figure 2.5 Upgrade in Two Stages

A repeater facilitates the exchange of data packets among its various clients. The repeater is very fast and can create the electronic illusion that all its clients are connected to a common shared bus. It accomplishes this trick by following one very simple rule: When a packet arrives, immediately forward it to *all other links*. A repeater copies incoming packets, without modification or unnecessary delay, to *all* its output ports.[8]

A repeater can serve any number of ports. Each port typically connects to one client with a point-to-point link. The client may be a PC, workstation, server, bridge, switch, or even another repeater.

---

[8] Technically, a repeater forwards all signals, whether they be packets, collision fragments, jam signals, or bursts of noise. It also amplifies and reshapes the incoming signals, sending them on their way in pristine condition.

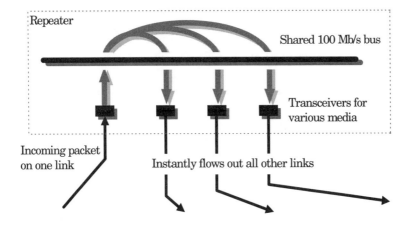

Figure 2.6 Repeater (Shared Architecture)

The repeater operates like an old-fashioned telephone party line: when one person talks, everybody listens. Any local area network with the party-line property is called a shared-media LAN. Ethernet, Token Ring, and FDDI are all examples of shared-media LANs.

Any LAN with the shared-media architecture can successfully process only one transmission at a time. In Ethernet, the CSMA/CD protocol enforces the one-at-a-time rule (see *The Ethernet Control System* in Chapter 1). When two clients attempt simultaneous transmission, the repeater detects the resulting collision and notifies all ports.[9] Errant devices see the notification, quickly cease transmission, and clear the network for the next packet. Collisions in Fast Ethernet clear themselves within about 5 *micro*seconds (we said it was fast!).

Because any two devices connected to a repeater can collide, we say that the repeater provides one *collision domain*. Repeaters (and collision domains) must obey certain timing constraints, which limit the possible ways they may be connected.[10] A complete set of rules for configuring repeaters appears in Chapter 3, *Topology*. Here is one of the more important rules:[11]

---

[9] The collision notification is called a *jam* signal.

[10] A *collision domain* is a collection of Ethernet devices (nodes) connected by any number of repeaters. Only one node at a time may transmit inside a collision domain. See Chapter 7.

[11] Assumes 100 m twisted-pair links. With shorter links, three repeaters are possible. See Chapter 3, *Topology* for more information about configuration rules.

*With 100 m client links, only two Fast Ethernet repeaters may
reside in the same collision domain.*

This rule sounds very restrictive, but there is a simple way around
it. Basically, the configuration rules do not apply across switching
devices. Any switch, bridge, or router breaks the collision domain rule,
permitting virtually unlimited expansion. Large Fast Ethernet networks
are built using switches.

In a collision domain, since only one device is active at a time, the
total bandwidth of a shared architecture product (10 or 100 Mb/s)
spreads out among all the clients connected to it. For example, a
100 Mb/s repeater with 50 clients attached provides 2 Mb/s of average
available bandwidth per client. The attached clients *share* the
bandwidth; thus a repeater is said to have a *shared* architecture. The
iconic representation of a shared-architecture repeater is the heavy
horizontal bus drawn in Figure 2.6.

The shared-architecture 100 Mb/s repeater in Figure 2.7 serves
four 100 Mb/s clients.[12] All the 100 Mb/s clients share the same 100 Mb/s
collision domain. In addition to 100 Mb/s services, this product has a

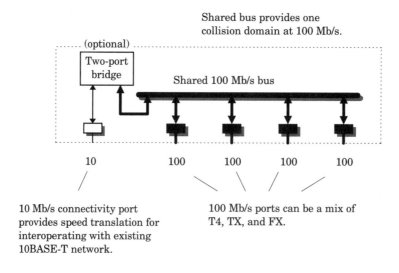

Figure 2.7 100 Mb/s Repeater with Connectivity Port

---

[12] A large repeater might support hundreds of ports.

special connectivity feature. It provides a 10 Mb/s port. The 10 Mb/s port (shown on the left side) connects through an internal 10/100 speed translating bridge to the main 100 Mb/s repeating bus. Such a port is called a 10 Mb/s *switched* port. Any 10 Mb/s Ethernet service may attach to this connectivity port. Fast Ethernet repeaters may theoretically provide any number of such 10 Mb/s connectivity ports.

The shared-architecture 100 Mb/s repeater in Figure 2.8 serves four 100 Mb/s clients. Like the previous example, all the 100 Mb/s clients share a single 100 Mb/s collision domain. The special feature on this switch is an optional switched expansion port. The switched expansion port (shown on the right side) runs at a full 100 Mb/s. It connects through an internal bridge to the main 100 Mb/s repeating bus. The switched expansion port can attach to the next higher repeater in a large hierarchical array of repeaters. Because it is a true switched port, the expansion port circumvents the collision domain timing limitations (collision domains don't penetrate switches, bridges or routers). A virtually unlimited array of switched-expansion-port repeaters may be assembled.

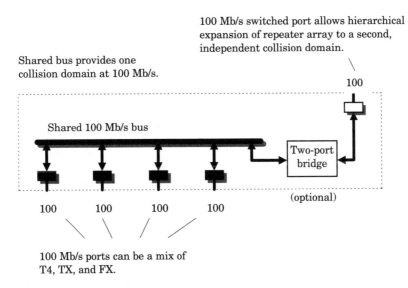

Figure 2.8 100 Mb/s Repeater with Expansion Port

Switch Architecture

Compared to a repeater, a switch costs more, but boosts system performance. Where a repeater is simple, a switch is more complex. Where a repeater is dumb, a switch is smart. The switch includes a big CPU and lots of memory to help it do its job. The extra memory and CPU horsepower are what make it more expensive.

Switching hubs improve Ethernet performance by overcoming the basic limitations of its shared-media architecture. These basic limitations are mostly related to the one-at-a-time nature of shared access: when one user talks, everyone listens.

Imagine if everyone in a large corporation had to sit around a big table where only one person talked at a time. Nothing would ever get done! Parallel processing is what makes businesses work today and it is the wave of the future for computer networking. Everybody does their own thing, all at the same time. Switching applies the power of parallel processing to the problem of network performance. Here is how it works.

In a switching system, messages pass *only* to those clients who need them. Other clients remain free to exchange additional traffic. Like a phone system. We do not get our neighbors' calls (at least not very often). A phone system can process many calls at once.

Switching brings with it the same terrific advantage: *all the clients can be active at the same time.* A nonblocking switch can receive, process, and forward packets on all lines independently. For example, at one instant half of the clients can be transmitting packets while the other half are receiving. Each of the transmitters can be talking to a different receiver.

With a *full-duplex* switch the throughput is even higher. With full duplex, every client can both transmit *and* receive simultaneously. Full-duplex switching generates an explosion of bandwidth throughout the system.

Figure 2.9 depicts the architecture of a typical switch. Transceivers in a switch connect to a switching fabric, instead of a shared bus. Each port has its own independent connection to the switching fabric. When a data packet arrives, it is first routed into the fabric, where it is stored. When the switch has received enough of the packet to decide where to send it, the fabric routes the packet back out to the destination port. This is the most important point: *a switch only sends packets where they*

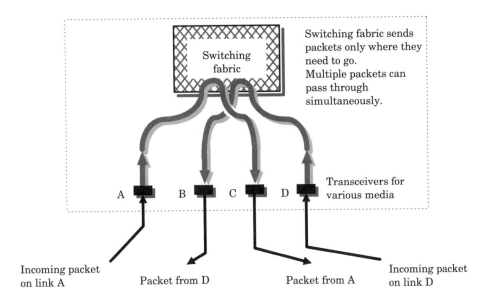

Figure 2.9 Switch Architecture

need to go. [13] In contrast, a repeater forwards all packets to all links, wasting a lot of bandwidth.

The prime advantage of a switch is its ability to simultaneously receive multiple packets. A repeater cannot. A repeater, which forwards incoming packets immediately to all ports, effectively blocks off other incoming traffic. The switch keeps the other lines clear. It can simultaneously receive on many ports, transferring all packets into memory inside the switching fabric. Even more amazing, it can transmit out to several destinations at once, while *still receiving* on unused ports.

The example in Figure 2.9 shows two packets in transit. One packet from link A is moving through the switching fabric out port C. Meanwhile, a packet from link D is also moving through the switching fabric to port B. Inside the switching fabric, the packets cross effortlessly, without hitting one another. The iconic representation of a switch is the cross-hatched switching fabric bus drawn in Figure 2.9.

Because incoming packets on different links do not collide, we say the switch provides a separate *collision domain* on each port. The switch

---

[13] Sophisticated switches use the spanning tree algorithm, just like bridges, to determine where to route packets.

isolates collisions on each link so that they will not interfere with each other. That boosts performance. It also raises an interesting point about how Ethernet works.

Normally, in the event of a collision, the Ethernet *Media Access Control* (MAC) tries again (it re-transmits the packet). It continues doing so until the packet gets through to its ultimate destination. In the switching world, collisions work differently. In a switching environment, a packet travels first from a client into the switch memory, where it may wait in queue before going on to the server. In this case, since there was no immediate collision, the transmitting MAC *forgets about the packet*. It is now the responsibility of the switch. If the switch experiences a collision outbound on the way to the server, it is the responsibility of the switch, not the original MAC, to re-transmit it. The original MAC does not see any collisions that happen on the far side of the switching fabric. The switch partitions the network into independent, noninteracting collision domains.

In this way, a cascaded network of switches acts like a fish ladder. Once a packet makes it through a given collision domain, it never swims back to the previous pool. Each packet keeps jumping along until it reaches its final destination (Figure 2.10).

A key component of a switching fabric is its memory, or buffer, capacity. The memory helps ride through situations where many devices are transmitting to the same receiver (for instance, a server). Packets can back up in the memory for a while and then burst out to the destination device. More memory makes buffer overflow occur less frequently.

Switches are also rated in terms of their address filtering sophistication. Address filtering determines how a switch knows which packets to forward to which port. Switches that support many physical addresses per port are very flexible. For example, they may participate in hierarchical arrays.

Address filtering is important in a hierarchical array because each port in the array must support many devices elsewhere in the hierarchy. A packet destined for *any* of these devices must be forwarded in the appropriate direction. Some early products that could only support one physical address per port would not be able to perform this function.

As far as the repeater configuration rules go, a switch port looks like a DTE. Configuration constraints, like the two-repeater rule, do not penetrate the switch. For example, any switch port may legally connect to a collision domain which *already* contains two Class-II repeaters.

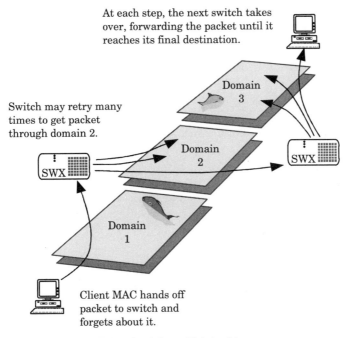

At each step, the next switch takes over, forwarding the packet until it reaches its final destination.

Switch may retry many times to get packet through domain 2.

Domain 3

Domain 2

SWX

SWX

Domain 1

Client MAC hands off packet to switch and forgets about it.

Figure 2.10 Switches Behaving Like a Fish Ladder

In a switch, many ports can operate at once. In a *nonblocking* switch, *all* the ports can operate at once (either transmitting or receiving). In a non-blocking *full-duplex* switch, all the ports can both transmit and receive simultaneously. Theoretically, the total system bandwidth equals the number of ports times the bit rate per port. In practice, depending on traffic patterns and the capabilities of the switch, the maximum available bandwidth may not be attained.

Regarding switch architecture, you may hear the terms *cut-through* and *store-and-forward*. A cut-through switch begins forwarding a packet as soon as it figures out the correct destination. Only the packet preamble and header need arrive before the packet can be sped on its way. Cut-through action is good for low latency.

A store-and-forward switch receives the entire packet (and validates the CRC)[14] before sending it to its destination. The

---

[14] The CRC, also called a frame check sequence (FCS), is a 4-octet error detection code appended to every packet. It helps identify any errors that may happen during transmission.

store-and-forward technique takes longer, but it does not propagate collision fragments to its destination ports. It therefore helps control congestion.

Figure 2.11 depicts a 10 Mb/s switch. Each 10 Mb/s port provides an independent collision domain. In addition to its 10 Mb/s ports, this switch provides a special 100 Mb/s port. The 100 Mb/s port pumps data directly into the switching fabric. Packets passing from the 100 Mb/s world to the 10 Mb/s world automatically change speeds as they pass through the switching fabric.

The switch in Figure 2.11 is a terrific transition product. It exists to help migrate users from 10 to 100 Mb/s performance. This switch, since it provides 10 Mb/s links to each client, works with ordinary 10BASE-T client adapters. This is a key advantage. The switching architecture provides the immediate benefit of expanded system bandwidth for the 10 Mb/s users.

Another big benefit of this switch is its ability to combat congestion on a file server. Imagine a server connected, using Fast Ethernet, to the 100 Mb/s switch port. The switch can funnel traffic from many 10 Mb/s clients onto the 100 Mb/s file server link. Because the file server link is ten times faster than the individual client links, it will not tend to choke up with client traffic.

Of course, now the *server* is so fast it could theoretically overload a

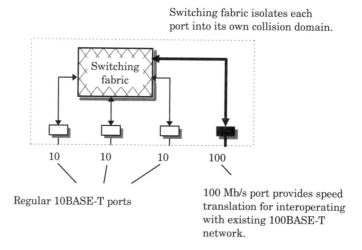

Figure 2.11 10 Mb/s Switch Architecture (with Fast Ethernet Port)

client link with traffic. Fortunately, this effect is handled by transport layer software. The transport layer throttles the server back to a rate of transmission acceptable to each client.

This switch architecture was among the earliest of Fast Ethernet products released, because of its importance in the migration of 10 Mb/s systems. A specific example of performance achieved with this architecture appears in the section entitled *Real Network Performance*, at the end of this chapter.

The switch in Figure 2.12 looks almost identical to the switch in Figure 2.11. The difference is that in Figure 2.12 most of the ports are 100 Mb/s (not 10), and the switching matrix is correspondingly faster.

The switch in Figure 2.12 provides an independent 100 Mb/s collision domain on each 100 Mb/s port. In addition, this switch includes a special port for 10 Mb/s connectivity. The connectivity port brings 10 Mb/s traffic directly into its central switching fabric. The 10 Mb/s port hooks together the 100 and 10 Mb/s networking worlds. Such compatibility is an essential feature of Fast Ethernet.

Because a switch is in reality a very fast multiport bridge, each switch port needs several packets worth of buffer memory and substantial amounts of CPU horsepower to do its job. These extra parts make switched ports more expensive than their simpler, bit-repeating

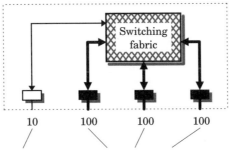

Switching fabric isolates each port into its own collision domain.

10

100 100 100

10 Mb/s port provides speed translation for interoperating with existing 10BASE-T network.

100 Mb/s ports can be a mix of T4, TX, and FX.

Figure 2.12 100 Mb/s Switch Architecture

cousins, the repeater ports. To combat the increased cost, some vendors have proposed hybrid products.

These hybrid products provide several shared (repeatered) ports connected to each true switched port. This hybrid architecture delivers some of the advantages of switching, but does not cost as much as a true bridge-per-port architecture. Figure 2.13 depicts a hybrid product with three repeater ports per true switch port. The importance of this configuration and its relation to the Class II repeater limits, are described in Chapter 3, 100BASE-T *Repeater: Distinguishing Features, Allowed Topologies.*

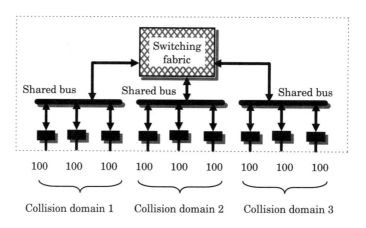

Switching fabric isolates each of the shared buses into its own collision domain.

Within each collision domain, contention exists and bandwidth is shared.

Ports can be a mix of T4, TX, and FX.

Figure 2.13 Hybrid Switch/Repeater Architecture

Points to Remember

- All new, fast PCs should be configured with dual-speed 10/100 adapters.
- Fast Ethernet hubs are available as repeaters, switches, and many combinations in between.
- Repeaters are simple, dumb, and cheap.

- Repeaters are subject to configuration rules.
- With a repeater, the average available bandwidth per port shrinks as devices are added to the network.
- Switching costs more, but boosts system bandwidth.
- Switches are immune from most topology rules.
- Switches, with sufficient address filtering capability, may be configured in virtually unlimited hierarchical arrays.
- With a switch, the total system bandwidth grows in proportion to the number of attached devices.
- Some 100 Mb/s hubs include a 10 Mb/s speed-translational port.
- Some 100 Mb/s repeaters include a 100 Mb/s switched port for hierarchical expansion.

APPLICATION OF FAST ETHERNET

Between 10BASE-T and 100BASE-T there are as many migration paths as there are users. Factors influencing the pace of migration include those given in Table 2.6.

As you can see, the factors involved in choosing a migration path are complex. Whatever happens, if you have already installed dual speed adapters, your work will be easier. The following examples illustrate some of the issues involved in selecting an appropriate migration path for your installation.

Table 2.6 Factors Influencing Migration

Issue	Considerations
Need for 100 Mb/s	Only needed for some clients
	Only needed for some servers
	Only needed at some sites
Budget	Dollars are limited today...
	...but I have to plan now for future upgrades
Logistics	Not enough network technicians to go around
	Cannot upgrade all at once
	Want to try it out before committing
	Have to retain compatibility with existing 10 Mb/s users

Implementing a Mixed 10/100 Mb/s Network

The examples in this section assume that you wish to introduce 100 Mb/s service gradually. The focus is on maintaining compatibility with the existing 10 Mb/s services as other parts of the network change. Subsequent sections will discuss full-blown, start-from-scratch 100BASE-T networks.

There are two basic products that can gradually introduce 100 Mb/s networking into an existing 10 Mb/s environment:

1. 100 Mb/s repeater
2. 10 Mb/s switch

Both increase total system performance. Both benefit the user community, but in different ways. The 100 Mb/s repeater provides full 100 Mb/s access to a fixed number of users. It is a good approach for turbocharging the performance of a few clients in a network that is otherwise performing adequately. The 10 Mb/s switch benefits all users, without requiring any upgrades to their existing computer hardware. It is a good approach for attacking widespread network congestion. Either product may be installed incrementally, upgrading only those users directly connected to 100 Mb/s services.

The 100 Mb/s repeater shown in Figure 2.14 creates a single, shared 100 Mb/s collision domain. All the high-performance workstations and the server share this single domain. Users connected to the new 100BASE-T repeater will experience a dramatic improvement in performance.

Along with its 100 Mb/s ports (thick lines), this particular repeater provides one 10BASE-T port (thin lines). The 10BASE-T port bridges internally to the 100 Mb/s services. The bridging function is speed translational. This special port (called a 10 Mb/s *switched* port) is marked with a crosshatched switching icon in Figure 2.14.

In this example, the 10 Mb/s switched port connects to existing portions of a 10 Mb/s network (a 10BASE-T repeater). Users connected to the 10BASE-T repeater should see little or no change in overall server performance. The 10 Mb/s switched port provides connectivity to 10BASE-T, but no improvement in its performance. Performance gains in this installation are reserved for the high-performance workstations.

In another installation, the same 10 Mb/s switched port might connect to an existing 10 Mb/s campus backbone or to some other 10 Mb/s service.

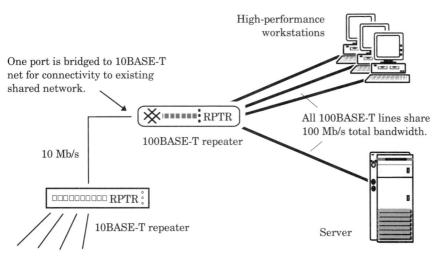

High-performance
workstations

One port is bridged to 10BASE-T
net for connectivity to existing
shared network.

All 100BASE-T lines share
100 Mb/s total bandwidth.

100BASE-T repeater

10 Mb/s

RPTR

10BASE-T repeater

Server

Figure 2.14 Using a 100 Mb/s Repeater

Not all 100BASE-T repeaters have a 10 Mb/s switched port. Ask
your vendors if they have this feature.

The 100 Mb/s repeater illustrated in Figure 2.15 has an expansion
port. The expansion port is a switched 100 Mb/s port. It does not share
the same collision domain as the other ports and so is immune to the
topology constraints of Class I and II repeaters. In other words, the
expansion port can be used to cascade repeaters in a virtually unlimited
hierarchy. The special expansion ports are marked with a crosshatched
switching icon in Figure 2.15.

In this example, the expansion port is used to create a two-level
hierarchy of repeaters. This greatly expands the port capacity of the
network. Furthermore, devices on the right side of the drawing are
isolated by the switching action from devices on the left, so the traffic
patterns do not interfere. The total available system bandwidth is
greater than 100 Mb/s.

Hierarchical expansion ports can increase both the scope and
performance of a 100BASE-T network. The resulting 100 Mb/s
sub-network may still be connected through a speed-translating bridged
port to an existing 10 Mb/s network.

In the next example, let's try using a 10 Mb/s switch.

The 10 Mb/s switching hub shown in Figure 2.16 provides 10 Mb/s
switched lines to a group of high-performance workstations (thin lines).
The switch funnels traffic from these workstations into a 100BASE-T

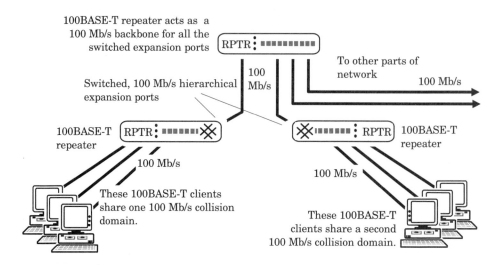

Figure 2.15 100 Mb/s Repeaters with Switched Expansion Ports

line running to a high-performance server (thick line). In the reverse direction, the server feeds 100 Mb/s into the 100BASE-T switched port, which the hub fans out as needed to the workstations at 10 Mb/s each. Server link performance has been increased ten fold.

Also shown in this diagram is a 10BASE-T repeater. This repeater represents an existing 10 Mb/s network. One of the 10 Mb/s switched ports on a switching hub often connects to a 10BASE-T repeater.

The 10 Mb/s switch is a simple and effective way to introduce Fast Ethernet to an existing 10 Mb/s site. All the devices connected to the switch experience an immediate boost in server performance, even though they retain their 10 Mb/s client links.

Once 100 Mb/s networking has been introduced to a site, there are many mechanisms for increasing its prevalence. One of the most useful mechanisms involves use of a 100 Mb/s switch. The 100 Mb/s switch can perform four functions:

  A) Consolidate links from other switches into a server pool
  B) Consolidate links from 100 Mb/s repeaters into a server pool
  C) Directly attach 100 Mb/s clients and servers
  D) Provide long-distance connectivity to other sites

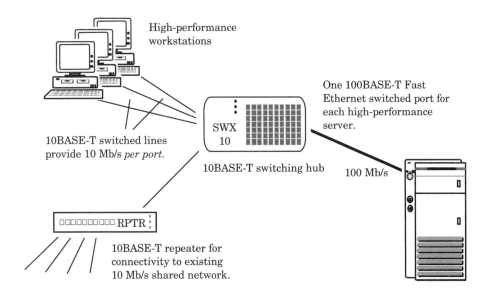

High-performance
workstations

One 100BASE-T Fast
Ethernet switched port for
each high-performance
server.

SWX
10

10BASE-T switched lines
provide 10 Mb/s *per port.*

10BASE-T switching hub   100 Mb/s

RPTR

10BASE-T repeater for
connectivity to existing
10 Mb/s shared network.

Figure 2.16 Using a 10 Mb/s Switch

The configuration in Figure 2.17 illustrates all four functions. The 10BASE-T workstations at the top of the figure connect through an ordinary 10BASE-T repeater to a single shared 10 Mb/s collision domain. The 10BASE-T repeater in turn connects to one port of a 10BASE-T switch. The 10BASE-T switch provides an isolated 10 Mb/s collision domain on each port. High-performance workstations (second group) connect to the remaining ports on the 10BASE-T switch. These workstations each get a dedicated 10 Mb/s port.

All the 10 Mb/s ports on the 10BASE-T switch funnel their traffic onto its 100BASE-T port. This port drops down to a 100 Mb/s port on the 100BASE-T switch. In this part of the example, the 100BASE-T switch is performing function *A)*, consolidating a link from another switch (a 10BASE-T switch, in this case).

The third group of workstations, labeled *higher performance*, hook to a 100BASE-T repeater. This repeater provides a single shared 100 Mb/s collision domain. All workstations connected to this repeater share the same 100 Mb/s of bandwidth. One port on the 100BASE-T repeater drops down to a 100 Mb/s port on the 100BASE-T switch. In this part of the example, the 100BASE-T switch is performing function *B)*, consolidating a link from a 100BASE-T repeater.

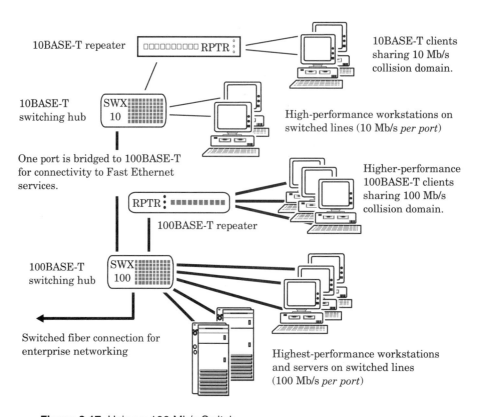

Figure 2.17 Using a 100 Mb/s Switch

The fourth group of workstations, the highest performance group, directly attach to 100BASE-T switching ports. This provides each workstation with a dedicated 100 Mb/s connection, function *C)*. The same mode of attachment is used for the servers.

Function *D)*, long distance connectivity, is represented by the line at the bottom left. This 100 Mb/s line represents a switched fiber connection, leading to other parts of the enterprise network. A switched fiber line may be as long as 2 km if used in full-duplex mode, or 412 m otherwise. Check with your vendor to see if their switched fiber port has a full-duplex mode. See *100BASE-FX: Distances* in Chapter 3.

Long-range adapters are a life-saver in some applications, but watch your step. Fiber optic long-range adapters use special single-mode fiber optic transmitters and receivers and operate only over single-mode fiber optic cable. A significant amount of engineering is required to install these types of lines. They also cost a bundle. Check with your vendor to see if they can recommend a model known to be compatible with their transceiver.[15]

Implementing a Pure 100 Mb/s Network

This section shows how to grow a large 100BASE-T network from scratch. Although the emphasis is on growth of 100 Mb/s components, the configurations shown here will interoperate with 10 Mb/s systems as well. Combining ideas from this section and the previous section, users can construct very large networks, spanning several kilometers and serving thousands of users with an arbitrary mix of 10 and 100 Mb/s services. These scenarios will be presented cumulatively, with each building on the previous example.

The most basic 100 Mb/s network starts with one 100 Mb/s repeater (Figure 2.18). As the network grows, the first repeater will eventually run out of ports. At that point, you have three basic choices:

1. Add a second repeater.
2. Buy a larger, stackable repeater.
3. Combine several repeaters with hierarchical expansion ports.

Let's look at the two-repeater alternative first. It sounds simple, and is, but there is a catch: *not all repeaters can be used in a two-repeater*

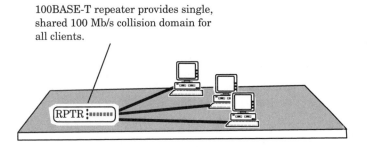

100BASE-T repeater provides single, shared 100 Mb/s collision domain for all clients.

Figure 2.18 Basic 100 Mb/s Repeater Configuration

---

[15] Geoff Thompson, a long-time member of 802.3 from Bay Networks, Inc., suggests that a 100BASE-FX product with integrated single mode optics would be perfect for long-range applications. It should use the FDDI SM-PMD. Would somebody please build one?

configuration. This catch is a consequence of the CSMA/CD *collision constraint,* which dictates network timing (see Chapter 3, 100BASE-T *Repeater: Distinguishing Features,* and Chapter 3, *Topology*).

Fortunately, each repeater is labeled with a *class mark* (I or II), which indicates whether or not a repeater may be used in a two-repeater configuration. A Class II repeater works fine in a two-repeater configuration. A Class I repeater does not (see Table 2.7).

Table 2.7 Fast Ethernet Repeater Classes

Repeater Class	Number of Repeaters Allowed in Collision Domain Assuming 100-m Client Links
I	1
II	2[a]

[a] More are possible with reduced link lengths; see Chapter 3, *Topology.*

Subtle differences separate the Class I and Class II repeaters. These differences involve timing delay, and feature content. Basically, the timing delay of a Class II repeater is less than the timing delay of a Class I repeater. This reduced timing delay does *not* mean that a Class II network has greater throughput, or better performance, than a Class I network. It *does* mean that two Class II repeaters will fit within the timing budget prescribed by the collision constraint, whereas two Class I repeaters will not.

Because the Class I repeater has been allocated a greater budget for timing delay, it may accommodate more features than a Class II repeater. These features may include stacking and translation (see Chapter 3, *Repeaters*).

Always check with your vendor to make sure that you understand the class of the repeater that you are buying. Violation of the class restrictions may result in numerous late collisions, which affect performance and clutter network management with diagnostic alarms. Late collisions can also cause undetected frame errors (although the probability of this happening is extremely remote).

The configuration in Figure 2.19 depicts two repeaters (both Class II). In this example, they are positioned adjacent to each other. In Fast Ethernet, the technique of cascading repeaters doubles the total

100BASE-T Class II repeaters may be
connected in tandem, doubling effective
capacity.

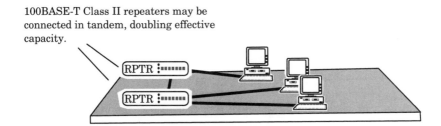

Figure 2.19 Adding a Second Repeater

port capacity, but does not enlarge the collision domain diameter. The
DTEs in Figure 2.19 are still separated by only 200 m. To enlarge the
collision domain diameter, one uses bridges, routers, or switches. Other
uses for a Class II repeater are discussed in Chapter 3, 100BASE-T
Repeater: Distinguishing Features, Allowed Topologies.

If two repeaters are not enough, try using a *stackable repeater*. The
term stackable repeater refers to any type of modular, expandable
repeater. There are several popular stackable architectures. For
example, some stackable products incorporate a backplane that
accommodates expansion cards. Each card can serve multiple clients.
Other stackable products, like flat ribbon cable, provide a means to
flexibly interconnect several boxes, aggregating them into a single large
repeater unit. Each box can serve multiple clients. Stacking
architectures can exchange data very efficiently, with low delay,
between their modules. The overall delay of a stacked product is usually
more than the delay of a single Class II repeater, but not as great as a
series combination of two Class II repeaters. Stackable products almost
always carry a Class I delay mark. Stackable repeaters of either type
can easily serve up to hundreds of users.

Stackable repeaters, being generally more flexible than
fixed-chassis repeaters, are more likely to include a 10 Mb/s bridged
connection for interoperability with existing 10 Mb/s services.

The stackable repeater in Figure 2.20 sports a fiber interface,
which becomes important when we begin to build larger systems. As
noted in Figure 2.20, fiber connections can exceed 100 m (see *Topology*
in Chapter 3). Ask your vendor if the repeater they carry has a fiber port
and how far it will go. Growth of a network through the use of
hierarchical expansion ports was explained in Figure 2.15 and its
associated text.

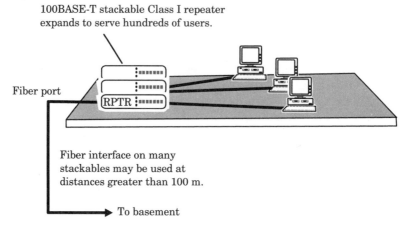

Figure 2.20 Using a Stackable Repeater

To construct very large networks, Fast Ethernet uses switching. In a typical switching configuration, several repeaters connect to a switch, which in turn connects to a pool of network data servers. Fast Ethernet repeaters of any type, fixed or stackable, can connect to a 100 Mb/s switch.

Figure 2.21 depicts a switching scenario. In this figure, vertical links from the repeaters drop down to a 100 Mb/s main switch in the basement. The server pool connects to the main switch. This is a popular way to configure very large networks.

Besides serving as a central connection point for the server pool, the basement switch in this example provides several other functions. First, the switch partitions the network into several independent collision domains. This improves system robustness, and at the same time increases total system bandwidth. Because the collision domains are separated, a network on one floor can crash and burn without affecting anyone else's service.

Second, the switch consolidates links from all floors. Although the drawing shows each repeater serving only one floor, in reality a stackable repeater can easily serve users spread throughout multiple floors in a large building. Configuration rules require only that each user be located within 100 m of their repeater. For example, one repeater centrally located on a building's sixth floor might serve floors 1 through 12, totaling 300,000 square feet of office space. In any case, the basement switch consolidates traffic from throughout the building.

Finally, the switch provides long-distance connectivity to other sites. At the bottom of Figure 2.21, a long fiber leads off to the right. This fiber connects to the remainder of the enterprise network. Presumably, there is another switch (or bridge or router) at the other end of the fiber. The fiber used in this link, if it runs between switches in full-duplex mode, can span 2 km (412 meters without full duplex). This is sufficient to span the distance between buildings in even the largest campus. See *100BASE-FX: Distances* in Chapter 3.

In very large buildings, a hierarchy of switches can be used to consolidate traffic from groups of floors (Figure 2.22). The second-level switch on the top floor provides a switched, point-to-point fiber link to the basement. Because a switch is present at each end of such a link, it can span 2 km in full-duplex mode (412 m without full duplex, see *100BASE-FX: Distances* in Chapter 3), which is more than enough for

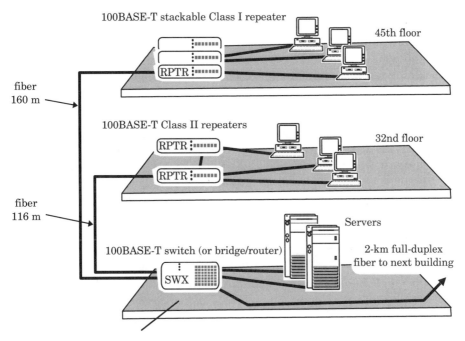

The hub consolidates independent nets from each floor into the server pool.

Figure 2.21 Switch Used for Consolidation

the tallest building. A hierarchy of 100 Mb/s switches can also service very high-performance applications that demand individual 100 Mb/s switched service to every desktop.

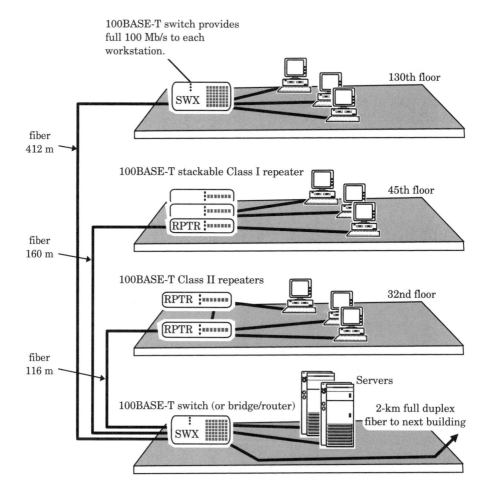

Figure 2.22 Switching Hierarchy in a Large Building

Points to Remember

- Fast Ethernet hubs support many modes of migration from 10 to 100 Mb/s.
- Hubs with speed translation ports can support both 10 Mb/s and 100 Mb/s.
- Fast Ethernet repeaters are rated as Class I or Class II.
- Stackable repeaters can grow to serve hundreds of users.
- A switch can consolidate traffic in a large building or campus environment.
- Switches can support very long fiber connections.

NETWORK PERFORMANCE

The subject of network performance involves the use of statistics.[16] The best network managers avoid overreliance on network statistics. Talking to end users and watching the port indicators on a busy switch are equally valid means of diagnosing network problems.

Finding the Bottlenecks Is Hard

To speed up a network, first look for the bottlenecks. Every system has a few bottlenecks. Improve them and the whole network performs better.

Typical approaches to identifying bottlenecks usually begin with some form of performance measurements. This is a delicate issue because, as we shall demonstrate, it is rather difficult, in a functioning network, to obtain an *accurate* measurement of performance. Here is why.

The first thing to remember about a large network is that *every user perceives the network differently*. Some users have good connections to their server. Others connect through Rio, Tibet, and Hong Kong. Some users run applications designed for efficient networking. Some run older *disk chugging* applications that worked poorly *before* the network existed. What seems slow to one user is fast to another. Every site is different, every server is different, and every user on every workstation is different. There just is not a good way to characterize

---

[16] The same sorts of statistics are used to predict the weather, the economy, and the outcome of presidential elections. Let this serve as a warning.

overall network performance in an accurate, easy to understand, standard manner. On top of that, user behavior fluctuates in crazy patterns.

In the face of fluctuating user behavior, the instantaneous network load gyrates wildly from moment to moment. Technically, it is even worse than random, it is actually *chaotic* (see box).

The chaotic behavior of networks implies that almost no precision exists in our ability to practically measure the performance of a system working in the field. It also means that measurements made one day are likely to differ widely from measurements made the next day. Worst of all, with chaotic data, averaging over long periods of time does not improve the accuracy of the observations.[17]

In nature, chaotic processes are very common. One familiar

Ethernet Is a Chaotic Process

As Leland, Taqqu, Willinger, and Wilson explain in their 1994 paper,[18] Ethernet traffic has what mathematicians call a *self-similar* nature. This means that it is bursty across all scales of time. In the short term, little pips of traffic go by. In the medium term, you get bursts of little pips. In the long term, you get huge surges of bursts, and so on.

The pattern resembles ocean waves, another well-known self-similar phenomenon. Networks experience random storms of activity where data traffic will exceed all previous maximums and then, like the tide, recede to a lower level. On a long-term scale, the network looks as random as it does on a short-term scale. There is no grand scale across which behavior averages out. A truly self-similar process has no average, normal, or steady-state behavior. Everything remains in a constant state of change.

Self-similar patterns are sometimes generated by *chaotic* processes. Chaos theory is the branch of mathematics that attempts to study these processes. Chaotic behavior is often the result of nonlinear, coupled systems that face a maximum cutoff point, or threshold, beyond which they cannot proceed. Ethernet is such a system.

---

[17] As with any general rule, there are exceptions. Manufacturers of closed-loop control systems for aerospace, transportation, and manufacturing operations often construct networks with predictable, repetitive traffic patterns. Such networks are not chaotic; office networks are.

[18] Will E. Leland, Murad S. Taqqu, Walter Willinger, and Daniel V. Wilson, "On the Self-Similar Nature of Ethernet Traffic," *ACM Transactions on Networking*, Feb. 1994.

example of a chaotic process is the Dow Jones Industrial Average.[19] Try looking at the Dow every hour, on the hour, for a week; then predict where it will be in a year. This is the sort of problem network managers face when they attempt to predict the performance of tomorrow's networks based on today's measurements.

Characterizing a Network

If there were a way to smooth out network traffic, to calm its chaotic nature, then the bottlenecks and sticking points would become obvious. This is the "big idea" behind network modeling.

The modeling process starts like this:

- Build an abstract model of your network.
- Apply synthetic data to it, called the *offered load.*
- Simulate its performance with the synthetic data.
- Take measurements from the simulation.

The simulator predicts a number of important variables including delay, buffering requirements, and packet loss due to congestion.

The next step in the modeling process is usually to apply some new element to the network model, perhaps a bridge, router, switch, Fast Ethernet upgrade, or some other change. Then the network is resimulated with the same traffic to show the improved performance.

Some simulators are sophisticated enough to automatically increment the offered load until the network reaches some predefined critical level of congestion. The simulator then reports the throughput attained. With such a simulator, after inserting the new elements, one would expect the reported capacity to increase. Presumably, the simulated results coincide with what would really happen in your network were it to experience traffic patterns corresponding to the synthetic data model.

The accuracy of the modeling process hinges on three factors:

1. **Was the model put together correctly?** In large networks, it is difficult to get an accurate description of who connects where to what. The configuration may even change while you are in your office doing the simulation. Fortunately, this is not

---

[19] Peters, Edgar, E., *Chaos and Order in the Capital Markets*, John Wiley & Sons, Inc., New York, NY: 1991.

a critical factor. If you get the main servers and user pools in the right places, little changes in traffic will not make that much difference to your conclusions.

2. **Does the synthetic data represent actual network data?** This is a key concern. Simulated data patterns often represent a heavy, continuous load (such as a Poisson traffic model).[20] Real data packets are chaotic. The difference in many cases invalidates the simulation.

3. **Is the simulator itself accurate?** The least of your worries. Modern simulator programs are themselves extremely accurate. The problem is with the data fed to them, not their internal operations. As they say in the mainframe world, *Garbage In, Garbage Out (GIGO).*

Vendors of simulation software have invented many clever schemes to combat the GIGO problem. One scheme involves capturing data from your actual working network. These traffic patterns are captured on disk and then played back through the simulator in non-real time. The data playback approach permits the simulation of before-and-after comparisons using real packet traffic from your actual system.

At first look, this approach appears to circumvent the "chaotic data" representation problem. It captures real patterns of traffic and then uses them to represent your network. The problem is that real network traffic is chaotic. A sampling of network traffic does not even begin to adequately represent a real network. For example, traffic collected on Friday afternoon may little resemble the traffic on Monday morning. The representation problem is almost completely intractable. Sampling your network traffic is no more accurate than asking users if they are experiencing delays, congestion, and aggravation.

It is important to realize that even the most sophisticated modeling tools provide little more than an educated guess about actual network performance.

Characterizing Part of a Network

Prospects for characterizing one piece of a network, as opposed to a whole network, are considerably brighter. For example, the performance

---

[20] The Poisson model, though random over short intervals, averages out to a smooth, continuous, and very predictable amount of traffic in the long term. This is the opposite of chaotic data packets, which have no such long-term average.

of a client-server link, with no other network traffic, is very repeatable and easily measured. Measuring the performance of one link is easy. Predicting overall network performance is hard.

There are (at least) four ways to characterize the speed of a common client—server configuration (see Table 2.8).

Table 2.8 Ways to Characterize a Client-Server Link

Parameter or Test	Test Conditions
Maximum instantaneous data transfer speed	Transceiver data transmission speed is 100 Mb/s for all 100BASE-T transceivers.
Non-contested transmission rate	Measured from client (or server) into the ether. No one requests, receives, or acknowledges these packets. Result is plotted versus packet size.
Perform-3 Point-to-point mode	A point-to-point file transmission test between client and server. These measurements are taken versus file size. A full request/acknowledgment protocol is used.
Perform-3 Multipoint mode	From one server, data packets fan out to N clients. Measurements are taken versus file size. A full request/acknowledgment protocol is used.

The first test is not really a test at all, it is just a data sheet specification. As such, it specifies the maximum possible throughput we could ever get on a link. For all 100BASE-T transceivers, the maximum instantaneous data transfer speed is 100 Mb/s. The throughput attained in actual practice depends on other factors in the system.

The second test is a little more realistic. This test measures the unused space, called *interpacket gap*, between packets. If there is no gap, the network is maximally efficient, and the non-contested transmission rate equals the maximum instantaneous rate. The results generally appear in a graph showing the non-contested transmission rate as a function of packet size. At smaller sizes, the network is less efficient, because at small packet sizes the ever-present gaps form a larger percentage of each packet. Note that this test measures only transmission efficiency and has nothing to do with the receiver. An example graph showing non-contested transmission rate versus packet size for one of the first Fast Ethernet prototype adapters appears in Figure 2.23.[21]

One factor that causes gaps between packets is the Ethernet MAC protocol itself. The MAC enforces a gap of 96 bits between packets. In addition, the MAC uses 208 more bits to encode the preamble, address, length, and CRC fields. The packets counted in the throughput measurement exclude the gap, preamble, address, length, and CRC fields. These fields cause efficiency to suffer at small packet sizes.[22] The best case efficiency for a packet of N bits is therefore $N/(N + 96 + 208)$.

Other factors causing inefficiencies include buffering limitations in the MAC implementation and general slowness in the upper software layers. The transmit test usually creates one test packet in memory and retransmits it repeatedly, so disk speed rarely matters in this test.

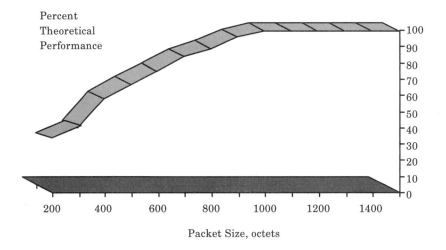

Figure 2.23 Non-Contested Transmission Rate vs. Packet Size; Fast Ethernet Adapter with NDIS Driver (Data Courtesy of 3Com Corporation)

---

[21] This early data was taken in 1993. Development progress since that time has improved performance.

[22] Efficiency is the ratio of data throughput to maximum instantaneous data transfer speed.

The curve plotted in Figure 2.23 begins with a steep slope and then flattens as it approaches 100%. For packets larger than 1000 bytes, the gap becomes totally insignificant.

The third test, Perform-3, involves both transmitter and receiver. In this test, popularized by Novell, the server attempts to transfer complete files to and from a designated client. Each file is broken up into a number of packets, sent across the network, and reassembled at the far end. The average *delivered data* rate, as a function of file size, is plotted. The data packets in this test are usually quite large. The Perform-3 test is easy to run, and the results are often illuminating.

The point-to-point Perform-3 test involves a longer chain of events inside the client and server than do the previous two tests. Data must be retrieved from memory, transferred to the MAC, sent across the network, received, and stored at the far end. A bottleneck at any of these points will reduce efficiency. This test loads the network with request/acknowledge packets along with the data packets. Messages carried in the request/acknowledge packets do not count as delivered data in the reported statistics.

The fourth test may also be run using Novell's Perform-3 software. This test, in multipoint mode, fans data out from one server to multiple clients. This is the most realistic of the four tests. The file transfer rate from the server, as a function of file size, is plotted.

Figure 2.24 displays the results of Performs-3 testing as measured in both point-to-point (1 client) and multipoint (2 client) modes.[23] In both modes, performance climbs as packet size increases. The multipoint (2 client) results are better. This is natural, because there is less bottlenecking in the client adapters. As the number of clients in a multipoint test are increased, the performance results keep creeping up. Eventually, for very large numbers of clients, the test tends to measure only the performance of the server and the network. Individual client performance becomes irrelevant.

To supplement these basic tests, many network installers and consultants have devised their own ways of gauging performance. One general technique, called *stress testing*, directly addresses the problem of network congestion.

In a stress test, performance is measured while imposing some external stress on the system. The idea is to see how the system holds

---

[23] Using the same 3Com prototype hardware used for Figure 2.23.

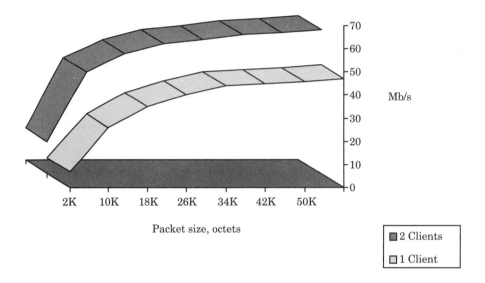

Mb/s

Packet size, octets

■ 2 Clients
□ 1 Client

Figure 2.24 Results of Perform-3 Testing with One or Two Clients (Data Courtesy of 3Com Corporation)

up while under stress. This gives you a feeling for how much excess capacity remains in the system.

Network experts induce stress in many ways. One simple way is to use a network analyzer. Configure the analyzer to blast out packets to a known destination. When the path of these test packets crosses the path of any client—server link involved in a Perform-3 test, the Perform-3 results should dip. The idea is to see how much stress (how many packets per second) the system can absorb before the Perform-3 results fall to, say, 50% of normal.

Network Planning Tip

When you are planning to expand an existing network, try stress testing the existing configuration. Dump in a few hundred extra packets per second and see if anyone complains. If no one notices, you can probably attach some more clients without worry. If you get complaints, you can comfort yourself with knowing that you found out the easy way.

Real Network Performance

Every system has a few bottlenecks. These are the points at which data must squeeze through some slow device. Typically, other devices in the network spend most of their time waiting on the bottlenecks. The bottleneck principle is universal. It applies to many systems, not just networks, that involve the flow of objects through constrained pathways.

The three simple rules given next comprise most of what is known about *Bottleneck Theory*.[24] The bottleneck model is a good way to visualize how networks really operate. This intuitive model, simple as it may sound, is quite effective. The rules apply to network components connected in series.

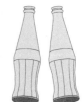

BT-1:   You can never exceed the speed of the slowest element in a path

BT-2:   Two elements in series go slower than one

BT-3:   All mixing devices are subject to congestion

Rule BT-1 is self-evident. Keep in mind that the slowest element may not always be a LAN segment, but may be a protocol stack, a client computer, or a server.

Rule BT-2 is slightly more powerful. Its most obvious application is in the case of cascaded switches. As more switches are added, network delays increase, and the transport protocols become less efficient. Performance goes down.

Rule BT-3 is a warning about mixing devices. A *mixing device* is any element, like a repeater, bridge, router, switch, or server, where traffic from several sources mixes together. This item reminds us that Perform-3 results are typically collected on an otherwise idle network. With other traffic present, results will always be worse.

Three real-world examples[25] suffice to explain how these principles work. In the first configuration (Figure 2.25), four users share one server using a simple 10BASE-T repeater. The purpose of this example was to establish a base line of Perform-3 measurements against which to measure the other configurations. All clients are continually exchanging data with the server. The Perform-3 result indicates the

---

[24] This theory was developed with the capable assistance of Mr. Colin Mick of Palo Alto, California, over a period of at least seven Margaritas.

[25] Data courtesy of the Fast Ethernet Alliance; taken from demonstration systems at Interop Fall 1994.

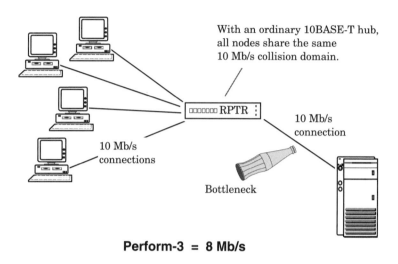

Perform-3 = 8 Mb/s

Figure 2.25 Perform-3 Testing: 10BASE-T Repeater

total effective system throughput. The total throughput in Perform-3 multipoint mode was 8 Mb/s.[26] The bottleneck here is the 10 Mb/s Ethernet link to the server. Its efficiency was 80%.

The second configuration (Figure 2.26) replaces the repeater with a 10 Mb/s switch. Switches are supposed to increase performance, and this is a perfect application for one. The switch in this example is a single-speed switch, meaning that all its ports operate at 10 Mb/s. The server connects, like the clients, to one of the 10 Mb/s switch ports.

In this experiment, a surprising thing happens. The Perform-3 multipoint mode throughput does not change. It is again 8 Mb/s. This example underscores an important point: *switch performance depends on patterns of data traffic*. Switching works best with random traffic. When everyone talks to one server (a very nonrandom case), all packets must traverse the server-to-switch link. The speed of this link then limits overall performance. In such a situation, a switch may perform no better than a repeater.

---

[26] We know, from previous experience, that the server and the clients are capable of operating at rates much higher than 8 Mb/s.

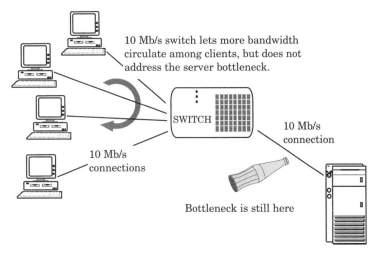

10 Mb/s switch lets more bandwidth
circulate among clients, but does not
address the server bottleneck.

SWITCH

10 Mb/s
connection

10 Mb/s
connections

Bottleneck is still here

Perform-3 = 8 Mb/s

Figure 2.26 Perform-3 Test: 10 Mb/s Switch

Single-speed switching hubs are most useful in peer-to-peer
networks where the access patterns between ports are random. A good
example of such an application might be a central switch serving several
autonomous repeater-based network segments.

The preceding example also establishes that the traffic-handling
capacity of the switch exceeds 8 Mb/s. We know this by applying the
converse of rule BT-2. Had the switch capacity been near 8 Mb/s, then it,
in series with the server link (also 8 Mb/s), would not have performed as
well as 8 Mb/s. In the example, the performance remained unchanged,
so we may assume that the switch must have been faster than 8 Mb/s.
The bottleneck is still the 10 Mb/s Ethernet server link. Its efficiency
remains at 80%.

The third and final configuration builds on an idea from the
previous example: *The speed of the server-to-switch link limits overall
performance*. If we could increase the speed of the server link, without
changing anything else, performance would increase. The right tool for
this job is called a *multirate switch* (Figure 2.27). A multirate switch
supports different speeds on its various ports. The third example uses a
multirate switch to upgrade the server connection to 100 Mb/s. Now we
have directly attacked the bottleneck.

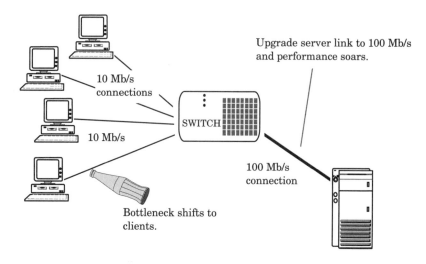

Perform-3 = 32 Mb/s

Figure 2.27 Perform-3 Test: Switch with Fast Ethernet Link

Perform-3 results, for multipoint mode, soar to 32 Mb/s. The bottleneck has shifted. It is now caused by the 10BASE-T links connected to the users. Each of these links tops out at 8 Mb/s. With each user contributing 8 Mb/s, the total system throughput equals 32 Mb/s. The numbers indicate that the switch is *still* not a bottleneck. The performance rating of 32 Mb/s (limited by the clients) indicates that this switch could support even higher throughput.

Many manufacturers now make multirate switches. These products typically have lots of switched 10 Mb/s 10BASE-T ports and a few fast 100 Mb/s ports. This convergence of switching and Fast Ethernet is very popular. The regular ports connect to the end users, and the fast ports connect to servers.

On the client side, a prime advantage of a multirate switch is that users may keep their existing 10 Mb/s 10BASE-T adapters. On the server side, the multirate switch provides more bandwidth exactly where it does the most good. A server can transmit at 100 Mb/s, and the switch will fan out the data at low speed to many clients. In the reverse direction, a number of clients can blast at 10 Mb/s, and the switch will aggregate their traffic onto the 100 Mb/s server link. A multirate switch is ideal for client—server computing.

Network Planning Tip

When planning a large Fast Ethernet installation, make sure you know the capabilities of the switch. Ask for widely accepted test results, such as the Scott Bradner reports or reports from an independent test lab. At a minimum, ask to see Perform-3 test results, with enough clients and servers connected to really see the switch limitations. Find out if the switch will be a bottleneck.

Points to Remember

- Avoid overreliance on network statistics.
- To speed up a network, first look for the bottlenecks.
- Perform-3 tests are easily run, and the results are often illuminating.
- You can never exceed the speed of the slowest element in a path.
- Two elements in series go slower than one.
- Mixing devices (like switches) are subject to congestion.

3

Detailed Guide to Fast Ethernet

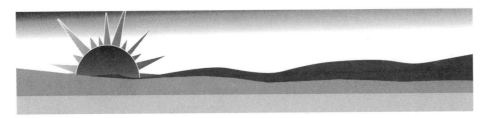

*T*he official IEEE 802.3 name for Fast Ethernet is 100BASE-T. It supplements the existing Ethernet standard, known as **IEEE Std 802.3**. Sweeping in scope, Fast Ethernet covers everything from physical-level transceivers to repeaters to management.

The full title of the Fast Ethernet supplement is:

IEEE Std 802.3u MAC Parameters, Physical Layer, Medium Attachment Units and Repeater for 100 Mb/s Operation.

The older, base Ethernet document which Fast Ethernet supplements is available as a joint ISO/IEC/ANSI/IEEE document. The latest version is dated 1993. A new version is slated for release in late 1995. The full title of the ISO edition of the base Ethernet document is:

ISO/IEC 8802-3 Carrier Sense Multiple Access with Collision Detection (CSMA/CD) Access Method & Physical Layer Specifications.

ORGANIZATION OF THE FAST ETHERNET STANDARD

This chapter reviews the major features of the Fast Ethernet (100BASE-T) standard. It shows how the parts of the standard relate to each other. It explains what options the standard allows. It will equip you with penetrating questions to ask your vendor about their new Fast Ethernet products, the kinds of questions that save money.

The technical depth presented here is not as great as in the real standard. This material is appropriate for users, buyers, strategic planners, and salespersons, not technical whiz kids. If you would like more details, please order a copy of the complete standard. See Chapter 8 for ordering details.

Before Fast Ethernet, the 802.3 standard contained twenty chapters (officially called clauses). The early clauses are numbered 1 through 20, in the order of their development. Each clause represents a different aspect of the Ethernet standard: thick coax, repeaters, Cheapernet, Broadband, 10BASE-T, fiber optic interfaces, and so on. Proponents of Fast Ethernet call the original set of twenty clauses the *base document*.

The Fast Ethernet supplement contains ten clauses. They have been assigned clause numbers 21 through 30. The package of all ten Fast Ethernet clauses is called supplement number **802.3u**, or just supplement **u**. Chapter 8 summarizes the contents of all thirty of the 802.3 clauses.

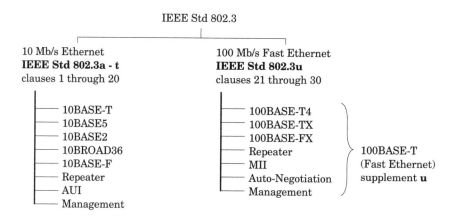

Figure 3.1 Relation of Fast Ethernet to 10 Mb/s Ethernet Standards

Because the standard is so complex, most people will not be very familiar with its details. This unfamiliarity leaves room for vendors to implement part, but not all, of the standard, without anyone noticing (at least for a while). Partial implementation is dangerous. Beware products that claim compliance to only part of the standard.

Fortunately, there is an easy way to tell if a manufacturer has implemented the complete standard. Just ask to see the *Protocol Implementation Conformance Statement* (PICS). The PICS is an official part of the standard. Every manufacturer claiming compliance with the standard must fill out a PICS. Instructions given in Clause 21 explain how to fill it out and how to interpret it. The PICS shows, clause by clause, precisely which features and options have been implemented.

Fast Ethernet Is a Supplement

Because it is a supplement, and not a separate standard, the authors of 100BASE-T took great care to guarantee exact interoperability between the old (Ethernet) parts and the new (Fast Ethernet) parts. This interoperability directly benefits users. For example, Clause 28 (Auto-Negotiation) provides a standard way for existing 10BASE-T and new Fast Ethernet devices to recognize each other and automatically switch to a mutually acceptable operating speed. Such interoperation among LAN standards is unprecedented.

There is a separate PICS for every clause of 100BASE-T (except Clauses 21, 29 and 30).

Clauses 21 through 30 each specify different aspects of Fast Ethernet operation. Figure 3.2 arranges the clauses into three groups, showing roughly how they relate to the basic 100BASE-T architecture.

As shown in Figure 3.2, the basic architecture is a hub-and-spoke configuration. From a central hub, point-to-point links radiate out to the client stations. Clause numbers appear next to the hub, cables, and clients. These numbers indicate where to find information about the various network elements. For example, Clauses 27, 29, and 30 mostly relate to the hub. Look there first for hub information. Clauses 23, 24, 25, 26, and 28 specify the physical transceivers used for various types of wire and fiber. The transceiver specifications apply equally to both

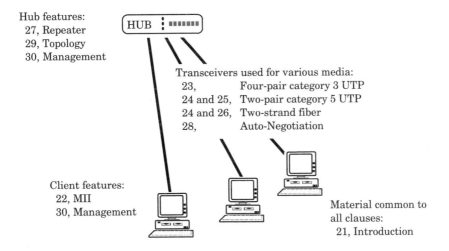

Hub features:
  27, Repeater
  29, Topology
  30, Management

HUB

Transceivers used for various media:
  23,   Four-pair category 3 UTP
  24 and 25, Two-pair category 5 UTP
  24 and 26, Two-strand fiber
  28,   Auto-Negotiation

Client features:
  22, MII
  30, Management

Material common to
all clauses:
  21, Introduction

Figure 3.2 Organization of 100BASE-T Standard

Fast Track Standard

Fast Ethernet astonished some old-time standards participants with the speed of its progress. Normally, a standard of this complexity endures years of withering debate. Fast Ethernet, in contrast, developed rather quickly. From inception (IEEE Project Authorization Request) to approval (working group ballot) took only 13 months.

Rather than fighting among themselves, the Fast Ethernet committee members displayed a rare combination of determination and cooperation. When the last vote was cast, most of the 132 representatives felt that they had participated in a timely and productive process.

---

client and hub end of every link. Clauses 22 and 30 involve the client stations. The introduction, Clause 21, contains information relevant to all parts of the system.

The remainder of this chapter explains the meaning of each clause, highlighting those aspects relevant to network equipment users. It is organized in sections, corresponding to the clauses of the Fast Ethernet standard.

Points to Remember

- Fast Ethernet and 100BASE-T are the same thing.
- Fast Ethernet is closely related to 802.3 Ethernet.
- The Fast Ethernet standard has ten clauses, organized by system area (transceivers, MII, repeaters, etc.).
- This chapter is organized into sections, corresponding to the clauses.

CHANGES TO PREVIOUS CLAUSES

An IEEE supplement can add new clauses to an existing standard, or it can change old ones. When a supplement provides significant new functionality, as does 100BASE-T, its authors often amend previous clauses to grant them the option of incorporating the new functionality. As long as the changes remain backward compatible with older equipment, no one complains.

To support 100BASE-T, changes were made in two areas of the existing 802.3 standard: Auto-Negotiation features and timing parameters. Both sets of changes appear in the front sections of supplement **802.3u**. When the supplement is eventually consolidated into a new base document, the change wording will be incorporated back into the affected clauses and stricken from the text of the supplement.

Changes Required by Auto-Negotiation

The supplement adds new wording to earlier sections granting them optional Auto-Negotiation capabilities. This wording permits the construction of dual-speed 10/100 Mb/s devices that can automatically interoperate with either existing 10BASE-T transceivers or with new, 100 Mb/s transceivers.

Changes to Timing Parameters of CSMA/CD MAC

Regarding timing parameters, the 10 Mb/s MAC specifies a bit time of 100 ns and an interpacket gap of 96 bit times, or 9.6 μs. Clause 21 defines new values for 100BASE-T. The new values specify a bit time of 10 ns and an interpacket gap of 96 bit times, now equal to 0.96 μs. These are the only adjustments required in the CSMA/CD MAC clause. These timing adjustments are trivial, all 100BASE-T products conform to them, and they are not optional. The CSMA/CD MAC algorithm is used unchanged.

Changes to Definitions, Abbreviations and References

Supplement **802.3u** contains an enormous number of definitions, abbreviations, and references. Don't panic. Not all this material relates to 100BASE-T. Supplement **802.3u** consolidates for the first time all the definitions, references, and abbreviations from previous 802.3 supplements. Items peculiar to 100BASE-T add to these rather lengthy lists.

If you have trouble locating a reference, please note that the reference section is broken into two pieces. The first piece, which specifies normative changes to Clause 1.3, contains references to CISPR, IEC, and ISO international documents. The second piece, which is formatted as an informative annex, contains references to ANSI, EIA, TIA, IEEE, FCC, UL, and other North-American standards. Supplement **802.3u** completely reworks both pieces, adding necessary 100BASE-T references at the same time.

Why Keep CSMA/CD?

At the time that 802.3 formed the Higher Speed Study Group, some members proposed radical changes to the low-level Media Access Control (MAC) protocol. After all, CSMA/CD had lasted roughly ten years, and there was a certain feeling that it was time for a change.

After a period of struggle, the 802.3 committee decided to retain CSMA/CD. There were many reasons for the decision, including these key points:

Large prior investment in CSMA/CD. Proponents of alternative MAC algorithms argued that, to users, the MAC protocol was irrelevant, but experienced network personnel knew better. It takes a long time to understand a protocol. Understanding is the only tool that really solves network problems. After many years, network managers, installers, and maintenance people really understand CSMA/CD. This knowledge is extremely valuable.

Uncertainty of change. With CSMA/CD, users would know what they were getting. With a new protocol, anything could happen. For example, FDDI underestimated the burden of station management. Token Ring overlooked technical problems with clock jitter. ATM argued for years about classes of guaranteed latency performance. New protocols always bring new problems. With something already developed (like CSMA/CD), such uncertainty would evaporate.

Lengthy development of MAC protocols. A standard that missed the market window would serve no one. Members predicted that reuse of the CSMA/CD protocol would cut months (perhaps years) off the development schedule. It did.

Points to Remember

- Fast Ethernet uses the CSMA/CD MAC unchanged.
- The standard permits construction of dual-speed 10/100 Mb/s devices.
- Supplement **u** consolidates all 802.3 definitions, references, and abbreviations.

100BASE-T INTRODUCTION (CLAUSE 21)

Clause 21 serves two purposes:

1. It positions 100BASE-T within the OSI reference model.
2. It contains information common to all 100BASE-T clauses.

OSI Reference Model

The relation of 100BASE-T to the OSI Reference Model appears in Figure 3.3. This figure has been adapted from Figure 21-1 in the standard.

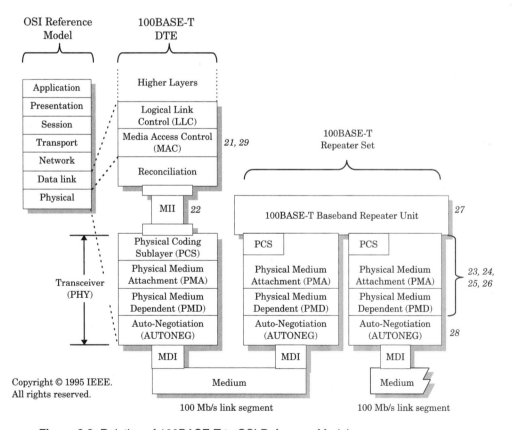

Figure 3.3 Relation of 100BASE-T to OSI Reference Model

The now-famous OSI seven-layer representation of network systems was standardized in 1984. All network standards tout their relation to it. The complete text for all seven layers may be found in **ISO 7498:1984**, *Information processing systems — open systems interconnection — Basic reference model*. The model calls out what types of functions are contained in each layer, but specifies neither the layers themselves nor the interfaces between them. It is a fuzzy document. Modern network operating systems rarely implement the top three layers (Application, Presentation, and Session). These are left to the discretion of application developers. Other layers (like the network layer) are sometimes skipped altogether.[1] The OSI model is useful mainly for comparing different network systems within a common framework.

Many people understandably confuse the source of this document, the *International Standards Organization* or ISO, with OSI, which stands for the Open Systems Interconnection model. This unfortunate choice of acronyms probably seemed cute to its authors. The confusion is not helped by the fact that the true name of ISO is not the International Standards Organization, but rather the *International Organization for Standards*.

In the OSI reference model, 100BASE-T Clauses 22 through 28 (MII, PHYs, Repeater and Auto-Negotiation) reside within the OSI Physical Layer. Clause 21 (which affects MAC timing) and Clause 29 (topology) mostly relate to the OSI Data Link layer. Clause 30 (management) is not represented in the OSI hierarchy.

The following terms and acronyms commonly appear in discussions of the OSI reference model:

Auto-Negotiation *(AUTONEG)*	This sublayer provides extensive support for determination of link options and optimal settings.[2] With Auto-Negotiation enabled, an adapter card may determine for itself what the capabilities are at the far end of the link and select the best operational mode as needed. See Clause 28.

---

[1] The characteristics of the seven layers are best described by Andrew S. Tanenbaum, *Computer Networks*, 2nd ed., Upper Saddle River, NJ. Prentice Hall:1988.

[2] In early drafts, this function was called *NWAY*.

Carrier Sense Multiple Access with Collision Detection (CSMA/CD)	MAC algorithm used in Ethernet. See Chapter 1, *Ethernet Control System*. Fast Ethernet uses the same CSMA/CD MAC protocol used in regular Ethernet, except for a 10 times faster bit rate. It connects to higher-layer protocols (that is, your computer I/O bus and NDIS driver) in precisely the same way as regular Ethernet.
Data Terminal Equipment (DTE)	A hoary old term that harks back to the early days of punch-card computing. It was originally used to differentiate between a remote computer terminal (DTE) and its associated modem (*data communications equipment*, or DCE). Today, generally, it refers to the computer on your desk. In Ethernet systems, specifically, it refers to any host system that contains a MAC. That could include a PC, workstation, server, switch port, bridge, or router.
ISO Model for Open Systems Interconnection (OSI)	A famous seven-layer representation of network systems. The complete text for all seven layers may be found in **ISO 7498:1984**, *Information processing systems — open systems interconnection — Basic reference model*.
Logical Link Control (LLC)	A protocol sublayer defined in a separate IEEE standard, called 802.2. The 100BASE-T system uses the LLC sublayer unchanged. Therefore, no references to the LLC appear in Clauses 21 through 30. The interface between LLC and MAC usually occurs in driver software just above the Ethernet adapter card in a client workstation.
Media Access Control (MAC)	A general term for any protocol sublayer used to control access to a shared communication medium. It determines who transmits, and when.
Media Independent Interface (MII)	A simple, inexpensive interconnection between a network adapter and an external Fast Ethernet transceiver. It supports all the standard 802.3 Fast Ethernet transceivers. The *Reconciliation sublayer* is an integral part of the MII. Its specification appears in Clause 22.
Medium	The 802.3 standard uses the word *medium* to refer to the wire (or fiber) that links nodes. Figure 3.3 shows one complete link from DTE to repeater and

one other link leading from the repeater to an unknown destination (jagged end on medium symbol). The word *media* is just the plural of *medium*.

Medium Dependent Interface (MDI)

A fancy name for *connector*. Connectors for T4, TX and FX are specified along with the PMD or PMA sublayer of each transceiver type.

Physical Coding Sublayer (PCS)

A sublayer of the PHY. Responsible for coding transmitted data into a form suitable for the physical medium and decoding it at the receiver.

Physical Layer Device (PHY)

Official term for *transceiver*. The PHY contains the analog circuitry necessary to communicate with the physical medium.

The PHY is a combination of the PCS, PMA, PMD, and AUTONEG sublayers. The PHY may be located either external to a host computer (external transceiver) or embedded onto an adapter.

Physical Medium Attachment Sublayer (PMA)

A sublayer of the PHY. In conjunction with the PMD, it is responsible for analog functions like transmit wave-shaping and receive data discrimination.

Physical Medium Dependent Sublayer (PMD)

A sublayer of the PHY. In TX and FX transceivers, this sublayer is borrowed from FDDI. In T4 transceivers, the PMD functionality resides within the PMA sublayer.

Repeater Set

An entire functional repeater, including the repeater unit (the core) and its associated transceivers. A repeater set couples together DTEs into a single collision domain.

Repeater Unit

This term is used in Clause 27 to refer to the logical inner workings of a repeater (the *core*). A repeater unit connects to the physical medium through many of the same sublayers used in the DTE.

Organization of T4 and X Clauses

Clause 21 introduces three *transceiver types*.[3] These transceivers go by the popular names T4, TX, and FX. The standard splits their definitions across Clauses 23 through 26. Figure 3.4 shows the relations between clauses and transceiver types

Clause 23 stands alone as a complete specification of the T4 transceiver. Clause 24, the opening clause for the X family of transceivers, specifies elements common to both TX and FX transceivers. Clauses 25 and 26 contain low-level specifications for TX and FX, respectively. These low-level specifications are borrowed from ANSI FDDI specifications. The collection of all three Clauses 24, 25, and 26, representing both TX and FX transceivers, is called 100BASE-X.

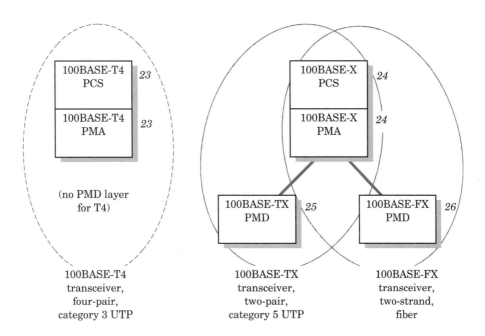

Figure 3.4 100BASE-T Physical Level Transceiver Standards

---

[3] The term *transceiver* refers to any *Physical Layer Device* (PHY), whether it be connected via an external MII interface, embedded in an adapter card, or integrated onto a computer motherboard.

The T4, TX, and FX transceivers are all quite different. They use different signaling conventions, require different numbers of wire pairs, and support different types of cabling.

Material Common to All Clauses

Clause 21 includes a list of abbreviations used by other clauses, defines terms used in the Protocol Implementation Conformance Statements (PICS), and explains how to interpret the Fast Ethernet state diagrams.

If the state diagrams in the standard interest you, take the time to read the typographical conventions listed in Clause 21.5. Some of the state diagram symbols have peculiar meanings, especially open-ended arrows.

Points to Remember

- 100BASE-T is a physical layer specification.
- 100BASE-T specifies multiple transceiver types: T4, TX, and FX.

MEDIA INDEPENDENT INTERFACE (CLAUSE 22)

Clause 22 consists of two parts: the *Media Independent Interface* (MII) and the *Reconciliation sublayer*. These two sublayers, working together, replace the older 10 Mb/s AUI standard. In 10 Mb/s Ethernet, the AUI provided a detachable point of interconnection between an adapter card and a transceiver. Any 10 Mb/s transceiver could plug into the adapter. The MII provides the same function in 100BASE-T. Any of the 100BASE-T transceivers can plug into an MII (see Figure 2.2). Figure 3.5 illustrates the relation of the Reconciliation sublayer and the MII to other protocol layers in a 100BASE-T DTE.

The terms and acronyms below are used when speaking about the MII:

Media Independent Interface (MII)	The MII specifies the signal characteristics, connectors, and cable lengths that convey information from the Reconciliation sublayer to the PHY.
Reconciliation sublayer	The Reconciliation sublayer is what we standards experts call a "weenie" sublayer. It translates the

terminology used in the MAC into the terminology appropriate for the MII sublayer. That's it. To the MAC, it is a transparent, functionless sublayer. Signals just pass through it. There are no options, configuration choices, or user-accessible features in the Reconciliation sublayer.

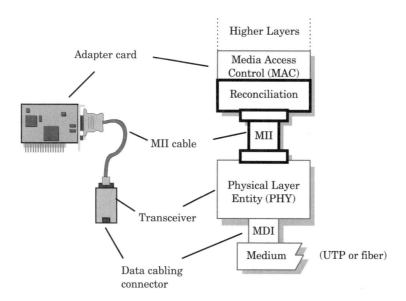

Figure 3.5 Where MII Fits in DTE Layer Stack

MII: New Features

The MII uses a clocked, nibble-wide (4-bit) data path in each direction. The clock rate for Fast Ethernet operation is 25 MHz. The MII data transfer speed is 4 bits x 25 MHz = 100 Mb/s. Compared to the older AUI interface, the MII has ten times the bandwidth. Physically, the MII provides a symmetrical interface, with data, clock, and control signals flowing in both directions. To carry all these signals, the MII connector uses 40 pins.

The MII incorporates some new error-control features. As a result, 100BASE-T can improve on the already extraordinary error robustness of Ethernet through the use of *block coding* (see box entitled *Block Coding*). Earlier Ethernet implementations had to wait for the 32-bit CRC at the end of a packet to detect errors. The 100BASE-T system uses the same 32-bit CRC, but can additionally use block coding to catch errors that happen midstream. Block coding errors are detected in the PHY sublayers.

The MII conveys block coding errors detected by the PHY to the MAC and management. It does so over two error-propagation signals new to Ethernet: RX_ER and TX_ER. In conjunction with block coding, these circuits make it virtually impossible for an erroneous packet to sneak through undetected. The circuits do not decrease the chances of a packet getting hit with noise; they just make sure that, if it does, the packet will be discarded by the MAC. The RX_ER signal is used by a DTE. When the PHY detects an error, RX_ER informs the MAC. The TX_ER signal is used by a repeater. It enforces propagation of block coding errors in order that they may be detected with certainty by the MAC in every receiving device.

Block Coding

100BASE-T uses a technology called *block coding*. Block coding improves the error-detecting properties of a data-transmission system.

Before transmission, block coding first links groups of bits into indivisible entities, called *code blocks*. The coding process then maps each block to a distinctive waveform pattern and transmits it. The receiver converts the waveform patterns back into code blocks. The error detection properties derive from the clever assignment of code blocks to waveform patterns.

A good block code defines many more possible waveform patterns than it needs. Only a fraction of the possible waveform patterns are used to represent valid code blocks. As a result, random errors often produce invalid waveform patterns. Detection of an invalid waveform pattern informs the receiver that an error has happened.

MII: Options

The entire MII is optional. If a manufacturer chooses to implement the MII, here are the MII options:

10/100 Mb/s

The MII specification supports dual-speed operation. Transceivers and adapter cards, however, may not. For dual-speed operation to work, both transceiver and adapter must also work at both speeds.

- MII clock for 100 Mb/s operation is 25.0 MHz.
- MII clock for 10 Mb/s operation is 2.5 MHz.

3.3V/5V logic

Every year, more vendors build low-voltage systems. Lower power supply voltages save power, prolonging battery life in portable products. Lower-voltage chips are smaller, reducing costs. Today, 5-V systems dominate. Tomorrow, the situation could change.

All logic signals on the MII support operation with either 3.3-V or 5-V logic. This permits use of the MII standard in future systems with low-voltage logic.

Regardless of the logic voltages used on either side of the MII, the MII standard calls for a fixed power voltage of +5 V. As 3.3-V systems become more common, this fixed specification will appear progressively more awkward. Eventually, some manufacturers may choose to circumvent this part of the standard. If you purchase a non-standard MII product that supplies 3.3-V power, make sure your transceivers will work with it.

Full duplex

Transmit and receive paths across the MII operate independently, so the MII naturally supports full-duplex operation. To gain the advantages of full-duplex operation, other system components must support full duplex as well:

- The local transceiver must have full-duplex capability.
- The local adapter must have full-duplex capability.
- The local transceiver must connect, by way of a point-to-point link, to another device with full-duplex capability.

Assuming that full-duplex capability *exists* at both ends of a link, it must also be *enabled* at both ends. For example, consider what happens if only one end of a link enables full-duplex mode. Full-duplex transmissions from one end would look like collisions to the other. The Auto-Negotiation standard (Clause 28) provides a useful way to manage the full-duplex settings, provided that both ends support that standard.

MII: Applications

Manufacturers are permitted, if they so choose, to squeeze all the DTE sublayers onto a single adapter card (or onto a computer motherboard). Such an implementation would not have an exposed MII. Only the data cabling connector (MDI) would appear on the adapter. There exists no standard name for such an implementation, although the terms *embedded transceiver*, *collapsed MII,* and *integrated adapter* are often used (Figure 3.6). Embedded MII designs enjoy the same cost advantages as embedded transceivers in Cheapernet and 10BASE-T (see *Cheapernet* in Chapter 1).

Adapters built to work with external transceivers always use the standard MII connector. An external transceiver has the option of providing a second MII connector, with polarity opposite that on the adapter, or of providing a permanently attached MII drop cord. If the external transceiver provides an MII connector, then an MII cable must be purchased to connect it to the adapter.

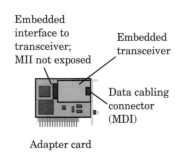

Embedded interface to transceiver; MII not exposed

Embedded transceiver

Data cabling connector (MDI)

Adapter card

Figure 3.6 Adapter with Embedded MII

Figure 3.7 depicts an MII connector. Symmetrical sets of transmit and receive signals cluster around the middle. The bottom row is all ground pins (except for +5V on the ends).

Although it looks like an RS-232 connector, it has more pins and will not work with an ordinary data break-out box. Adventurous network technicians who might like to construct their own custom break-out instrument should study the box entitled *MII Break-Out Box.*

The standard permits hot-plugging the MII connector (that is, plugging it in while power is applied to your computer). Beware that, while this may work, it is still good practice to power off your equipment while changing connectors.

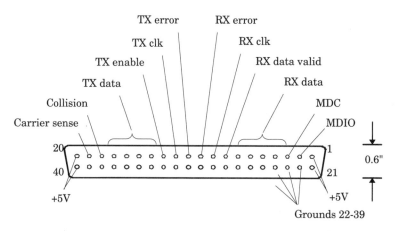

Figure 3.7 MII Connector

MII Break-Out Box

The MII signals can help debug broken transceivers and adapters, if you know what to observe. All signals use TTL logic levels with positive polarity.

The packet bursts happen very quickly. Use a pulse-stretching circuit to lengthen the bursts for display on LEDs.

Carrier sense. Indicates activity on the cable, either incoming or outgoing. Driven by the transceiver.

Collision. For half-duplex transceivers, indicates simultaneous transmission and reception. Full-duplex transceivers never activate this signal. Driven by the transceiver.

TX enable. Set by DTE or repeater while transmitting. *SET BY TX*

TX clk. 25 MHz for 100BASE-T. Driven by the transceiver. Runs continuously.

TX error. Set by repeater to force propagation of received errors. Never set by DTE.

RX error. Set by transceiver on detection of received error. The presence of errors often indicates bad wiring.

RX clk. 25 MHz for 100BASE-T. Driven by the transceiver. Runs continuously.

RX data valid. Set by transceiver while receiving a valid packet. The presence of carrier sense, but not RX data valid, indicates reception of broken packet headers, probably due to bad wiring or a broken transceiver.

MDC, MDIO. Serial management interface. MDC is driven by the adapter. MDIO is bi-directional.

MII: Management Features

The old AUI provided no way to interrogate or control a transceiver. By design, transceivers were rather simple, bit-repeating entities. The new MII is more intelligent and more flexible. It can be extended to support future transceiver options.

Every MII incorporates a simple, two-wire serial control bus, called the management interface. Using the management interface, an adapter card can gather status from a transceiver, and it can also control the transceiver. The management interface consists of the MDC and MDIO wires on the MII connector.

Transceivers embedded on an adapter card may also use the management interface. When buying an embedded transceiver, ask if it supports the management interface.

The management interface specifies a set of 32 registers divided into four groups (Table 3.1). Each register holds 16 bits. The management data model assumes that the registers reside in the transceiver (PHY). The interface allows the management entity, on the adapter side of the interface, to read and write the registers.

Table 3.1 Management Register Groups

Group	Register Addresses
Basic	0,1
Extended	2-7
Reserved	8-15
Vendor-specific	16-31

Every MII-based transceiver supports the basic register set. Definitions of the basic registers appear in Table 3.2. Extended registers 2 through 7 are optional. The extended registers provide, among other things, a unique PHY-type identifier and extensive control of the Auto-Negotiation process. The PHY-type identifier allows management to figure out how to interpret the vendor-specific registers.

The standard holds registers 8 through 15 in reserve for future applications. The standard exercises no control over registers 16 through 32. They are vendor specific.

Table 3.2 Basic Management Registers

Control Register 0. Written By Adapter.

Reg. Bit	Description
0.15	Reset transceiver.
0.14	Place transceiver in loop back mode for testing.
0.13	Speed selection: 10 or 100 Mb/s. Applies to transceivers with dual-speed capability.
0.12	Enable Auto-Negotiation process, if transceiver is so equipped.
0.11	Place transceiver in low power consumption state.
0.10	Electrically isolate transceiver from MII. Used in dual-transceiver configuration to enable only one transceiver.
0.09	Restart Auto-Negotiation.
0.08	Enable full-duplex mode, if transceiver is so equipped.
0.07	Test the collision signal.
0.00 – 06	Reserved

Status Register 1. Read By Adapter.

Reg. Bit	Description
1.15 – 11	Report transceiver capabilities: T4 or X, full or half duplex, 10 or 100 Mb/s.
1.06 – 10	Reserved
1.05	Indicates that Auto-Negotiation process is complete.
1.04	Indicates that a fault at the other end of the link (remote fault or far end fault) has been detected.
1.03	Indicates that transceiver has Auto-Negotiation capability.
1.02	Link status: up or down.
1.01	Jabber condition detected.
1.00	Indicates that transceiver supports extended management registers 2 through 7.

Every transceiver (PHY) implements its own set of registers. Each transceiver is also assigned a PHY address. The address feature permits one management entity to control many PHYs. Repeaters make good use of the address feature.

Another interesting use of the PHY management address feature is the *dual transceiver configuration* (see Figure 3.8). In this configuration, the adapter manufacturer has opted to include an embedded transceiver. The embedded transceiver is a 100BASE-TX transceiver (two-pair, category 5 UTP). The adapter also provides a standard MII port. This port may connect to a second external transceiver. The figure shows an external 100BASE-FX fiber transceiver connected to the MII port. Only one transceiver, or the other, may be activated at any given time.

In a dual-transceiver configuration, most vendors presume that if an external transceiver is connected it is the one you wish to use. Provisions are sometimes made to override this choice. Ask your vendor if you have to set a switch, push a button, or whatever, to override the automatic choice.

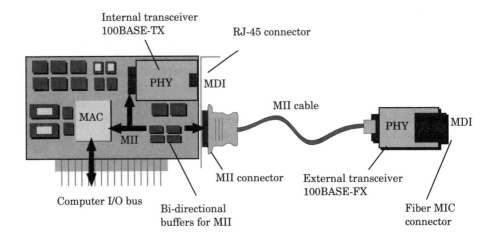

Figure 3.8 Dual Transceiver Configuration

Points to Remember

The MII always supports dual-speed operation, full duplex, and either 3.3-V or 5-V power. This is easy to do because it is just a connector. Other parts of the system must be checked carefully.

Questions to Ask

- Is the transceiver dual speed? Is the adapter?
- Does the transceiver have a full-duplex mode? Does the adapter?
- If both transceiver and adapter support full duplex, is Auto-Negotiation implemented? If not, what scheme determines when to switch to full duplex? Are jumper settings or software settings necessary?
- If the MII provides a non-standard power voltage (like 3.3 V) will the transceivers work at that voltage?
- Does the transceiver support the extended management registers 2 through 7? If yes, what is its PHY identifier?
- Does the transceiver support vendor-specific management registers 16 through 31? What do they do? Do they work with your adapter software?
- Does the adapter support a dual transceiver configuration? If so, are software settings or jumpers required to activate the external transceiver?

100BASE-T4 TRANSCEIVER (CLAUSE 23)

Clause 23 defines two sublayers, PCS and PMA, plus supporting information about cabling, connectors, timing, and other details. The combination of PCS and PMA sublayers is called the T4 transceiver, or 100BASE-T4 *Physical Layer Device* (PHY) in standards terminology.

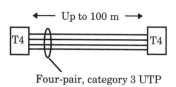

Four-pair, category 3 UTP

Relations between the T4 transceiver and other protocol sublayers are illustrated in Figure 3.9. In this figure, the T4 transceiver connects above to the Media Independent Interface (MII). It connects below to a piece of unshielded twisted-pair (UTP) cable.

In Figure 3.9, the block labeled MDI, standing between the transceiver and the cable, represents an ordinary RJ-45-type cable connector. The term MDI stands for *Medium Dependent Interface*.

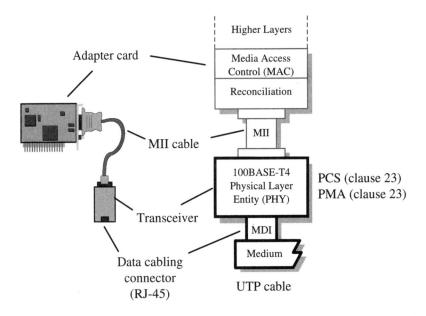

Figure 3.9 100BASE-T4 Layer Stack

100BASE-T4: Distinguishing Features

Cabling. The T4 transceiver requires 4 pairs of category 3, 4, or 5 unshielded twisted-pair cable. See section *100BASE-T4: Cables and Connectors* for more information.

Nominal Network Diameter. The maximum separation between any two T4 devices in the same collision domain is called the maximum collision domain diameter. The maximum collision domain diameter, for a pure T4 network, is about 200 m. This diameter may be increased somewhat by incorporating FX fiber links (see *Topology* this chapter).

The diameter limitation derives from a very simple rule: no T4 link may exceed 100 m. With a single repeater, the farthest separated T4 devices can be no more than 200 m apart. With more repeaters, it so happens that the maximum diameter does not improve.

Using a Class I repeater with translating capability, T4 devices may participate in the same collision domain with fiber links. Fiber links can be longer than 100 m. The use of fiber does increase the maximum diameter (see *Topology* this chapter).

Any repeater or switch may incorporate a full-duplex bridged connection to an FX fiber port that can span 2 km or more. See *100BASE-FX: Distances* later in this chapter.

Use of Wire Pairs. The T4 signaling scheme requires four wire pairs. It spreads the transmitted data out among several pairs, reducing the transmitted bandwidth on each. A reduced signaling bandwidth simplifies the circuitry needed to recover the data, making the system more robust. Figure 3.10 shows how the T4 transceiver manages the four twisted pairs at its disposal.

Figure 3.10 illustrates a complete T4 link, with a client device on the left and a hub on the right. Each side transmits data on three pairs. An important feature of the T4 transmission architecture is that the

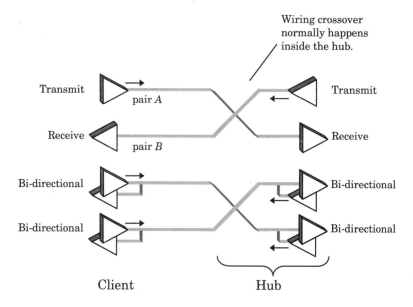

Figure 3.10 100BASE-T4 Use of Wire Pairs

client and hub transmit on *different sets of pairs*. In Figure 3.10, the client transmits on pair *A*, plus the bottom two pairs. The hub transmits on pair *B*, plus the bottom two pairs. Pairs *A* and *B* are used unidirectionally.

The uni-directional pairs ensure that each device can always hear the other, even while transmitting. For example, the client in Figure 3.10 can always hear the hub on its uni-directional receive pair. The client can, therefore, easily sense collisions.

The bi-directional pairs (bottom two pairs) do not provide higher throughput or improved collision resolution properties compared to other 100BASE-T transceivers. They just bring the T4 data rate up to a full 100 Mb/s.

Data Coding. T4 does not send data directly on each pair in binary format. It codes the data first. The coding scheme is called 8B6T coding. Coding accomplishes several objectives:

- Lowers the symbol transmission rate, making it easier for signals to pass through the cabling, and easier for products to pass internationally mandated radio-frequency emissions tests.
- Strips the signal of DC bias, permitting use of inexpensive transformer coupling without sophisticated DC restoration circuitry.
- Embeds enough transitions in the data to keep clock recovery locked.
- Establishes a signaling rate on each pair exactly equal to the MII clock rate of 25.00 MHz; as a result T4 needs no PLL circuitry for its transmit clock.

8B6T coding, as used with 100BASE-T4 signaling, first fans the data out onto three pairs (Figure 3.11). The effective data rate carried on each pair is one-third of 100 Mb/s, which is 33.333... Mb/s. On each pair, it then maps each octet to a pattern of six ternary symbols, called a 6T code group. The ternary symbol transmission rate on each pair is three-quarters times 33.33 Mb/s, or precisely 25.000 MHz.

Signals transmitted on each pair are ternary, meaning that at each signaling instant, or baud, the signal can have one of three levels. Such a signal can convey more information per baud than a binary, or two-level, signal (see Figure 3.12).

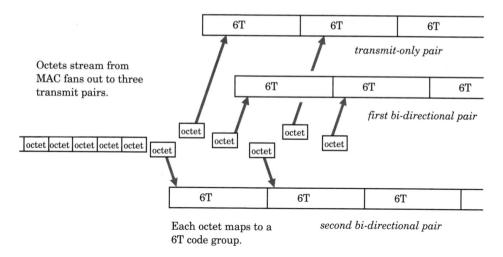

Figure 3.11 8B6T Coding

8B6T Coding Summary

The T4 transceiver accepts nibbles from the MII and assembles them in pairs into octets. The octets then fan out to the three transmit pairs in round robin-fashion. Before transmission, the transceiver applies 8B6T coding to each octet. The coding process maps each octet into a group of six ternary, or three-level, symbols. The receiver reverses the process.

The data rate per pair is one-third of 100 Mb/s, or 33.333 Mb/s. The transition rate on each pair is three-quarters of that rate, or 25.00 MHz.

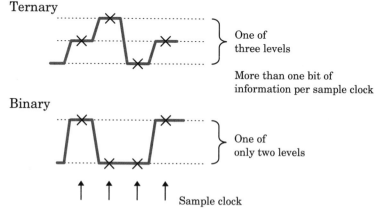

Figure 3.12 Ternary and Binary Signals

100BASE-T4: Other Features

We have already discussed cabling, network diameter, and data coding. Next let's look at carrier detection, link integrity, and error robustness. Figure 3.13 depicts where these functions fit inside a T4 transceiver.

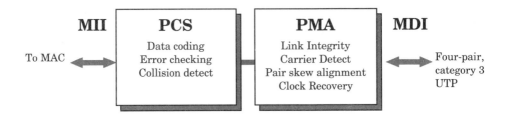

Figure 3.13 Functional Block Diagram of T4 PHY

Carrier Detection. The T4 transceiver incorporates a smart squelch algorithm. This function prevents the transceiver from activating its carrier signal until the incoming signal has qualified itself with a battery of three tests (see box entitled *Smart Squelch—100BASE-T4*). The three tests prevent spurious activation of carrier upon the occurrence of impulse noise that may occasionally be present on the wires. The same tests also prevent the receiver activating carrier upon reception of valid link integrity pulses from the far end.

Link Integrity. The link integrity function protects the network from the consequences of a critical failure of the wiring. When such a failure is detected, the link integrity function disables the transceiver.

In the absence of a link integrity function, a transceiver could conceivably transmit without regard to colliding traffic, clogging the

---

Smart Squelch—100BASE-T4

To activate the carrier, an incoming signal must first transcend 750 mV, then fall more negative than -250 mV, and finally exceed the 750-mV threshold once again.

From an idle condition, it takes errors on at least three symbols to cause a false carrier event. Such a pattern of errors is rather improbable.

network with late collisions. Such a scenario could happen if, for example, pair B in Figure 3.10 failed. If that pair failed, then the client, which uses it to sense incoming traffic, would have no way to sense collisions. The client might then transmit at the wrong times. The link integrity function prevents this scenario from happening.

The link integrity function comprises two operations: transmission and reception of link integrity pulses.

Each transceiver sends link integrity pulses continuously on its primary transmit pair (pair A or B in Figure 3.10). These pulses occur about 1 ms apart.[4] The transceiver stuffs them into the gaps between packets.

Every transceiver watches for the presence of link integrity pulses from the far end. If present, the transceiver activates. The beauty of this scheme is that if the collision detection wire breaks the pulses do not arrive, and the transceiver reverts to an inactivated state. No transmissions (except for the continuous link integrity pulses) emanate from an inactivated transceiver.

The names of the activated and inactivated states are LINK_OK and LINK_FAIL, respectively.

Error Robustness. Special error-detection circuits exist in every T4 transceiver. These circuits can detect many errors that happen in the middle of a data packet without relying on the CRC. Other more subtle error patterns must await CRC detection in the MAC. In conjunction with the CRC, T4 can detect these specific types of errors:

- Every error affecting one symbol
- Every pattern of errors affecting two symbols
- Virtually all patterns of three-symbol errors

The residual probability of a T4 receiver failing to detect any combination of errors is extremely small. Assuming a uniform line error rate of one part in 10^8, the mean time between undetected packet errors would be 307 million billion years (3.07×10^{17}). Numbers this large are

---

[4] The 1 ms spacing is one-tenth the spacing used for link integrity pulses in 10BASE-T, which makes the 10BASE-T and 100BASE-T4 link integrity pulses intentionally incompatible. Neither system will respond if accidentally cross-connected. The 1 ms spacing is intentionally much longer than the spacing between pulses of an Auto-Negotiation *Fast Link Pulse* (FLP) sequence, for similar reasons.

difficult to comprehend. Imagine that there were 100 million T4 transceivers in the world, all blasting packets at the maximum possible rate, under worst-case noise conditions. On average, undetected errors would occur only once every 3 billion years. Will you experience an undetected packet error at your site? It is more likely New Jersey will be invaded by beings from planet Geldar-23.

100BASE-T4: Frame Structure and Encapsulation

Figure 3.14 shows how T4 synchronizes ternary symbols on the three transmit pairs. Time proceeds from left to right in the figure.

The following frame elements appear in Figure 3.14:

- **SOSA.** An alternating pattern of +1, -1 symbols. The T4 transceiver substitutes this pattern for the first 5 octets of preamble.
- **SOSB.** A special pattern used to establish the beginning of data on each pair.
- **P3.** Same as SOSA, but only two symbols long.
- **P4.** Same as SOSA, but four symbols long.
- **DATA.** The 8B6T coded result of a data octet.
- **EOP1-5.** Special end-of-packet markers.

The preamble of every 802.3 packet contains exactly 8 octets. During transmission through 100BASE-T repeaters, this exact preamble length remains constant.[5] During the preamble, a T4 transmitter substitutes a special pattern designed to help the receiver locate the beginning of data on each pair. The receiver strips this pattern and returns an ordinary preamble to the MAC.

The special pattern used by T4 consists of 5 octets of pattern SOSA, followed by 3 more octets of pattern SOSB. The SOSB pattern is duplicated on each pair. On each pair, directly following the SOSB, the flow of data commences.

End-of-packet markers are duplicated on each pair as well. There are five markers, EOP1 through 5. The end-of-packet marker patterns

---

[5] 10 Mb/s repeaters have a different property. A packet preamble may gain or lose a few bits when passing through a 10 Mb/s repeater.

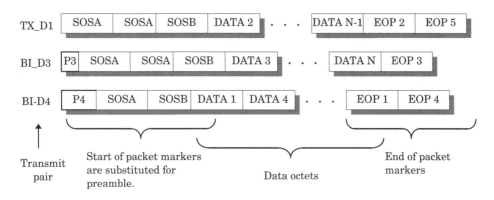

Figure 3.14 T4 Frame Structure

look very unlike data, making it extremely improbable that a series of data errors could cause premature packet termination.[6]

In Figure 3.14, the last 6T code group, DATA N, appears on transmit pair BI_D3. It could have appeared on any of the three transmit pairs. Wherever it appears, the five code groups EOP1 through EOP5 follow as the next five octets in sequence. For the purpose of measuring the *interpacket gap* (IPG), the end of packet is defined as the first ternary symbol of EOP1.

Figure 3.14 illustrates the frame structure as it is leaving a transmitter. The three independent data streams appear exactly aligned. At the receiver, the frame structure looks different. At the receiver, the three data streams have traversed different wire pairs. Any differences in the speed of propagation among those three pairs will shift the time of arrival of the streams relative to each other. Such a shift is called a *skew*.

The T4 receiver contains a special processing block, called the ALIGN function, that combats skew. The ALIGN function will correct a skew of up to 60 ns between any two pairs. This is more skew than will likely ever occur on any four-pair category 3, 4, or 5 cable.

NOTE: In every T4 link, all four wire pairs *must* share a common jacket. Do not use two two-pair cables or mix one pair from a spare cable. The cable lengths will likely be different, creating too much skew,

---

[6] For example, EOP1 contains six ternary 1s. No other 8B6T data pattern contains more than three 1s.

and the ALIGN function will not be able to compensate. A difference in cable lengths of only 10 m will defeat the ALIGN function. Smaller differences erode the ALIGN function's margin of safety.

100BASE-T4: Options

The T4 PICS authorizes five specific options:

Exposed MII	Vendors may place the T4 transceiver on an adapter, or a system motherboard, omitting the exposed MII interface (see *MII: Applications*).
PCS and PMA	Technically, transceivers embedded inside a repeater may do funny things with the PCS and PMA sublayers. These options matter only to repeater developers.
Internal crossover	Each interface may be equipped with the normal pin assignment, or a complementary one called an *internal crossover* pin assignment. See C*rossover Wiring* in Chapter 4.
Support for Auto-Negotiation	The T4 specification defines low-level interface primitives used by Auto-Negotiation. Use of the Auto-Negotiation algorithm itself is optional.
Installation/cable	This option code in the PICS identifies those requirements incumbent upon the installer. Adapter and hub manufacturers never check this option.

In addition, manufacturers often provide a few extras of their own:

DTE-to-DTE communication	Not really an option. Any two T4 interfaces will operate in point-to-point mode if cross connected to each other. Explicit crossover of the wiring is generally required in this case (see Chapter 4, *Crossover Wiring*).
Polarity reversal	Polarity reversal refers to the swapping of the two wires within a given pair. It is different from a wiring crossover, which, for example, swaps pair 2 with pair 3. The T4 line coding scheme permits construction of interfaces smart enough to recognize polarity reversal. The standard does not require this function, but many manufacturers

provide it. Your installation people will thank you if you insist on it.

Full duplex   Not an option. The T4 line coding scheme does not permit full-duplex operation.

100BASE-T4: Features Not Needed

Previous 802.3 transceivers included functions called *SQE test* and *jabber*. Neither function applies to 100BASE-T4 transceivers.

SQE test, in 10 Mb/s transceivers, tests the collision-detection circuits. Collision detection had traditionally been difficult in Ethernet, since early implementations both transmitted and received on the same physical wire. The collision-detection circuits were tricky.

With T4, collision detection depends merely on sensing incoming signal energy on the dedicated collision detection pair. T4 transceivers test the collision function in two ways. First, the Link Integrity function verifies that it can hear signals from the far end of the cable. Then a special MII test specifically verifies the operation of the MII collision-detect wire. No additional testing need be performed.

The jabber function, in 10 Mb/s transceivers, senses when a MAC or DTE has gone crazy and begun continuously transmitting. In previous Ethernet systems, this watchdog function resided in the last stages of each transmitting DTE. T4 places that same jabber function in the repeater core, not in the transceiver. When the repeater senses a continuously jabbering port, it turns it off. Because the repeater does this function, the T4 transceiver does not need a jabber function.

100BASE-T4: Cables and Connectors

The T4 transceiver requires four pairs of category 3, 4, or 5 unshielded twisted-pair cable, installed according to **ISO/IEC 11801**. Minor exceptions to the ISO installation practices appear in the next section.

T4 transceivers use the same RJ-45-type 8-pin data connector used for 10BASE-T and other UTP LANs. The RJ-45 connector goes by many names (see Table 3.3 and Figure 3.15). In standard practice, work area cables use this same RJ-45 connector at the wall outlet.

8 pins   Looks like a 6-pin telephone jack, but has 8 pins.

Figure 3.15 RJ-45 Connector

Table 3.3 Different Names for the RJ-45 Connector

Name	Description
RJ-45	Common name for the traditional 8-pin data plug or jack. This is the name most used by data installers.
ISO 8877	An ISO connector specification to which RJ-45 conforms.
IEC 603-7, Detail Specification for Connectors, 8-Way	The latest IEC specification of the RJ-45 connector. It adds new mechanical characteristics to **ISO 8877**.

Pin assignments for the eight RJ-45 pins appear in Table 3.4. Pins marked RX_ can only receive and the TX_ pins can only transmit. Pins marked BI_ work bi-directionally. Note that Table 3.4 provides two different pin assignment listings, for devices with and without an internal crossover. Any Fast Ethernet port equipped with an internal crossover pin assignment will be marked with an "X" symbol.

The normal wiring arrangement pre-supposes a hub port equipped with internal crossover, and a client port without. In this case the pins are wired straight through, from pin 1 to pin 1, 2 to 2, et cetera. The

Table 3.4 100BASE-T4 MDI Contact Assignments

RJ-45 Contact	Four-Pair Category 3 UTP	
	No Internal Crossover	With Internal Crossover
1	TX_D1+	RX_D2+
2	TX_D1-	RX_D2-
3	RX_D2+	TX_D1+
4	BI_D3+	BI_D4+
5	BI_D3-	BI_D4-
6	RX_D2-	TX_D1-
7	BI_D4+	BI_D3+
8	BI_D4-	BI_D3-

customary correspondence between connector pins and the wiring color-code, for North America, appears in Table 3.5. Take care when wiring to keep pairs [1, 2], [3, 6], [4, 5], and [7, 8] routed on distinct pairs throughout.

Table 3.5 RJ-45 Color-Code
Assignments for North America

RJ-45 Pin	UTP Colors
1	GRN/WHT
2	WHT/GRN
3	ORG/WHT
4	BLU/WHT
5	WHT/BLU
6	WHT/ORG
7	BRN/WHT
8	WHT/BRN

If the connectors at both ends of a link are marked with an "X", or neither is marked, then an external crossover is required, as explained in Chapter 4, *Crossover Wiring*.

Some systems tolerate *polarity reversal*, or interchange, of the two wires within each pair. This feature makes installation easier. One of the most common installation errors involves accidentally swapping the two wires of a pair, for example BLU/WHT and WHT/BLU. Ask your vendor if their adapter supports polarity reversal. The standard does not require this feature.

A Warning About RJ-45 Wiring

You may violate the color code by consistently substituting one colored pair for another. Such a substitution has no impact on the electrical performance of the wiring. If your system supports polarity reversal, you may even swap the individual wires in any colored pair. But never, never, split the pairs apart. For example, the wires on pins [4, 5] must remain on a physically distinct twisted pair for the entire length of the cable. The same applies for pin combinations [3, 6], [1, 2], and [7, 8]. When the pairs separate, results are unpredictable. Service providers will charge a lot to debug a pair-splitting error.

100BASE-T4: Exceptions to ISO 11801 Wiring Practice

T4 stipulates that the wires behind a category 3 connector at the wall plate or punch-down block not be untwisted, or separated, for more than 1 inch (see Clause 23.6 and additional notes in Chapter 4). Any connector installed with reasonable care already meets this limit. By controlling the amount of untwisting, T4 controls the amount of crosstalk (see box entitled *Controlling Crosstalk in Connectors*).

Surprisingly, ISO specifications currently permit unlimited amounts of untwisting behind a category 3 connector. Such installation practice, besides being sloppy, introduces too much crosstalk between wire pairs. The T4 standard therefore took the approach of limiting the untwisting.

The one-inch untwisting limit is the same specification ISO presently uses for category 4 connectors. What benefits category 4 benefits category 3 as well. You should know that the original studies behind this specification indicated the T4 system would work with untwisted loops as big as 3 inches, in the presence of absolute worst case cable. There is a substantial margin built in to the specification.

The untwisting specification reduces the amount of crosstalk expected in a worst case category 3 cabling plant. At the same time, it also improves the attenuation. As a result, link attenuation and crosstalk specifications for T4 differ slightly from ISO values. Up to 12.5 MHz, T4 requires no more than 12 dB of attenuation, and at least $26 - 15\log(f/10)$ dB of crosstalk loss. T4 additionally assumes mandatory compliance with the ISO cable delay guideline of 5.7 ns/m.

Other than the restriction on the installation of category 3 connectors, and the delay requirement, T4 conforms in all other ways to the **ISO 11801** category 3 wiring specification.

Installation hint: If a particular T4 link won't quite meet the near-end crosstalk specification, try using it with a category 5 jumper cord. The better jumper cord noticeably improves overall link crosstalk performance.

Controlling Crosstalk in Connectors

The purpose of twisting wires into pairs is to reduce crosstalk. Well-twisted pairs exhibit little crosstalk. Wherever the wires of a pair separate, crosstalk increases. By holding the wires together at the connector, crosstalk is improved. Limiting the untwisting is just plain good installation practice.

100BASE-T4: Signal Levels, Comparison to 10BASE-T

T4 transmits larger signals than 10BASE-T. These larger signals make up for the increased cable attenuation expected at higher speeds and the use of three signal levels for T4 signaling, compared to two in 10BASE-T. T4 receivers also use adaptive equalization, which markedly improves the susceptibility to external noise.

The T4 transmitted signal is nominally 7 V peak-to-peak. T4 signaling uses three transmitted signal levels.

100BASE-T4: Safety

Clause 23.9, the safety clause, implores users to follow all relevant local safety guidelines. Of course, there are so many that the IEEE cannot possible list what all those guidelines might be. Nor does it say where to find them. Is this useful, or what?

The safety clause makes more sense once you realize that it has little to do with your safety or protection. On the contrary, it is designed to protect the folks at the IEEE from legal liability should your network cables inadvertently contact a high voltage and kill someone. If that happens, the IEEE can just say, "We told you so."

For my own protection, I will reiterate here the intent of Clause 23.9:

Always follow local safety codes and guidelines. Do not mix
power and data cables.

Clause 23.5.1.1 (Isolation Requirements) provides some useful safety features. Basically, it says that should some unwitting technician hook your 100BASE-T4 transceiver wiring up to 440 VAC power wiring, your computer will not explode. It won't work any more, but it won't explode, either. It also protects you against lightning surges of less than a few kilovolts. That number may sound low, but it ties in with the way lightning arresters work in many buildings.

First, a word about lightning. The energy in a lightning bolt is unbelievably huge. Have you ever seen an old oak tree split in two by a lightning bolt? If your data wiring suffers a direct strike, you can kiss your computers good-bye (and everything tied to them). Fortunately, buildings rarely sustain direct hits. Much more often, lightning hits a mile or more away, or is diverted to ground by a lightning rod, or some other structure. The electricity that flows into the building wiring is a mere shadow of the bolt's true power. These are the cases that can be saved by proper installation of lightning arresters.

Most building codes call for the installation of lightning arresters on all outside wiring. The lightning arresters (zinc oxide or spark gap type) are installed near the point where the cables enter the building. Properly installed, they will short out moderately high-voltage transients from nearby, but not direct, lightning strikes. Unfortunately, arresters are not perfect. When lightning strikes, a residual voltage in the kilovolt range still appears on inside building wires (especially on phone wires that come from the outside). These kilovolt-level surges can couple from telephone wiring to data wiring if they run close together (a good reason to keep the two separate). Clause 23.5.1.1 protects your equipment against such surges.

This brings up an important point: do not run 100BASE-T4 cables, or any other data cables, out of doors suspended on poles. Use underground conduits. Underground conduits shield your wiring from most lightning strikes. Better yet, use fiber.[7]

Hint: To check out the lightning immunity of a piece of equipment, ask to speak with users in Florida. They get regular thunderstorms in the afternoons that generate massive amounts of lightning. If the equipment has a problem with lightning, people in Florida will know about it.

100BASE-T4: Confusion with Telephone Wiring

Phone wire looks just like data wire. It uses similar connectors. Phone and data wires often get cross connected in the wiring closet.

When you connect a T4 adapter to an analog phone system, the telephone ringing voltage will probably blow out the adapter. No safety hazard will be created (that is, nothing will catch on fire), but if the phone rings, your adapter is dead.

The phone system will survive the abuse undamaged. The symptoms, as observed by both ends, will be as follows. The T4 data port will remain in the LINK_FAIL state until the phone rings. After that, who knows what will happen. The telephone port, if it is an analog phone interface, will probably think the phone is in use (busy).

---

[7] Fiber is also a good choice for links that traverse different AC power grids inside a large building. STP, because its shield can pick up massive 60-Hz currents, is the worst choice for long connections.

When you connect a T4 adapter to a digital phone system, the chances for equipment survival are greater. The T4 data port will likely remain in the LINK_FAIL state. To the PBX, the digital phone will appear dead (or disconnected).

100BASE-T4: 120-Ω Wiring

The North American building cabling standard **EIA/TIA 568-A** does not authorize use of 120-Ω cabling. Internationally, **ISO/IEC 11801** does permit use of 120-Ω cabling (see Chapter 4, *Horizontal Cabling*). Some T4 transceivers, although designed for operation over 100-Ω cabling, will also work with 120-Ω cabling. Check with your vendor.

The remarkable ability of some T4 transceivers to tolerate 120-Ω cabling allows people that already have 120-Ω cabling (mostly installed in France) to use the T4 system without modifying their cable plant.

There are advantages to 120-Ω cable. For one, typical 120-Ω cable generally qualifies as category 4. It has better attenuation and crosstalk ratings than category 3 cable. These properties make it better.[8]

For T4 applications, as well as 10BASE-T, there is also a disadvantage. The cable impedance is wrong (see box entitled *Cable*

Cable Impedance

The *impedance* of a cable, measured in ohms (Ω), specifies how signals propagate along the cable. Technically, it measures the ratio of voltage to current in the cable. Impedance also controls how and when signals reflect, or bounce around, in a cable plant. Here is how it works.

The impedance of an ordinary cable is uniform along its length. Signals propagate normally through such a cable. Where two cables with the same impedance are joined, signals flow smoothly from one cable into the next. If the impedances differ, signals do not flow smoothly. A fraction of the incoming signal bounces off the joint, traveling back toward its source. Such a joint is called an *impedance discontinuity*.

In a link with multiple impedance discontinuities, signals change direction several times, bouncing back and forth between the joints. When these reverberations finally arrive at their destination, they have become de-synchronized from the original signal. At the receiver, the reverberations interfere with the true signal, just like noise.

---

[8] But not as good as category 5 cable, which is required for use with TX transceivers.

Impedance). T4 transceivers are designed for operation with 100-Ω cable, not 120-Ω.

During the 802.3 committee meetings, one representative from France exhaustively proved that the advantages outweighed the disadvantages. He demonstrated that, under worst-case assumptions, a system using 120-Ω cabling was no worse than a system using 100-Ω cabling. If the system worked with worst-case 100-Ω cable (which it did), then it should work with 120-Ω cable. The same basic reasoning applied to 10BASE-T, although details of the proof differed.

So far, so good. 120-Ω cable does not exacerbated the worst case. But how about the average case? In other words, what will likely happen in your cable plant?

Use of 120-Ω cables, on average, reduces the system operating margin. Even though the absolute worst case doesn't get any worse, the average case (the case you probably have) deteriorates. Why risk it? If you do not have 120-Ω cabling now, do not install any. If you have some, but can replace it, do so. If you must use 120-Ω cabling with T4, here are the rules:

- Use of category 4 120-Ω cabling, when used with short 120-Ω jumper cords and patch cords, is permitted.
- Use of category 5 120-Ω cabling is permitted with short jumper cables and patch cords of either 120 or 100 Ω.
- Never join a long section of 120-Ω cable with a long section of 100-Ω cable.
- Ask your vendor if the transceiver they carry will work with 120-Ω cables. Some do and some do not.

Points to Remember

- T4 works with 100 m of four-pair category 3 or better UTP.
- Do not use two two-pair cables or mix one pair from a spare cable.
- If the untwisted wiring loops behind your wall plate and punch-down blocks exceed 3 inches, you should reinstall them, or install category 4 connectors.
- A T4 transceiver may included an internal crossover. If so, it will be marked with an "X".

- Does the transceiver tolerate polarity reversal?
- Does the transceiver work with 120-Ω wiring?
- Does the transceiver support Auto-Negotiation?

100BASE-X TRANSCEIVER (CLAUSE 24)

Clause 24 defines two sublayers, PCS and PMA, plus supporting information about cabling, connectors, timing, and other details. The combination of PCS and PMA sublayers, plus the PMD sublayer from either Clause 25 or 26, is called an X transceiver, or 100BASE-X *Physical Layer Device* (PHY), in standards terminology. When combined with the Clause 25 PMD we get a 100BASE-TX twisted-pair transceiver. When combined with the Clause 26 PMD, we get a 100BASE-FX fiber transceiver.

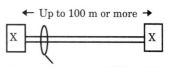

Two-pair, category 5 UTP, STP, or two-strand fiber

Relations between the X transceiver and other protocol sublayers are illustrated in Figure 3.16. In this figure, the X transceiver connects above to the Media Independent Interface (MII). It connects below to the data cabling. The block standing between the transceiver and the cable, labeled MDI, represents the data cabling connector. The term MDI stands for *Medium Dependent Interface*.

100BASE-X: Relation to ANSI FDDI Standards

The X standard joins together the best parts of two different standards worlds. It crisscrosses between the Ethernet and FDDI standards, picking up the MAC and high-level control from one and the low-level transceiver design from another.

Early presentations about X depicted the two standards with a big X bridging between them (Figure 3.17). This mental image is brilliant in its simplicity. Both Ethernet and FDDI already share a great deal of similarity because both use the IEEE 802.2 Logical Link Control (LLC) sublayer. They just have different MACs and transceivers. The X approach stitches together the IEEE CSMA/CD MAC on the left with the ANSI PMD hardware (transceiver) on the right. The result is a

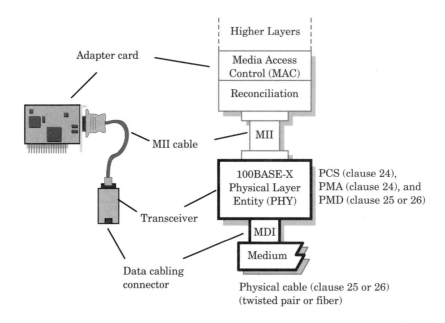

Figure 3.16 100BASE-X Layer Stack

network that conforms to the Ethernet MAC, but uses FDDI transceiver standards.

The X translation sublayer presently accommodates two of the FDDI transceivers (twisted pair and multimode fiber). If ANSI chooses to certify additional transceivers, the X scheme may adopt them as well.

Clause 24 serves as the glue between the MII (Clause 22) and the two ANSI PMD sublayers defined to date (Clauses 25 and 26). Clauses 25 and 26 do not actually define the PMD sublayers; they merely incorporate the corresponding FDDI sublayers by reference.

Please note that the X system has nothing to do with bridging Ethernet and FDDI packets (a common misconception). The X system really has little to do with FDDI. It merely uses portions of the existing FDDI physical layer standards to define a new, stand-alone, 100 Mb/s Ethernet standard.

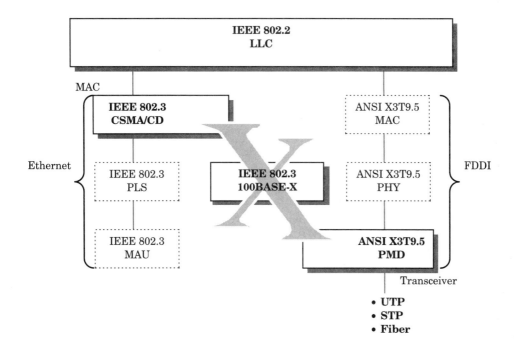

Figure 3.17 100BASE-X Joins Two Standards

100BASE-X: Distinguishing Features

Cabling. 100BASE-X could, in theory, support any high-speed full-duplex medium. The specific media choices provided in the standard appear in Table 3.6. See *100BASE-TX, Cables and Connectors* and *100BASE-FX, Cables and Connectors* later in this chapter for more information about the cables used by Clauses 25 and 26, respectively.

Nominal Network Diameter. The maximum separation between any two X devices in the same collision domain is called the maximum collision domain diameter. The maximum collision domain diameter, for a pure TX network on category 5 UTP, is about 200 m. This diameter may be increased somewhat by incorporating fiber links (see *Topology* this chapter).

    The diameter limitation for TX derives from a very simple rule: no TX link may exceed 100 m. With a single repeater, the farthest separated TX devices can be no more than 200 m apart. With more repeaters, it so happens that the diameter does not improve.

Table 3.6 Cabling Options for 100BASE-X

Cabling	Transceiver Designation	Covered by Which 100BASE-T Clause	Defined in Which FDDI Standard
Two-pair 100-Ω category 5 UTP	100BASE-TX	25	**ANSI X3.263 TP-PMD**, Revision 2.2 (1 March 1995) Not yet approved by ISO.
150-Ω STP	100BASE-TX	25	**ANSI X3.263 TP-PMD**, Revision 2.2 (1 March 1995) Not yet approved by ISO.
Two-strand 62.5/ 125 μm fiber	100BASE-FX	26	**ISO 9314-3 (1990)**

Rules for FX operation are more generous. Optical signals traveling in fiber links tend to go much farther than 100 m. That is one of the beautiful things about the FX transceiver. Unfortunately, FX does not enjoy the full benefit of its fiber capability. The timing of CSMA/CD fiber optic communications, not signal propagation, limits the allowable distances.[9] The timing rules do permit connection *long fiber drops* in a collision domain. A long fiber drop may span much farther than 100 m, depending on other aspects of the system configuration and timing (see Clause 29 and the discussion in *Topology* this chapter). Applications of long fiber drops are illustrated in Figures 2.20 through 2.22.

A repeater or switch may incorporate a full-duplex bridged connection to an FX fiber port that can span 2 km or more. See *100BASE-FX: Distances* this chapter.

Use of Wire Pairs. The X signaling scheme concentrates all its data on two signaling channels, one for each direction. Each carries a full

---

[9] The collision domain timing constraint applies.

100 Mb/s payload. The channels are symmetric, meaning that neither end of the physical channel acts as master or slave.

The X architecture preserves the full-duplex nature of the underlying channel (Figure 3.18). Any X transceiver, if connected to a full-duplex MAC, may be used for full-duplex communications.

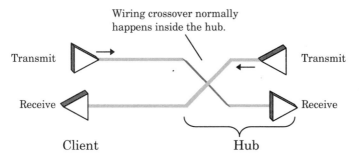

Figure 3.18 100BASE-X Use of Wire Pairs

Data Coding. X does not send data directly on each pair in binary format. It codes the data first. The coding scheme is called 4B5B coding (see Figure 3.19). Coding accomplishes several objectives:

- Provides several extra patterns, unused by ordinary data transmission, for signaling the start and end of each packet.
- Strips the signal of most of its DC bias, permitting use of inexpensive AC coupling.
- Embeds enough transitions in the data to keep clock recovery locked.
- In the case of TX, coding scrambles the transmitted data, spreading out electromagnetic emissions and make it easier for products to pass internationally mandated radio-frequency emissions tests.[10]

---

[10] T4 needs no scrambling because its signal transmission frequencies lie below the bands controlled by tough FCC and VDE regulations. X transmission frequencies per wire range up to five times higher (125 million transitions per second vs. 25 million for T4). FX needs no scrambling because it uses fiber.

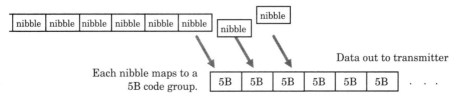

Nibble stream from MAC
feeds single transmit pair.

| nibble | nibble | nibble | nibble | nibble | nibble |

nibble

nibble

Data out to transmitter

Each nibble maps to a
5B code group.

| 5B | 5B | 5B | 5B | 5B | 5B | . . .

Figure 3.19 4B5B Coding

After 4B5B coding, the X transceiver uses one of two signaling schemes, depending on the PMD type, to send the 5B code groups. TX transceivers use MLT-3 ternary signaling, meaning that at each signaling instant, or baud, the signal can have one of three levels. In the TX signaling scheme, a change from one level to the next marks a logical 1. Intervals where the signal remains constant represent logical 0s. The transmitted signal circulates endlessly among the three possible signal values, always in the same order: [+1, 0, -1, 0, +1, 0,...]. This system uses three levels, but at each stage it can only do one of two things, either advance to the next level or stay where it is (see Figure 3.20). Each sample clock, therefore, conveys exactly one bit of information.

FX transceivers transmit the 5B code groups as binary, or two-leveled, signals with NRZI coding. An NRZI code transmits each logical one as a change of state.

In both TX and FX, idle symbols run continuously between packets. The transmitters always stay on.

MLT-3

NRZI

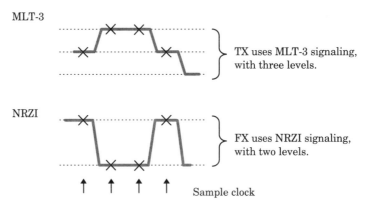

TX uses MLT-3 signaling,
with three levels.

FX uses NRZI signaling,
with two levels.

Sample clock

Figure 3.20 Ternary and Binary Signals

4B5B Coding Summary

The X transceiver accepts nibbles from the MII. Before transmission, the transceiver applies 4B5B coding to each nibble. The coding process maps each nibble into a group of 5 binary, or two-level, symbols. The receiver reverses the process.

The data rate per pair is 100 Mb/s. The transition rate on each pair is five-fourths of that rate, or 125.00 MHz.

100BASE-X: Other Features

We have already discussed cabling, network diameter, and data coding. Next let's look at carrier detection, the link monitor, and error robustness and where these functions fit inside an X transceiver.

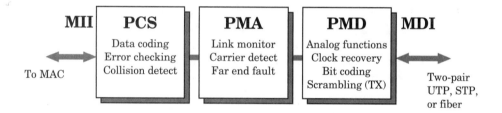

MII **PCS**   **PMA**   **PMD**   **MDI**

	Data coding	Link monitor	Analog functions	
To MAC	Error checking	Carrier detect	Clock recovery	
	Collision detect	Far end fault	Bit coding	Two-pair
			Scrambling (TX)	UTP, STP,
				or fiber

Figure 3.21 Functional Block Diagram of X PHY

Carrier Detect. The X transceiver incorporates a *digital squelch* algorithm. This function prevents the transceiver from activating its carrier signal until the incoming signal has qualified itself (see box entitled *Digital Squelch—100BASE-X*). This qualification procedure prevents spurious activation of the carrier upon the occurrence of impulse noise that may occasionally be present on the wires.

Link Monitor. The Link Monitor process evaluates the reliability of the physical-level channel. If it detects something wrong, it shuts down the receiver.

The Link Monitor process watches the medium for indications of a strong, healthy, continuous signal. The signal must remain strong and healthy for at least 33,000 bits (330 μs) before the Link Monitor enables reception.

Digital Squelch—100BASE-X

Every receiver recognizes the idle pattern. When a bit arrives that does not fit the idle pattern, the receiver notices right away, but does not activate the carrier.

To activate the carrier, two out of ten incoming bits must be non-idle. It therefore takes errors on at least two symbols to cause a false carrier event. Such a pattern of errors in an otherwise idle channel is rather improbable.

The Link Monitor protects the system against broken wires, unplugged cables, and other related service problems.

Error Robustness. Special error-detection circuits exist in every X transceiver. These circuits can detect many errors that happen in the middle of a data packet, without relying on the CRC. Other more subtle error patterns must await CRC detection in the MAC. In conjunction with the CRC, the X system can detect the following specific errors:

- Every error affecting one symbol
- Every pattern of errors affecting two symbols
- Virtually all patterns of three-symbol errors

The residual probability of an X receiver failing to detect any combination of errors is extremely small. Assuming a uniform line error rate of one part in 2.5×10^{10}, the mean time between undetected packet errors is 31 million billion years (3.16×10^{16}). Numbers this large are difficult to comprehend. Imagine that there were 100 million TX transceivers in the world, all blasting packets at the maximum possible rate, under worst case noise conditions. On average, an undetected error would occur only once every 3 hundred million years. Will an undetected error affect your site? You are more likely to learn that you have won the lottery while simultaneously being struck by lightning.

Far End Fault. Auto-Negotiation (Clause 28) provides a Remote Fault capability useful for detection of some types of link failures. It flags links that fail in one direction but not the other.

Unfortunately, Auto-Negotiation works only with copper media, such as TX and T4. Auto-Negotiation does not work with fiber. The Auto-Negotiation Remote Fault capability is therefore unavailable with fiber.

The FX transceiver makes up this deficiency by supplying its own Far End Fault function. Detection of Far End Faults over fiber is particularly useful for two reasons:

1. Fiber links can be very long. A Far End Fault detection feature can save travel time.
2. Fiber links often serve as backbones. Well-designed systems may use the Far End Fault indication to reconfigure to a backup link.

When the ever-present incoming IDLE signal is missing, the Far End Fault feature sends a special Far End Fault indication to its far end peer. The Far End Fault indication looks very much like ordinary IDLE. Receivers equipped with Far End Fault detection circuits can pick up the indication. Receivers without Far End Fault capability just ignore it.

The Far End Fault and Remote Fault indications have slightly different meanings. Far End Fault specifically indicates that the far end transceiver cannot hear transmission from the local device. Remote Fault is a general-purpose indication of any type of error at the far end.

For management reporting purposes, both indications are consolidated, along with other factors, under the umbrella term MediaAvailable.

100BASE-X: Frame Structure and Encapsulation

The structure of frames as physically transmitted on X closely parallels the 802.3 MAC frame structure. Differences include the substitution of a JK pattern for the first octet of preamble, the addition of a TR pattern following the last octet of the CRC, and the inclusion of an IDLE pattern between frames.

The following frame elements appear in Figure 3.22:

- **JK.** A pattern used to establish the beginning of data on each pair.
- **TR.** A pattern used to mark the end-of packet.
- **DATA.** The 4B5B coded result of a data octet.
- **IDLE.** Continuous idle signal transmitted between packets.

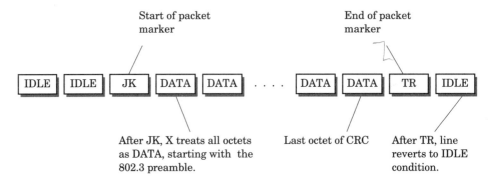

Figure 3.22 X Frame Structure

The preamble of an 802.3 packet contains exactly 8 octets. During transmission through 100BASE-T repeaters, this exact preamble length remains constant.[11] During the first octet of the preamble, the TX transmitter substitutes the JK pattern. This pattern helps the receiver locate the beginning of the preamble. The receiver strips this pattern and returns an ordinary preamble to the MAC. The TR, added after the last octet of data, is stripped by the receiver as well. During reception of IDLE characters, the MAC carrier indication remains off.

100BASE-X: Options

The 100BASE-X PICS authorizes six specific options:

Exposed MII	Vendors may place the TX or FX transceiver on an adapter, or a system motherboard, omitting the exposed MII interface (see *MII: Applications*).
PCS and PMA	Technically, transceivers embedded inside a repeater may do funny things with the PCS and PMA sublayers. These options matter only to repeater developers.
Internal crossover	Each interface may be equipped with the normal pin assignment, or a complementary one called an *internal crossover* pin assignment. See C*rossover Wiring* in Chapter 4.

---

[11] 10 Mb/s repeaters have a different property. A packet preamble may gain or lose a few bits when passing through a 10 Mb/s repeater.

Support for Auto-Negotiation	The X specification defines low-level interface primitives used by Auto-Negotiation. Use of the Auto-Negotiation algorithm itself is optional, provided that it is defined for use with the physical medium (see next item).
Medium supports Auto-Negotiation	Auto-Negotiation is defined for use with TX systems that use 100-Ω UTP, but not 150-Ω STP or fiber.
Far End Fault	An optional feature helpful for debugging cabling problems with fiber (see *100BASE-X: Other Features*, earlier in this chapter).

In addition, manufacturers often provide a few extras of their own:

DTE-to-DTE communication	Not really an option. Any two X interfaces will operate in point-to-point mode if cross-connected to each other. Explicit crossover of the wiring is generally required in this case (see Chapter 4, *Crossover Wiring*).
Polarity reversal	Polarity reversal refers to the swapping of the two wires within a given pair. It is different from a wiring crossover, which, for example, swaps pair 2 with pair 3. The TX line coding scheme permits construction of interfaces smart enough to recognize polarity reversal. The standard does not require this function, but many manufacturers provide it. Your installation people will thank you if you insist on it.
Full duplex	All TX and FX interfaces naturally have full-duplex capability. If connected to a full-duplex MAC, they can be placed in a full-duplex operating mode. For switch-to-switch links, this mode is highly desirable.
	Unfortunately, at the time of publication, the complete benefits of full-duplex operation have not been realized due to a lack of standard flow control mechanisms. Flow control, while not required, will improve the performance of large networks of full-duplex switches. The 802.3 committee opened a project in 1995 to standardize flow control for full-duplex links (see Chapter 5, *Flow Control*).

100BASE-X: Features Not Needed

Previous 802.3 PMAs included functions called *SQE test* and *jabber*. Neither function applies to 100BASE-X transceivers.

SQE test, in 10 Mb/s transceivers, tests the collision-detection circuits. Collision detection had traditionally been difficult in Ethernet, since early implementations both transmitted and received on the same physical wire. The collision-detection circuits were tricky.

With 100BASE-X, collision detection depends only on the health of the receive channel. By checking the ability to properly receive signals from the low-level hardware, the Link Monitor function effectively replaces SQE test.

The jabber function, in 10 Mb/s transceivers, senses when a MAC or DTE has gone crazy and begun continuously transmitting. In previous Ethernet systems, this watchdog function resided in the last stages of each transmitting DTE. 100BASE-X places that same jabber function in the repeater core, not in the transceiver. When the repeater senses a continuously jabbering port, it turns it off. Because the repeater does this function, the X transceiver does not need a jabber function.

Points to Remember

- 100BASE-X works with two pairs of category 5 UTP, type 1 STP or fiber.
- A TX transceiver may include an embedded crossover. If so, it should be marked with an "X".
- Auto-Negotiation is optional with TX.
- Auto-Negotiation does not work with fiber or STP.
- FX may or may not include optional Far End Fault sensing.

Questions to Ask

- Does a TX transceiver tolerate polarity reversal?
- For adapters that support full duplex, ask if Auto-Negotiation is implemented. If not, what other scheme determines when to switch to full duplex? Are jumper settings or software settings necessary?
- Full duplex does not require flow control, but it works better with it. For full-duplex mode, what flow control mechanism, if any, is employed?

TX PMD (CLAUSE 25)

Clause 25 defines the low-level analog functions, called the PMD sublayer, of a 100BASE-TX transceiver. It specifies the wiring, connectors, signaling levels, safety requirements, and other aspects of system operation relevant to physical communications (Figure 3.23).

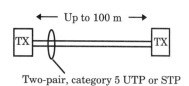

Two-pair, category 5 UTP or STP

Clause 25 incorporates most of these functions by reference. It references an ANSI document previously defined for FDDI. That document is:[12]

ANSI X3.263 TP-PMD, Revision 2.2: 1 March 1995, Fibre Distributed Data Interface (FDDI) — Part: Token Ring Twisted Pair Physical Layer Medium Dependent (TP-PMD)

The ANSI document defines a complete, functional, full-duplex signaling system for twisted-pair wiring.

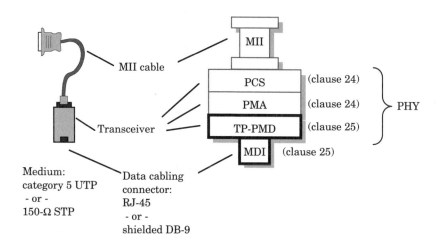

Figure 3.23 100BASE-TX Transceiver

---

[12] Available from: American National Standards Institute, 11 West 42nd Street, 13th Floor, New York, NY 10036. See Chapter 8 for ordering details.

Please note that the X system has nothing to do with bridging Ethernet and FDDI packets (a common misperception). The X system really has little to do with FDDI. It merely uses portions of the existing FDDI physical layer standards to define a new, stand-alone, 100 Mb/s Ethernet standard.

The ANSI TP-PMD sublayer, coupled with the PCS and PMA sublayers of Clause 24, makes a whole, working 100BASE-TX transceiver.

100BASE-TX: Cables and Connectors

The TX transceiver supports either of two cable types.

1. Two-pair category 5 unshielded twisted-pair cable (UTP), installed according to **ISO 11801**
2. Two-pair 150-Ω shielded twisted-pair cable (STP), installed according to **ISO 11801**

8 pins   Looks like a 6-pin telephone jack, but has 8 pins.

Figure 3.24 RJ-45 Connector

The physical connectors and cable impedances specified for these two cables are different. A given transceiver will support one type of cabling or the other, but not both. The choice of cable support is the only option in the Clause 25 PICS. See additional comments in Chapter 4 about cabling.

A TX transceiver supporting UTP uses the familiar RJ-45 8-pin modular connector (Figure 3.24). The RJ-45 connector goes by many names, as shown previously in Table 3.3. In standard practice, work area cables use this same RJ-45 connector at the wall outlet.

A TX transceiver supporting STP uses a shielded DB-9 connector (Figure 3.25). This connector goes by many names as well (see Table 3.7). In standard practice, work area cables used with 150-Ω STP use a shielded DB-9 at one end, and a Token Ring style data connector at the wall outlet (same as the IBM Cabling System Data Connector, **IEC 807-8**).

Figure 3.25 Shielded DB-9

Table 3.7 Different Names for the Shielded DB-9 Connector

Name	Description
Shielded DB-9	Industry name for generic part type. Most people recognize this name.
9-pin D-subminiature shielded	Nomenclature used by some manufacturers (including AMP and MOLEX).
EIA/TIA 574:1990 Section 2	The EIA/TIA connector specification to DB-9 connectors conform.
82034-0010	Example Molex part number for connector housing; this housing also requires nine crimp pins, a metal shell, and two screws.

Table 3.8 gives pinouts for both UTP and STP connectors. Note that Table 3.8 provides two different pin assignment listings, for devices with and without an internal crossover. Any Fast Ethernet port equipped with an internal crossover pin assignment will be marked with an "X" symbol.

Table 3.8 100BASE-TX MDI Contact Assignments

| Contact | Four-Pair Category-5 UTP (2 Pairs Used) | | Two-Pair 150-Ω STP | |
	No Internal Crossover	With Internal Crossover	No Internal Crossover	With Internal Crossover
1	Transmit +	Receive +	Receive +	Transmit +
2	Transmit –	Receive –		
3	Receive +	Transmit +		
4				
5			Transmit +	Receive +
6	Receive –	Transmit –	Receive –	Transmit –
7				
8				
9	N/A	N/A	Transmit –	Receive –
Shell	N/A	N/A	Chassis	Chassis

The normal wiring arrangement pre-supposes a hub port equipped with internal crossover, and a client port without. In this case the pins are wired straight through, from pin one to pin one, two to two, et cetera. The customary correspondence between connector pins and the wiring color-code, for North America, appear in Table 3.5 and Table 3.9. On an RJ-45 connector, take care when wiring to keep pairs [1, 2], [3, 6], [4, 5], and [7, 8] routed on distinct pairs throughout. On a DB-9 connector, the correct pair assignments are [1, 6] and [5, 9].

If the connectors at both ends of a link are marked with an "X", or neither is marked, then an external crossover is required, as explained in Chapter 4, *Crossover Wiring*.

Table 3.9 DB-9 Color-Code Assignments for 150-Ω STP

DB-9 Pin	STP Wire Color
1	Orange
2	
3	
4	
5	Red
6	Black
7	
8	
9	Green
Shell	Cable sheath

Installation Tip

Although TX uses only two pairs, any other pairs in the same sheath should not be used for another high-speed application, including 10BASE-T. Digital or analog phones are OK, but not high-speed data.

100BASE-TX: Exceptions to ANSI TP-PMD

Clause 25 directly references the ANSI TP-PMD specification. It then calls out a few differences required to make it play with 100BASE-T.

The only difference relevant to users of the system pertains to pin assignments. When the FDDI TP-PMD was first developed, it chose pin assignments incompatible with 10BASE-T. Use of the FDDI pin assignments would make it difficult to construct a system that could perform either 10BASE-T or FDDI functions using the same connector. At the time, no one cared about such functionality.

The world of Fast Ethernet now cares very much about dual functionality. Dual-speed devices lie at the heart of many customers' migration strategies. A tremendous demand has built for devices that operate either in 10BASE-T mode or in an advanced Fast Ethernet mode.

When the TX system was designed, its architects faced a choice. They could adopt the popular 10BASE-T pin assignments, or they could adopt the FDDI TP-PMD pin assignments. They wisely chose the 10BASE-T pin assignments.

For UTP cable, TX uses the same pin assignments as 10BASE-T. For STP cable, which has only two pairs, TX accepts the FDDI pin assignments (Table 3.8).

Further Technical Differences Between 100BASE-TX and TP-PMD

100BASE-X includes none of the FDDI Station Management (SMT) functions. That simplifies the PMD considerably.

FDDI permits multiple PMD circuits to service a single PMA, 100BASE-X does not. Again, a simplification. 100BASE-X accomplishes a similar function at the MII level. Several PHY circuits may serve one MII (one at a time), but only one PMD may serve each PMA.

Lastly, 100BASE-X imposes additional delay constraints that are not relevant to FDDI.

100BASE-TX: Signal Levels, Comparison to 10BASE-T

TX transmits smaller signals than 10BASE-T. At the same time, TX receivers experience far less noise. The category 5 UTP (or 150-Ω STP) cables used for TX transmission provide much greater noise immunity than the category 3 cables typically used for 10BASE-T. The greater noise immunity of the cables more than makes up for the reduced signal levels and increased bandwidth of the TX signals. The TX transmitted signal amplitude is 2V peak-to-peak. TX signaling uses three transmitted signal levels.

100BASE-TX: Safety

The FDDI TP-PMD specification does not explicitly address safety and installation guidelines, but this book will:

Always follow local safety codes and guidelines. Do not mix power and data cables.

Section 8.4.1 of the FDDI TP-PMD (UTP Isolation Requirements) provides some useful safety features. Basically, it says that should some unwitting technician hook your 100BASE-TX transceiver wiring up to 440 VAC power wiring, your computer will not explode. It is allowed to slowly melt, but not actually explode or catch fire.

It also protects you against lightning surges of less than a few kilovolts. This number may sound low, but it ties in with the way lightning arresters work in many buildings (see *100BASE-T4: Safety* earlier in this chapter).

This brings up an important point: do not run 100BASE-TX cables, or any other data cables, out of doors suspended on poles. Use underground conduits. Underground conduits shield your wiring from most lightning strikes. Better yet, use fiber.[13]

100BASE-TX: Confusion with Telephone Wiring

Phone wire looks just like data wire. It uses similar connectors. Phone and data wires often get cross connected in the wiring closet.

When you connect a TX adapter to an analog phone system, the telephone ringing voltage will probably blow out the adapter. No safety hazard will be created (that is, nothing will catch on fire), but if the phone rings, your adapter is dead.

The phone system will survive the abuse undamaged. The symptoms, as observed by both ends, will be as follows. The TX data port will remain in the LINK_FAIL state until the phone rings. After that, who knows what will happen. The telephone port, if it is an analog phone interface, will probably think the phone is in use (busy).

When you connect a TX adapter to a digital phone system, the chances for equipment survival are greater. The TX data port will likely remain in the LINK_FAIL state. To the PBX, the digital phone will appear dead (or disconnected).

---

[13] Fiber is also a good choice for links that traverse different AC power grids inside a large building. STP, because its shield can pick up massive 60-Hz currents, is the worst choice for long connections.

Points to Remember

- 100BASE-TX works with two pairs of category 5 UTP or two pairs of 150-Ω STP.
- The pin assignments for UTP are the same as for 10BASE-T. These differ from FDDI assignments.
- A TX transceiver may included an embedded crossover. If so, it will be marked with an "X".

FX PMD (CLAUSE 26)

Clause 26 defines the low-level analog functions, called the PMD sublayer, of a 100BASE-FX transceiver. It specifies the wiring, connectors, signaling levels, safety requirements, and other aspects of system operation relevant to physical communications.

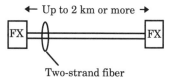

Clause 26 incorporates most of these functions by reference. It references an ANSI document previously defined for FDDI, called the Fiber-PMD. That document is:[14]

ISO 9314-3: 1990, Information Processing Systems — Fibre Distributed Data Interface (FDDI) — Part 3: Physical Layer Medium Dependent (PMD)

The ANSI document defines a complete, functional, full-duplex signaling system for multimode fiber.

Please note that the X system has nothing to do with bridging Ethernet and FDDI packets (a common misperception). The X system really has little to do with FDDI. It merely uses portions of the existing FDDI physical layer standards to define a new, stand-alone, 100 Mb/s Ethernet standard.

---

[14] ANSI is the primary source and official sales agent for ISO standards in North America: American National Standards Institute, 11 West 42nd Street, 13th Floor, New York, NY 10036. Outside of North America, contact: International Organization for Standardization, Case Postale 56, CH-1211, Genève 20, Switzerland. See Chapter 8 for ordering details.

The ANSI Fiber-PMD sublayer, coupled with the PCS and PMA sublayers of Clause 24, makes a whole, working 100BASE-TX transceiver (Figure 3.26).

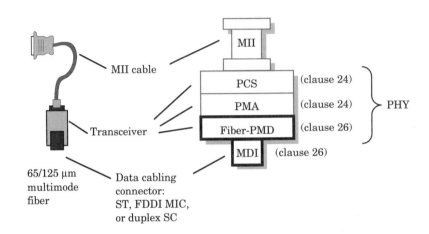

Figure 3.26 100BASE-FX Transceiver

100BASE-FX: Cables and Connectors

FX is designed for 1300 nm operation over two strands of 62.5/125 μm graded-index multimode fiber. Both EIA and ISO standards for building cabling provide fiber specifications suitable for use with FX.

In North America, use EIA-568-A *horizontal 62.5/125 μm optical fiber cable* (**ANSI/EIA/TIA-492AAAA**). The same grade of fiber is also authorized by EIA for backbone applications.

Internationally, use **ISO/IEC 11801** *62.5/125 μm multimode optical fibre* (IEC 793-2 type A1b, with 1.0 dB/km attenuation and 500 MHz/km bandwidth). For FX applications, the slight differences between this and the EIA fiber may safely be ignored.

If your fiber does not meet either of these standards, **ISO/IEC 9314-3**, the FDDI Fiber-PMD document cited by FX, recommends at least meeting the detailed parameters below:

- Two strands
- 62.5/125 μm multimode fiber
- Numerical aperture 0.275
- 11 dB total link budget

- 500 MHz-km modal bandwidth
- Zero dispersion wavelength 1295 to 1365 nm
- Dispersion slope less than 0.093 ps/nm^2-km

Adherence to these parameters will guarantee operation up to 2 km. Operation at lesser distances is possible with poorer fiber. Finally, **ISO/IEC 9314-3** Annex C provides useful information about engineering an FX link to use other multimode fiber sizes, including:

- 50/125 μm multimode fiber, two strands
- 85/125 μm multimode fiber, two strands
- 100/125 μm multimode fiber, two strands

Exact specifications for all allowed fiber types appear in the base Fiber-PMD document (**ISO 9314-3, 1990**).

At the present time, FX permits use of the following three fiber optic connectors:

1. ST®
2. FDDI MIC
3. Duplex SC™

From time to time, arguments flare among users about which fiber connector is best, although most users agree that none of these choices is ideal. As the fiber optic industry matures, better connectors will undoubtedly emerge, and 100BASE-FX will be modified to permit their use.

The ST-type connector, also called BFOC/2.5, is the most widely installed at this time. This is the same connector specified for use in the IEEE 10BASE-F standard.[15] It uses separate bayonet-style connectors for transmit and receive fibers (Figure 3.27). Adapters exist to convert between ST connectors and the newer SC versions.

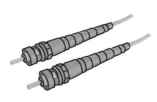

Figure 3.27 ST Connector

The fiber MIC connector was originally developed for FDDI.[16] It houses both transmit

[15] **IEEE Std 802.3**, Clause 15 (supplement **j**).

[16] **ISO/IEC 9314-3: 1990**, Information Processing Systems - Fibre Distributed Data Interface (FDDI)—Part 3: Physical Layer Medium Dependent (PMD).

Figure 3.28 FDDI MIC Connector

and receiver connectors in a shared plastic housing. It is a keyed connector, which neatly solves the problem of accidentally swapping the ST transmit and receive fibers. On the other hand, it is a rather large connector and takes up a lot of circuit board area. (Figure 3.28).

The duplex SC connector shown in Figure 3.29 improves on the basic FDDI fiber MIC design. It is smaller, and takes up less circuit board area. FDDI specifications permit use of this connector with the *FDDI low-cost fiber* transceiver.[17] It is also used by ATM and Fiber Channel. The SC duplex connector, also known as a duplex SCFOC/2.5, is designated as the preferred connection for new systems by both building cabling standards **ISO/IEC 11801** and **EIA/TIA 568-A**.

At this time, for Fast Ethernet, ST is the most widely used connector. ISO has designated SC as the connector of choice for future system designs, but Fast Ethernet vendors will stick with ST, because ST is used for fiber in 10 Mb/s Ethernet.

Figure 3.29 Duplex SC Connector

The duplex SC is slowly gaining in popularity for adapter cards. It is perceived as the best combination of low cost, ease of use, small size and reliability.

Fiber and Sharp Corners

Do not bend fiber around sharp corners. Each manufacturer specifies a minimum bending radius for their fiber. Violate this limit and the light will literally spill out the side of the fiber into the dark jacket. Communications will be interrupted.

A fiber power meter can easily demonstrate this effect. Strip back the jacket on a section of fiber, exposing about 12 inches of bare strand. Connect one end of the strand to a transmitter and the other end to the meter. Now wrap the strand several times tightly around a pencil or other small object. As you wrap, the received power will drop.

---

[17] **ANSI X3T9.5 LCF-PMD** Rev 1.3 (1 September 1992), sections 7.1–7.3.

Whatever connector is used, 100BASE-FX always uses the same star configuration used by T4 and TX.[18] Each client station connects to the central hub with two fibers (transmit and receive).

Every fiber link needs an explicit, external crossover.[19] In other words, the transmit port of one interface must wire to the receive port of the opposite interface, and vice versa. The crossover must be explicitly implemented somewhere in the cabling.

See additional comments in Chapter 4 about cabling.

100BASE-FX: Exceptions to ANSI Fiber-PMD

FX permits the use of ST connectors, which are not permitted by the ANSI Fiber PMD specification.

FX permits the use of duplex SC connectors, which are not permitted by the ANSI Fiber PMD specification. Both ST and duplex SC connectors are permitted by a different ANSI standard, called the FDDI *Low Cost Fiber* (LCF) PMD. These two connectors are the only elements of the LCF-PMD used by 100BASE-FX. The FX transceiver does not authorize use of the LCF-PMD reduced power output specifications.

100BASE-FX: Signal Levels

The peak optical transmission power from a 100BASE-FX interface is between 200 and 400 µW. Transmissions include approximately equal numbers of 1s and 0s (light ON and OFF), so the average power ranges from 100 to 200 µW. These figures specify the light coupled into a 62.5/125 µm fiber. Larger fibers generally capture more light.

100BASE-FX: Distances

An FX fiber link may be implemented as part of a shared-media Fast Ethernet configuration, or as a stand-along full-duplex link. When used as a shared-media segment the FX link participates with other segments in a collision domain. It is therefore subject to timing restrictions that limit its maximum range to 412 m or less. These limitations are discussed in *Topology*. A shared-media FX link never uses full-duplex mode.

---

[18] Passive star couplers, à la 10BASE-FP, are not permitted.

[19] Technically, the requirement is for an odd number of crossovers.

An FX link between two switches, or a switch and a DTE, may use full-duplex mode (if the devices at each end are so equipped).[20] When used as a full-duplex link, FX breaks free from the strictures of collision domain timing. The only remaining factors limiting the distance attained by a full-duplex FX link involve the performance of its optical components. The primary optical factors are the attenuation of the fiber itself, and the modal bandwidth and chromatic dispersion of the fiber. With either the EIA or ISO recommended fibers (see above) FX will span at least 2 km. Additional information about application of FX with fiber that exceeds the minimum EIA or ISO performance specification appears in the base Fiber-PMD document (**ISO 9314-3, 1990**). Also see notes regarding extended distances in *100BASE-FX: Use of Single-Mode Fiber.*

100BASE-FX: Environmental Specifications

Fiber-optic links use photons, not electrons. As a result, fiber optic links operate free from interference due to radio waves, power line noise, lightning, and all other electromagnetic effects. This makes fiber links perfect for communication between buildings.

Fiber links may run near power lines and other communication lines without fear of interference. They may be bundled tightly together without limit.

One thing you should never do with a fiber is look into the end of it. The FX system (like most fiber communication systems) uses infrared light. The human eye cannot see it, but it is very, very bright. The surface brightness, over the tiny active cross-section of the fiber, can rival that of an oven heating element on full broil. While it is true that there are no internationally recognized safety guidelines for multimode LED emitters in the FX power range, it is still never a good idea to look directly into the end of an active fiber.

This author will always remember the warning he found posted near the transmit port of one early fiber optic transmitter: "Do not look into this orifice with your remaining good eye."

---

[20] Full duplex is an optional feature available on some equipment. In full-duplex mode, a link may transmit and receive at the same time. In this mode, the collision detection circuitry is disabled, freeing the link from the constraints of collision timing.

100BASE-FX: Use of Single-Mode Fiber

Single-mode fiber is not explicitly provided for in the 100BASE-FX standard, but it can be made to work. The prime advantage of single-mode fiber is that signals, once launched, travel much farther than in multimode fiber. Distances in excess of 20 km are attainable.

The prime disadvantage of single-mode fiber is the difficulty of launching signals into it. The cross-section of a single-mode fiber core spans as little as 5 µm, much less than the 62.5 µm core used in multimode fiber. As a result, single-mode fiber requires an expensive laser diode with a narrow output beam, as opposed to the relatively cheap but wide-beamed LED optics used with multimode fiber. Single-mode fiber, because of its tiny core diameter, also needs more precise connectors.

To use single-mode fiber, a 100BASE-X installation requires an outboard conversion device at both ends of the link. The outboard device converts from either the standard TX copper interface or the standard FX multimode fiber interface into a proprietary single-mode format. Such devices were originally developed for FDDI. Because 100BASE-FX uses the same low-level signaling, clocking, and optical specifications as FDDI, those old conversion devices will work fine.[21] Once converted, the signals will travel on the order of 20 km in good-quality fiber.

Very long fiber links (longer than 412 m) always require use of full-duplex mode.

Points to Remember

- 100BASE-FX works with two strands of 62.5/125 µm multimode fiber.
- With additional engineering, 50, 85, or even 100 µm fiber may be used.
- FX uses an external crossover in every link.
- FX supports three alternative fiber connectors: ST, FDDI MIC, and duplex SC.

---

[21] Components appropriate for single-mode conversion are available from Meret Optical Communications, Inc., 1800 Stewart Street, Santa Monica, CA 90404.

REPEATERS (CLAUSE 27)

Repeaters are the building blocks of modern local area networks. Using repeaters, customers can aggregate small, easily managed network segments into larger network structures.

Repeaters have historically been made to work with both coaxial and unshielded twisted-pair (UTP) wiring. Even though the basic repeater functions are the same, the terminology and topology associated with these two applications differ.

In the original thick coax system, many devices could connect to a single coaxial cable. Each length of coaxial cable, with its attached devices, was called an Ethernet *segment*. A large coaxial Ethernet network could contain several segments. Repeaters were used to tie the segments together into a coherent network (Figure 3.30). The earliest coaxial repeaters had only two ports.

Systems based on UTP are architected differently. They use the hub-and-spoke wiring model. In this model, UTP wires radiate out from a central repeater to the various clients. A typical hub-and-spoke type of repeater has many ports.[22] A UTP repeater is commonly called a hub, rather than a repeater. In a hub-oriented network, only one device typically resides at the end of each wire. Each wire, with a hub on one end and an attached device at the other, is called a link.

In Ethernet terminology, UTP networks use hubs to interconnect their links (Figure 3.31). Coax networks use repeaters to interconnect their segments. The terms differ, but the UTP hubs and the old thick coax repeaters share many similarities.

- UTP hubs and thick coax repeaters both amplify and reshape incoming signals, passing them along in pristine condition to all other links (or segments) to which they connect.
- They are both bit-oriented low-level devices. As bits come in from one packet, they flow through, without modification or delay, to the outputs.[23]
- They both increase the physical extent of the network beyond the distance limitations imposed by any single segment or link.

---

[22] Eight, 12, and 24 are popular numbers of ports.

[23] In contrast to a switch (or bridge) which operates on whole packets, rather than individual bits, and may incorporate substantially larger delays.

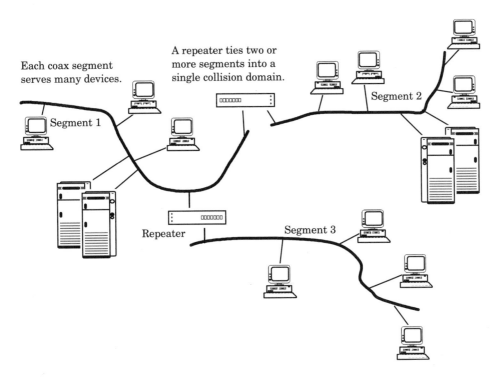

Each coax segment serves many devices.

A repeater ties two or more segments into a single collision domain.

Segment 1

Segment 2

Repeater

Segment 3

Figure 3.30 10 Mb/s Thick Coax Topology

The same sorts of specifications cover both UTP hubs and thick coax repeaters. These are really two realizations of the same device, targeted at different markets (coax versus UTP). Although hubs are often called repeaters, an old two-port coaxial repeater is almost never called a hub.

Repeaters and hubs commonly support the interoperation of different signaling interfaces. For example, a 10 Mb/s repeater may interconnect thick Ethernet (10BASE5), thin Ethernet (10BASE2), UTP (10BASE-T), and fiber optic (FOIRL) interfaces. As long as the speed and packet format are the same, a repeater may translate packets freely from one form of signaling to another. Packets flowing into one repeater port flow through to all other ports in real time. The repeater automatically handles signaling translations.

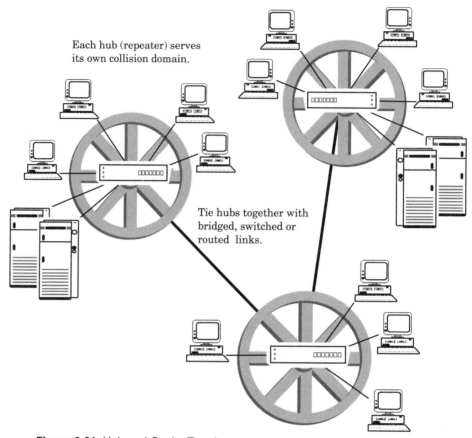

Each hub (repeater) serves
its own collision domain.

Tie hubs together with
bridged, switched or
routed links.

Figure 3.31 Hub-and-Spoke Topology

Repeaters differ from switches, bridges, and routers in their handling of packet forwarding. A repeater follows one simple, well-defined rule: *Forward each incoming packet,*[24] *without modification or unnecessary delay, to all output ports.* In a network of several repeaters, each packet flows instantly through the repeaters to all devices in the network. A switch, bridge, or router follows a more complex set of forwarding rules and acts in a data-dependent manner (see *Switch Architecture* in Chapter 2).

---

[24] Technically, a repeater forwards *all* signals, whether they be packets, collision fragments, jam signals, or bursts of noise.

The repeater rule is rather mindless, leading to certain inefficiencies. On the other hand it is a simple rule, which makes repeaters very inexpensive.

We say that all devices in a repeatered network exist in the same *collision domain* (see *What is a Collision Domain?* in Chapter 7 and *Repeater Architecture* in Chapter 2). Only one device in a repeatered network can successfully communicate at a time. That is the nature of a shared-media LAN.

As a rule, repeaters can only connect identical LANs. For example, while a repeater may translate between thick Ethernet and UTP, it cannot also translate to Token Ring. That action, because it involves changes to the base packet format, requires a bridge.

Repeaters incorporate special features to disconnect, or partition, malfunctioning segments from the rest of the network. This approach prevents equipment failures in one part of the network from spilling over into other parts.

100BASE-T Repeater: Distinguishing Features

Translation Capabilities. Fast Ethernet repeaters are permitted to translate among the following device types:

- 100BASE-T4
- 100BASE-TX
- 100BASE-FX

Not all repeaters have full translation capability. Some support only one device type, or a limited range of device types. Others may include support for additional proprietary device types.

Keep in mind that two repeaters may be interconnected with an inter-repeater link only if they share some common interface type. For example, a pure T4 repeater and a pure TX repeater cannot be directly connected unless one translates to the other's format.

Translation affects repeater timing. When translating a packet from one device type to another, the more the two coding styles differ, the more time the repeater needs to accomplish the translation. Because TX and FX are so similar, a repeater that translates only among TX and FX enjoys certain timing advantages. As a result, the possible interconnection topologies for mixed TX/FX repeaters are more flexible than those for mixed T4/FX repeaters (see *Topology* later in this chapter).

Limitations. The timing requirements in Clause 29 place certain restrictions on how repeaters may be connected:

- Unless the links are shortened to less than 100 m, no more than two repeaters may coexist in a collision domain. This precludes construction of multilayer hierarchies of widely separated repeaters, a common practice in the 10BASE-T hub market. NOTE: Repeaters having a switched expansion port (see *Repeater Architecture* in Chapter 2) may circumvent this limitation. They may be cascaded in virtually unlimited hierarchies.
- Between two repeaters, the inter-repeater link in the most general case cannot exceed 5 m. In effect, the repeaters must sit side by side (see topology rules in *Topology* later in this chapter, and in Clause 29). NOTE: Sacrifice of client link distances will permit longer inter-repeater links.

Although at first these sound like draconian limitations, in practice they have little impact. Why? Because, at the start of the Fast Ethernet project, the 802.3 working group came to a major realization, from which all other system requirements flowed:

Switching is good for longer distance connections.

Modern switching hardware is cheap, efficient, and very fast. Switched ports are routinely implemented as single-chip devices. Contrary to conditions just a few years ago, adding a switched expansion port to a repeater does not significantly raise the cost. The 802.3 working group decided that switching was an effective way to couple together Fast Ethernet repeaters.

Once the decision was made to couple repeaters using switched ports, no need remained to support multitiered hierarchies of widely separated repeaters in the same collision domain. With full-sized 100-m links, only two are allowed. Beyond two, Fast Ethernet uses switching. Many repeater manufacturers now provide switched expansion ports on their repeaters for the purpose of implementing switched, multitiered hierarchies (see *Repeater Architecture* in Chapter 2).

Class I and Class II Repeaters. Fast Ethernet defines two classes of repeaters, called Class I and Class II (see Table 3.10). The classes differ in their timing and feature content. Their timing differences affect how many of each class may be configured in a single collision domain.

Basically, the timing delay of a Class II repeater is less than the timing delay of a Class I repeater. This reduced timing delay does *not* mean that a Class II network has greater throughput, or better performance, than a Class I network. It *does* mean that two Class II repeaters will fit within the timing budget prescribed by the collision constraint, whereas two Class I repeaters will not.

With full-length links, two Class II repeaters are permitted in a collision domain. Only one Class I repeater is permitted in a collision domain. Although not mentioned in the standard, when link lengths are reduced to less than 100 m, up to three Class II repeaters may be configured in a single collision domain (see *Topology* later in this chapter).

The greater delay budget of a Class I repeaters carries with it certain advantages, mostly related to feature content. Additional features possible in a Class I repeater include stacking and translation.

In general, translation between T4 and the X family of transceivers requires a Class I repeater. Translation between TX and FX, because their signaling formats are so similar, may be accomplished within the timing budget of a Class II repeater. This fact establishes TX as a privileged interface type, because it can more easily translate to FX, the

Table 3.10 Repeater Capabilities

Class	Number of Repeaters in Collision Domain	Notes
I	One permitted	Relaxed timing budget; translation, stacking, and other features are easily achieved.
II	Two permitted[a]	Tight timing budget; translation between T4 and the X family is probably precluded; stacking is not as flexible as in Class I.

[a] With reduced link lengths, more than two are possible. See *Topology* later in this chapter.

Transceiver Timing Budgets: T4 Versus X

T4 uses relatively slow speed transmitters working across multiple parallel paths. In each path, the delays internal to a T4 transceiver are multiples of the symbol transmission rate, which is 25 MHz. By comparison, the symbol transmission rate of an X transceiver is 125 MHz, or five times faster. For the same number of processing steps, more time must be allocated in the timing budget for a T4 transceiver than for an X transceiver.

The additional processing time required for T4 transceivers takes away from the T4 repeater budget. The T4 Class II repeater budget contains little space for additional repeater features, such as translation and stacking.

---

fiber protocol. Class II TX repeaters can have fiber ports. Class II T4 repeaters will probably never have fiber ports.[25]

The standard requires that repeaters display a visible marking indicating their class. The official designations are a Roman numeral I in a circle (Class I), and a Roman numeral II in a circle (Class II). In addition, the standard recommends (but does not require) that the product display certain timing information relevant to topology calculations (see *Topology* later in this chapter).

Allowed Topologies. The Fast Ethernet standard permits only three basic topologies *using a single collision domain*. Remember that the standard limits itself to discussion of a single collision domain. It does not address the issue of switching. Switched ports may always be used to enlarge the system diameter and richness of interconnection, but are not discussed in the 802.3 standard, because each switched port creates a new, independent collision domain. Switching is addressed by a different IEEE standard (see **IEEE Std 802.1d**). The three single-collision-domain topologies referenced in the Fast Ethernet standard correspond to zero, one, and two repeaters, respectively.

Figure 3.32 shows the only possible configuration with zero repeaters. It connects two devices. This configuration is useful between a server and a switch port, a client and a switch port, or two switches.

The single-repeater configuration in Figure 3.33 depicts a typical repeater setup. There is only one repeater, and all devices connect to it. The single repeater setup is an essential part of the Fast Ethernet standard. Without it, we wouldn't have a network.

---

[25] Some doubt remains as to whether the timing restrictions will ever permit practical construction of a Class II T4 repeater.

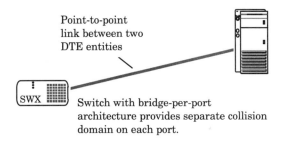

Point-to-point
link between two
DTE entities

SWX

Switch with bridge-per-port
architecture provides separate collision
domain on each port.

Figure 3.32 Point-To-Point Configuration

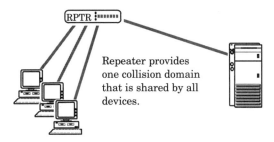

Repeater provides
one collision domain
that is shared by all
devices.

Figure 3.33 Single-Repeater Configuration

The value of the dual repeater setup in Figure 3.34 is less obvious. As a connection between two stand-alone repeaters, it doubles the system port capacity, but makes no practical difference in the allowed system diameter. This is a useful, cheap way to stack two repeaters, but not a critical system feature.

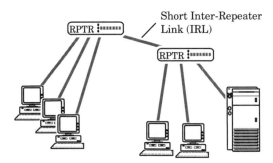

Short Inter-Repeater
Link (IRL)

Working together, two repeaters provide a single
collision domain that is shared by all devices.

Figure 3.34 Two-Repeater Configuration

A better justification for the dual-repeater scenario appears in Figure 3.35. This figure shows the hybrid switch–repeater topology from Figure 2.13, with a new twist. As discussed in Chapter 2, each of the internal switch ports (*A, B* and *C*) provides an independent 100 Mb/s collision domain. Internally connected to each of those ports is a built-in 3-port repeater. The average available bandwidth provided by this hybrid architecture, on a per port basis, is 33 Mb/s.

Now for the good part. The ordinary Class II repeater cascaded below the main switch expands the ratio of devices per switched port. This combination of hybrid switch–repeater, with additional repeaters cascaded below, is a powerful and flexible architecture. A large external expansion repeater creates a large number of ports with relatively low average bandwidth. Direct use of the native built-in repeater ports provides a modest 33 Mb/s average bandwidth per port. Using only one port from each internal switch section, a full 100 Mb/s may be provided.

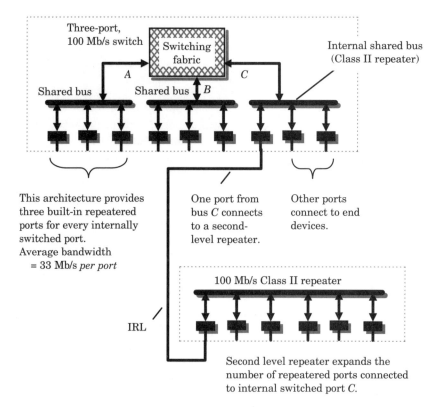

Figure 3.35 Hybrid Switch–Repeater with External Port Expansion

This flexibility lets customers match the average available bandwidth to the capabilities of their attached devices. This sort of super-flexible switch—repeater architecture is made possible by the existence of Class II repeaters.

Figure 3.36 illustrates another useful two-repeater configuration. In this example, a server pool is located some distance away from its clients. The customer has implemented one repeater near the clients, and another near the server pool. The server links, all being in the same room, are very short. Their compactness allows deployment of a long inter-repeater link. The overall network diameter (A + B + C) is limited in this case to 205 m (see *Topology, Simplified Constraint System* later in this chapter).

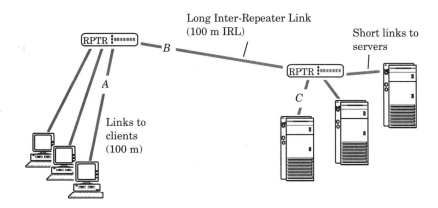

Figure 3.36 Two-Repeater Configuration with Remote Server Pool

100BASE-T Repeater: Other Features

Stackable Class I Repeater Architecture. Class I repeaters are in many cases stackable. A stackable product is one that can be expanded by hooking together many boxes using a proprietary link (often a ribbon cable). Stackable products provide more flexibility and grow to larger sizes than fixed-sized products.

The disadvantage of a stackable product, compared to a fixed one, is its higher initial purchase cost. Even when equipped with the minimum number of ports, it comes with an expansion connector, special management features, and other items not needed on a minimal, fixed-sized product.

For a fixed-sized network, buy fixed-sized repeaters. For networks that need to grow, consider stackable repeaters.

Partitioning. Fast Ethernet repeaters provide three features to help isolate faulty links. These features are the partition function, the jabber function, and the carrier integrity monitor.

If a link experiences 60 or more collisions in a row, the repeater removes the link from service (that is, it *partitions* the link). If a link is continuously active for more than 75,000 bit times (that is, the link *jabbers*), the repeater disconnects the link. If a TX or FX link experiences carrier detection problems indicating a broken wire or disconnected interface (that is, three consecutive *false carrier* events or one false carrier event of extraordinary duration) the repeater disconnects the link. In all cases, the repeater disconnects the problem segment, while other segments keep functioning normally.

Fiber Optic Links. Fast Ethernet and 10BASE-T treat the subject of fiber optic links differently. Fast Ethernet defines one 100 Mb/s fiber optic link, 100BASE-FX, that may be used for any purpose, including links between repeaters. 10 Mb/s Ethernet specifies several flavors of fiber optic links used for different purposes. The most popular of the 10 Mb/s optical links is a special link used for connecting repeaters. This link is called the Fiber Optic Inter Repeater Link (FOIRL).[26] The Fast Ethernet FX link is not compatible with the FOIRL (they run at different speeds).

Allowable link distances for 100BASE-FX inter-repeater links depend on the application. In most cases, timing considerations, not signal strength, limit the maximum achievable distances (see *Topology* later in this chapter).

No Half-Repeaters. The term half-repeater was used very early in the development of the 10 Mb/s Ethernet market. It referred to either end of a repeater system that has been split down the middle and stretched across the landscape through the use of some non-Ethernet transmission technology. A half-repeater connected two Ethernet

---

[26] The newer 10BASE-FL standard is compatible with the FOIRL.

segments in remote locations. This term is no longer in current usage. Fast Ethernet accomplishes the half-repeater function with bridging.

Switching. Switching and bridging both lie beyond the scope of the 802.3u standard, but definitely not beyond the scope of real Fast Ethernet products. See *Switch Architecture* in Chapter 2, and *Switching*, Chapter 5. Standards for *MAC-level bridging* apply to switches, because a switch is, among other things, a multiport bridge. MAC-level bridging standards are produced by the IEEE 802.1 working group. In particular, see **IEEE Std 802.1d**.

100BASE-T Repeater: Options

The Clause 27 PICS authorizes these specific options:

Links	T4, TX, and FX (see the preceding section *Translation Capabilities*)
Topology	Class I or Class II (see the preceding section *Class I and Class II Repeaters*)

In addition, manufacturers often provide a few extras of their own:

Auto-Negotiation	Not specifically mentioned in the repeater clause, but may be implemented at the manufacturer's option.
Cascading	Many repeater architectures provide a 100 Mb/s switched port. Such ports permit many interesting configurations, including multitiered hierarchies (see Chapter 2, *Repeater Architecture*).
Crossover correction	Some repeaters in the 10 Mb/s market can detect inadvertent interchange of the transmit and receive pairs, and fix the problem themselves.
Full duplex	This feature makes sense only between switches, not repeaters. It may appear on TX or FX links used as a cascading port.
Polarity reversal	All Fast Ethernet coding schemes permit construction of interfaces smart enough to recognize polarity reversal. The standard does not require this function, but many manufacturers provide it. Your installation people will thank you if you insist on it.

Points to Remember

- Class I repeaters have more delay than Class II repeaters. A collision domain may contain only one Class I repeater or (with maximally long client links) two Class II repeaters.

Questions to Ask

- How many ports will the repeater support? Does it support stacking or other forms of expansion?
- What types of transceivers are supported? Will it accomplish translation between port types?
- Does it support 100BASE-FX fiber links?
- Does it have a switched port for hierarchical expansion? Does that port support fiber?
- Does the switched port support full duplex? Full-duplex fiber?
- Is there a bridged port for connecting to 10 Mb/s networks?
- What management features are provided (see the section that follows, *Management*)?
- Do the ports tolerate polarity reversal?

AUTO-NEGOTIATION (CLAUSE 28)

Auto-Negotiation is an ease-of-installation feature. Auto-Negotiation permits complete installation and configuration of one end of a network connection *without knowing what will be installed at the far end*. This property becomes important when installing dual-speed or multipurpose adapter cards. For example, a customer might order 200 PCs configured with dual-speed 10/100 adapter cards set up for use with two-pair category 5 cabling. Appropriate adapter cards would have at least two capabilities:

1. 10BASE-T (10 Mb/s two-pair category 3 or better)
2. 100BASE-TX (100 Mb/s two-pair category 5)

In this example, a technician at the shipping warehouse can install and test each adapter without specifying which of the two network capabilities will be used. Each PC may then be shipped in a fully operational configuration. At installation time, each PC may be connected to either a 10BASE-T hub or a 100BASE-TX hub. Auto-Negotiation automatically senses the capabilities of the far end and configures itself accordingly.

In this example, Auto-Negotiation also makes upgrading easier. If a PC is initially connected (via category 5 cabling) to a 10BASE-T hub, it may be later reconnected to a 100BASE-TX hub. When the hub connection is upgraded, Auto-Negotiation automatically configures the client for 100 Mb/s operation. A technician need visit only the wiring closet to accomplish the upgrade (a huge savings in labor compared to visiting all the client locations). If all the clients have dual-speed 10/100 adapters, upgrading a hub is a snap.

Other networks with fewer operational modes have less need for automatic configuration features. Fast Ethernet defines so many operating modes that automatic configuration has become necessary. In that sense, Fast Ethernet brought this problem on itself. In another sense, one could argue that Fast Ethernet is solving problems other LANs do not even have yet.

Auto-Negotiation: Distinguishing Features

Supported Modes. Auto-Negotiation is defined for all 802.3 LAN transceivers that use the 8-pin modular jack (RJ-45). This will include transceivers defined in the future. At the present time, it also includes some full-duplex operating modes that have not yet been completely standardized.

Auto-Negotiation works its magic every time a link is connected, powered on, or reset. Before enabling data transmission on the link, the Auto-Negotiation algorithm first exchanges information with the device at the far end. During the exchange, each device advertises its own capabilities and records the advertised capabilities of the device at the far end. Presumably, the device at one end or the other has been configured by the user to advertise only those capabilities supported by the installed cabling.

By the end of the exchange, the devices have determined the modes that they have in common. Of the common modes, both devices then select the highest priority mode, according to Table 3.11. The rationale behind Table 3.11 is this:

- Plain 10BASE-T, the lowest common denominator, is selected only if no other alternative is available.
- Any 100 Mb/s mode is higher in priority than any 10 Mb/s mode.
- The ordering of T4 and TX modes is almost moot, because they support different types of cable. Few, if any, devices will support both.
- Full duplex is always better than half duplex at the same speed.

Table 3.11 Priority Resolution Table

Transceiver Type	Cable	Duplex Mode	Auto-Negotiation Priority
100BASE-TX	Two-pair cat.5 UTP	Full	High
100BASE-T4	Four-pair cat.3 UTP	Half	
100BASE-TX	Two-pair cat.5 UTP	Half	
10BASE-T	Two-pair cat.3 UTP	Full	
10BASE-T	Two-pair cat.3 UTP	Half	Low

Knowledge of Cable Plant Required. Auto-Negotiation presumes the customer has knowledge of the installed cable. It can not determine by itself the type of cable in the walls. Neither can it determine the number of pairs. This is not a deficiency in Auto-Negotiation, it is a generic problem with the installation process.

For example, when working with single-capability devices, the customer must always ensure that the installed cable meets any special criteria required by that device. Presumably, the customer knows the type of cable, the number of pairs, and the requirements of the transceiver.

When working with multicapability devices, the situation is more complex. The customer must ensure that the installed cable supports *all* the modes advertised by a multicapability transceiver. Otherwise, the

Auto-Negotiation mechanism may select a mode not supported by the cable.

Many multicapability products provide means for telling the transceiver the type of cable that is installed. Auto-Negotiation will then advertise only those modes supported on the installed cable. Procedures for telling multicapability devices about installed cabling vary widely by manufacturer. Ask you vendor if this is possible, and if so, how to do it.

When installed with the wrong cable, Auto-Negotiation makes bad configuration choices (like enabling TX on category 3 cable or enabling T4 on two-pair cable). There are no safeguards against these errors. Of course, there are no safeguards in systems without Auto-Negotiation either. With bad cables, many transceivers just will not work.

Auto-Negotiation: Other Features

Compatibility with 10BASE-T. Auto-Negotiation communicates with a simple, low-rate sequence of pulses. This sequence is intentionally incompatible with the 10BASE-T link integrity test sequence. When connected to a dumb 10BASE-T interface, the dumb end of the link at first remains inactive. If the Auto-Negotiating device has 10BASE-T capability, then within a few hundred milliseconds Auto-Negotiation recognizes the 10BASE-T pulses from the far end and reciprocates by dropping into 10BASE-T mode. Thereafter, both ends of the link operate in ordinary 10 Mb/s, 10BASE-T mode.

Special Interfaces. Two Fast Ethernet transceiver types enjoy special status in the Auto-Negotiation hierarchy:

1. 100BASE-T4
2. 100BASE-TX

Their special status pertains to automatic recognition without use of the full Auto-Negotiation protocol. In these two cases, Auto-Negotiation permits automatic recognition of the far end device even if the far end does not support Auto-Negotiation. The native idle signals used by these two transceivers are sufficiently diverse to permit immediate recognition without further delay.

For example, let the device on the far end be a dumb, pure TX transceiver with no Auto-Negotiation capability. A suitably smart Auto-Negotiating device with TX capability can still lock onto it.

Future Fast Ethernet UTP transceiver types will likely not be granted special status, they will instead be required to support Auto-Negotiation.

Support for Full Duplex. Auto-Negotiation has reserved operating modes for full-duplex communications. These modes will probably be used in a future standard to enable full duplex in the simplest sense of the term, that is, with no means of automatic flow control. The 802.3 committee is currently reviewing the flow control issue, and may (or may not) standardize flow control issues related to full-duplex operation. For now, when Auto-Negotiation selects full duplex, it probably enables a connection with no flow control (or proprietary flow control).

Auto-Negotiation: Options

Implementation of Auto-Negotiation is entirely optional. Manufacturers may freely implement single-capability devices that do not respond to Auto-Negotiation signals, or even multicapability devices that do not respond to Auto-Negotiation signals (using, for example, a switch or a software setting to select operating modes).

For devices that claim compliance with Auto-Negotiation, the primary options include the following:

Transceiver capabilities	Can include 10BASE-T, 10BASE-T full duplex, 100BASE-T4, 100BASE-TX, and 100BASE-TX full duplex (full-duplex functionality to be defined).
Next page feature	A general mechanism for exchanging additional optional information, including a unique identifier code, as well as other vendor-specific information.
Remote fault indication	Auto-Negotiation allows signaling of any local fault condition to the other end.
Automatic recognition of some protocols	Auto-Negotiation permits automatic recognition of 10BASE-T, 100BASE-T4, and/or 100BASE-TX, even if the far end does not support Auto-Negotiation.

Points to Remember

- Auto-Negotiation encompasses three separate issues:

  1. A variety of transceiver capabilities
  2. Recognition of Auto-Negotiation pulses from the far end and determination of the best operating mode
  3. Optional automatic recognition of 10BASE-T, 100BASE-T4, and/or 100BASE-TX, even if the far end does not support Auto-Negotiation

- Accurate knowledge of the cable plant is required.
- Procedures for telling multicapability devices about installed cabling vary widely by manufacturer. Ask your vendor if this is possible, and if so, how to do it.

TOPOLOGY (CLAUSE 29)

Ethernet repeaters must obey certain timing rules. These rules limit the way that repeaters may be connected. Foremost among these rules is the *collision domain timing constraint*.[27] This constraint addresses the propagation delay of a network.

Because data signals travel at finite speed, the propagation delay through a network depends on its physical extent. As a network grows, the worst-case packet propagation time lengthens. If a network gets too large, it may violate the collision domain timing constraint. Violate this constraint, and a network will experience late collisions, lost packets, and generally poor performance.

Clause 29 lays down the rules of the road for 100 Mb/s networks, showing just how large a collision domain can be while still meeting both the spirit and the letter of all the Ethernet collision domain timing

---

[27] Ethernet devices connected by repeaters are said to exist within the same *collision domain*. Only one device at a time may successfully communicate inside a collision domain. Bridges, switches, and routers partition a network into independent collision domains across which the collision domain timing constraint does not apply. See general discussion in Chapter 2, *Repeater Architecture*, and further details in Chapter 7.

Network Delays Are Tiny, But Important
Typical network delays, by any objective measure, are very tiny. After all, signals propagate through a LAN at close to the speed of light. It seems as if these delays should not matter, but they do. Modern networks operate so fast that even the tiny delays involved in signal propagation can impair network performance.
Adherence to the collision constraint ensures that network delays will not cause problems.

constraints.[28] For reference, here is a simplified version of the primary *collision domain timing constraint* (or *collision constraint*) appropriate for 100BASE-T (for details see Chapter 7):

> *In any collision domain, the round-trip propagation delay*
> *must not exceed 512 bit times.*

For Fast Ethernet, the collision constraint is ten times more stringent than for regular Ethernet. This happens because bit times in Fast Ethernet are ten times smaller than corresponding bit times in 10 Mb/s Ethernet. Consequently, the collision constraint, which is about 512 bit times for both networks, shrinks by a factor of ten. To satisfy the collision constraint, collision domains in Fast Ethernet must be physically ten times smaller than their counterparts in 10 Mb/s Ethernet. The Fast Ethernet collision domain limit is 412 m for zero-repeater networks versus roughly 4 km for 10 Mb/s Ethernet.[29]

Note that the collision constraint limits the maximum physical extent of an *individual* collision domain, but not a whole network. Large networks use bridges, routers and switches to interconnect adjacent collision domains. Inside each collision domain, the collision constraint still prevails, but between collision domains it is irrelevant. Each bridge, router or switch partitions the network into separate collision domains across which the collision constraint no longer applies.

---

[28] Authoritative information about 10 Mb/s topologies may be found in **IEEE Std 802.3j** (that's supplement **j**). This supplement includes revisions and updates to the older material in 802.3 Clause 13. Supplement **j** will be consolidated into the next version of **ISO/IEC 8802-3**, due out in late 1995.

[29] A maximally configured 10BASE-T network spans just over 4 km.

With bridges, routers, and switches, Fast Ethernet networks can grow to arbitrary size. Limitations on link distances between switches are discussed in *100BASE-FX: Distances* (this chapter).

The following material pertains to systems composed of a single collision domain. It presents three different methods for determining the maximum practical extent of a network. They are all derived from Clause 29. The first method, *Basic Model 1 Topologies*, is appropriate if your system fits one of the four topology templates in Figure 3.37. The second method, *Bit Budget Calculation Method*, is a complete and comprehensive method of determining whether or not any particular configuration will work. It is the most powerful and general of the three techniques. The third method, *Simplified Constraint System*, is a simplification of the second method. Its main advantages are that it permits multiple fiber connections, and that it does not require any spreadsheet work.

Any configuration permitted by any one of the three methods is valid.

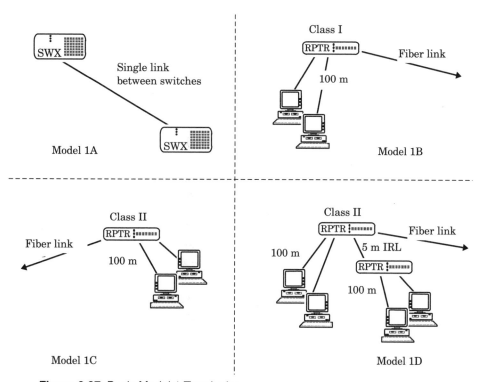

Figure 3.37 Basic Model 1 Topologies

Basic Model 1 Topologies (Single Collision Domain)

Clause 29 authorizes four specific example topologies. These topologies, referred to as Model 1 topologies, are summarized in Figure 3.37. Networks built according to these simple models always satisfy the timing constraints. No calculations are required.

The simple topologies each involve one long fiber connection, typically leading to a central switch (see examples of switch interconnection in *Implementing a Pure 100 Mb/s Network* Chapter 2). Table 3.12 summarizes the maximum permitted fiber length for each of the four Model 1 topologies. Multiple fiber links are permitted by each of the Model 1B, 1C and 1D topologies, but only one fiber may exceed 100 m in each case.

In the Model 1 topologies, twisted-pair TX or T4 connections are assumed to span no more than 100 m. The DTE devices drawn in Figure 3.37 as client workstations could be any type of DTE, including a client, workstation, PC, server, host computer, bridge, router, or switch port.

The direct DTE-to-DTE configuration is the simplest of the Model 1 topologies (top left, Model 1A of Figure 3.37). Only two devices reside in the collision domain. There is no repeater. The maximum link length varies from 412 m to more than 2 km, depending on the transceivers

Table 3.12 Summary of Basic Topologies

Topology	Maximum Fiber Length
Model 1A	
FX	412
FX full duplex[a]	2000
FX full duplex with single-mode optics[b]	20,000
Model 1B	
TX/FX only	160
If any T4 links are present	131
Model 1C	
TX/FX only	208
Model 1D	
TX/FX only	111

[a] Full-duplex links are not subject to collision domain timing rules.

[b] See *100BASE-FX: Distances* this chapter.

used (see Table 3.12).

A single Class I repeater (top right, Model 1B of Figure 3.37) supports T4 and TX links up to 100 m. A single fiber link, if present, may be as long as 160 m, or in some cases 131 m, as explained in Table 3.12. Such a link could be used, for example, to connect the repeater to a central switch.

A single Class II repeater (bottom left, Model 1C of Figure 3.37) produces a better fiber budget. The budget for Class II repeaters does not permit T4 to FX translation, so, If the fiber link is used, all the copper links must be type TX. The fiber link, if present, may as long as 208 m.

Two Class II repeaters (bottom right, Model 1D of Figure 3.37) produce the greatest flexibility. As in Model 1C, if the fiber link is used, all the copper links must be type TX. This configuration assumes a 5 m inter-repeater link (IRL). The fiber link, if present, may as long as 111 m.

Any of the repeater configurations shown in Figure 3.37 may be supplemented with one or more bridged (or switched) 100 Mb/s ports. Such a port may be used for the fiber connection. If a switched port is used for the fiber connection, it operates, for timing calculation, like a DTE. If the same switched port connects via fiber to a central switch, as opposed to a central repeater, the resulting DTE-to-DTE connection conforms to Model 1A and enjoys the rather generous fiber length budget listed in Table 3.12.

Bit Budget Calculation Method (Single Collision Domain)

The previous section illustrated four simple network models that always work. More complicated networks require bit budget analysis to see if they satisfy the Ethernet topology constraints.

Example questions answered by bit budget analysis include the following:

- The Y-Corp. Class I repeater timing budget is faster than Class I specifications. Can it use a longer fiber drop than indicated in Table 3.12?
- If cable delays are less than the maximum, will the system work with an inter-repeater link longer than 5 m?
- With two fiber drops on one repeater, what are the limitations?
- If I am willing to sacrifice on link lengths, can I employ more than two repeaters?

Bit budget analysis tells us whether or not a given configuration satisfies the Ethernet topology constraints. To check out a configuration, bit budget analysis examines the round-trip delay between every pair of DTEs in the configuration. No path between DTEs may have a round-trip delay greater than 512 bit times. If all path delays are less than 512 bit times, the configuration works. This calculation is called a *bit budget* calculation.

Figure 3.38 illustrates the generic components of a network used to perform a bit budget calculation. This figure depicts a single path between two devices. The client workstations shown in this figure could be any type of DTE including a client, workstation, PC, server, host computer, bridge, router, or switch. This generic path goes through two repeaters, although the bit budget process works with any number of repeaters. The alternatives for each part of the path are marked (link types, Class I or II repeaters, etc.).

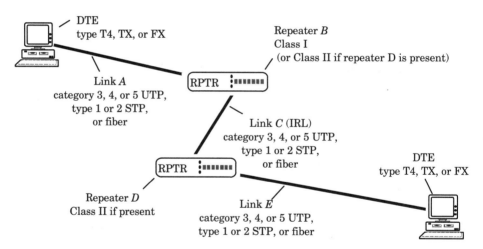

Figure 3.38 Standard Components for Bit Budget Calculation

Figure 3.39 illustrates a specific configuration, following the same general outline as Figure 3.38. Let's use the Bit Budget Worksheet in Table 3.13 to perform a bit budget calculation for the specific configuration in Figure 3.39. It has two repeaters (both Class II). The DTEs are both type TX. All the cable is category 5 UTP, and the cable manufacturer has assured us that the delay of this cable is no greater than 5.3 ns/m (a little faster than the worst case category 5 specification).

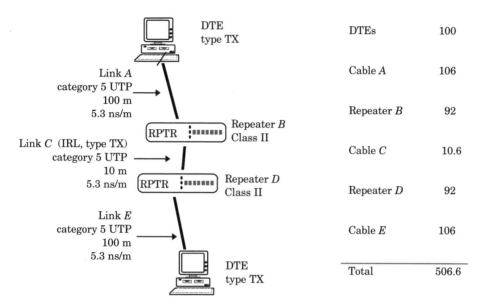

DTEs	100
Cable A	106
Repeater B	92
Cable C	10.6
Repeater D	92
Cable E	106
Total	506.6

Figure 3.39 Example Bit Budget Calculation

The Bit Budget Worksheet goes through each component of the system, adding up the path delays. At the bottom, the grand total had better come out to less than 512 bits. Go ahead and make a copy of the worksheet for this exercise.

The first section of the Bit Budget Worksheet concerns the DTE types. It lists three possibilities. Our example configuration has TX transceivers at both ends, so we place 100 bits in the rightmost column where it says "pick one above" (line [1]).

The next section concerns the cable segment labeled A in Figure 3.39. This is drawn in the figure as a 100 m cable. We know the actual cable probably isn't 100 m long, but since people rarely know the exact length, we will take the traditional precaution of using the maximum permitted length. Put 100 m on line [2].

The Bit Budget line labeled "round trip bits/m" is asking for the round trip delay of the cable, in units of bits per meter. The cable manufacturer has informed us that the one-way delay of the cable is 5.3 ns/m. We know that each bit time equals 10 ns, so this delay in units of bit times, equals 0.53 bits/m. The Bit Budget Worksheet asks for the *round trip* cable delay in bits/m, so we must double our figure to a final value of 1.06 bits/m round trip. Fill in the delay value of 1.06 bits/m on line [3].

Table 3.13 Bit Budget Worksheet

DTE types		
both T4	138	
any combination of TX and FX	100	
mix of T4 with either TX or FX	127	
pick one above:		[1]
Cable A		
length (m)	[2]	
round trip bits/m[a] X	[3]	
= cable delay:[b]		[4]
Repeater B		
Class I	140	
Class II with any mix of TX and FX ports, but no T4	92	
Class II with any port T4	67	
pick one above:[c]		[5]
Cable C (*N/A if only one repeater*)		
length (m)	[6]	
round trip bits/m X	[7]	
= cable delay:		[8]
Repeater D[d] (*N/A if only one repeater*)		
Class II with any mix of TX and FX ports, but no T4	92	
Class II with any port T4	67	
pick one above:		[9]
Cable E		
length (m)	[10]	
round trip bits/m X	[11]	
= cable delay:		[12]
	grand total:	[13]

a Use standard values from Table 3.14.
b Multiply length (m) times round-trip delay (bits/m) to get total delay in bit times.
c Or use better information from manufacturer, if available.
d The second repeater can by definition never be Class I.

If we hadn't already known the cable delay, we could have used the default delay values from Table 3.14. The default value for line [3] would have been 1.112 bits/m (category 5 UTP).

Table 3.14 Cabling Delays

Component	Round Trip Delay in Bits/meter[a]	Maximum Round Trip Delay in Bits
Cat. 3 cable	1.14	114 (100 meters)
Cat. 4 cable	1.14	114 (100 meters)
Cat. 5 cable	1.112	111.2 (100 meters)
STP cable	1.112	111.2 (100 meters)
Fiber optic cable	1.0	412 (412 meters)

[a] When cable speed is specified relative to the speed of light, the conversion to units of bit times per meter is: *(round trip bits / m) = (0.667128) / (speed relative to C)*.

Table adapted from Table 29-3 of 802.3u. Copyright © 1995 IEEE. All rights reserved.

Now multiply the length, line [2], times the delay per meter, line [3], to get the actual link delay. Place this figure (106. bits) on line [4].

In the next section, we note that repeater B is a Class II repeater, and that all of its ports are type TX. Place a value of 92 bits on line [5].

Cable section C is treated just like section A. Fill in line [6] = 10 m, and line [7] = 1.06 bits/m. Multiply lines [6] and [7] together to get 10.6 bits, which goes on line [8].

Repeater D is another Class II TX repeater. Place the value 92 on line [9]. If there had been no second repeater, we would have left sections C and D blank. If there had been three repeaters, we would have extended the spreadsheet to insert another section like the C and D calculations.

The last section, cable E, is again treated just like section A. Fill in line [10] = 100 m, and line [11] = 1.06 bits/m. Multiply lines [6] and [7] together to get 106. bits, which goes on line [8].

The grand total sums everything in the rightmost column. The correct total is 506.6 bits. The uppermost limit for bit budget calculations is 512 bits, so this system has a 5-bit timing margin. That completes the bit budget calculation for this path.

In a complex network, there are many paths. Technically, a complete bit budget calculation would check every possible path in the system. Practically, we need only check a few obviously long paths. All other paths being much shorter, this procedure proves the correct result while saving a lot of work. Note that there can be an unlimited number of other, shorter, paths. All that matters for the timing constraints is the worst-case longest path.

The longest path usually corresponds to a path between the two DTEs maximally separated from the central hub. Often it involves the farthest and next farthest of the DTEs. If there are two repeaters, the longest path usually, but not always, passes through both repeaters. If there is a long fiber drop, it is probably involved. When you are not sure which path is longest, evaluate several paths.

When performing these calculations, you may notice that *some components run faster than the permitted maximum delays.* If you have accurate information from your vendor, you may use it. If you use non-standard delay numbers, keep in mind that later changes of equipment may invalidate some long paths that previously worked. Stick to the worst case standard delays and it won't matter whose hardware you use.

Especially, check with your vendor about repeater delays. Repeaters without stacking or translation features generally run much faster than their more heavily feature-laden counterparts. Bear in mind that a faster repeater does not imply better network performance, it just means there are more bits available in the bit budget for attaching long fibers or long inter-repeater links.

The standard recommends, but does require, that manufacturers clearly label each repeater with its relevant delay information. Two delay numbers are needed for bit budget calculations: the *start of packet* (SOP) and *start of jam* (SOJ)[30] propagation delays. These two numbers are added together to determine the correct entry for line [5] or [9] of the Bit Budget Worksheet. In highly configurable products the SOP and SOJ numbers may depend on the installed complement of adapter cards.

Class II Repeater Budget

The Class II repeater budget varies depending on whether or not the repeater must support T4 transceivers. For technical reasons, the T4 DTE is slower than a TX or FX DTE. To compensate for the difference, the Class II T4 repeater specification was made that much faster.

---

[30] Also called the *start of collision* propagation delay.

Simplified Constraint System (Single Collision Domain)

The round-trip cable delay for fiber is only about 10% faster than category 5 cable. If we were willing to make the pessimistic assumption that their delays were the same (both 1.112 bits/m), then we could dramatically simplify the timing constraints at the expense of a mildly reduced fiber extent. To many users, this is a good trade. The resulting simplified rules appear in Table 3.15. This table restricts the maximum separation between DTEs under various assumptions about the types of devices in the network. Note that the number of repeater ports is irrelevant. All that matters is the worst case, maximum separation between DTEs.

Table 3.15 Simplified Constraint System

Individual link limits	
T4	100 m
TX	100 m
FX	412 m
FX full duplex	2000 m
FX full duplex with single-mode optics[a]	20 km
System limits for maximum separation between any two DTEs in a single collision domain	
T4-only with no repeater	100 m
T4/TX/FX with 1 Class I repeater	231 m
T4-only with 1 Class II repeater	200 m
T4-only with 2 Class II repeaters	209 m
T4-only with 3 Class II repeaters	151 m
TX/FX-only with no repeater.	412 m
TX/FX-only with 1 Class I repeater	260 m
TX/FX-only with 1 Class II repeater	308 m
TX/FX-only with 2 Class II repeaters	205 m
TX/FX-only with 3 Class II repeaters	122 m

[a] See *100BASE-FX: Distances* this chapter.

One advantage of these simplified rules over the Model 1 cases is that these rules permit the construction of all-fiber networks, for which more than one link exceeds 100 m. For example, with a single Class II repeater, the simplified rule set permits multiple fiber links spanning 154 m (yielding a maximum of precisely 308 between any two DTEs).

There is substantial reason to believe that, at this time, all category 5 cables have round trip delays no greater than 1.0 bit/m. If this rather favorable assumption were used, the last five figures in the right hand column of Table 3.15 would become 412/272/320/228/136. Beware that there are no internationally recognized standards mandating such an improved delay figure. That's just how cable is being made at present. According to ISO standards, category 5 cable is permitted a maximum (recommended) delay of as much as 1.112 bits/m.

Answers to Questions

The bit budget calculation examples below answer the questions raised at the beginning of *Bit Budget Calculation Method*. Note that these calculations include little or no margin. It is a good idea to include a few bits (perhaps five) of margin in real-world application calculations.

Question: The Y-Corp. Class I repeater timing budget is faster than Class I specifications. Can it use a longer fiber drop than indicated in Table 3.12?

Answer: Yes, it can. Assuming a specification for the Y Corp. Class I repeater of 128 bits, we may construct a bit budget showing 172 m of fiber.

Element	Delay (Bit Times)	Notes
DTE types	100	TX only
cable A	111.2	Table 3.14 cat.5 maximum
rptr B	128	Y Corp. Class I repeater
cable E	172	fiber, 172 m
grand total	511.2	

Question: If cable delays are less than the maximum, will the system work with an inter-repeater link longer than five meters?

Answer: Assume your cable vendor has guaranteed a category 5 cable delay of less than 5.0 ns/m (= 1 bit time per meter round-trip). The bit budget below permits an inter-repeater link (IRL) of 27 m.

Element	Delay (Bit Times)	Notes
DTE types	100	TX only
cable A	100	100 m at 1 bit/meter round-trip
rptr B	92	TX Class II
cable C	27	27 m IRL
rptr D	92	TX Class II
cable E	100	100 m at 1 bit/meter round-trip
grand total	511	

Question: With two fiber drops on one repeater, what are the limitations?

Answer: Assuming we have a single Class I repeater, the longest path will probably involve the two longest fiber runs. Let's make the two longest fiber runs equal length. This example shows a safe fiber length of 135 m. Any number of fibers this length or shorter may be connected to a Class I TX repeater.

Element	Delay (Bit Times)	Notes
DTE types	100	TX only
cable A	135	135 m fiber at 1.00 bit/m round-trip
rptr B	140	standard Class I repeater
cable E	135	135 m fiber at 1.00 bit/m round-trip
grand total	510	

Question: If I am willing to sacrifice on link lengths, can I employ more than two repeaters?

Answer: Yes, three repeaters are practical for networks of limited extent. The worst case path will traverse all three repeaters, so in the bit budget, we must add IRL cable C' and repeater D' to account for the extra repeater. The resulting system can tolerate client links of up to 56 m.

Element	Delay (Bit Times)	Notes
DTE types	100	TX only
cable A	62.3	56 m at 1.112 bit/meter round-trip from Table 3.14 (cat.5)
rptr B	92	standard TX Class II repeater
cable C	5.6	5 m IRL at 1.112 bit/meter
rptr D	92	standard TX Class II repeater
cable C'	5.6	5 m IRL at 1.112 bit/meter
rptr D'	92	standard TX Class II repeater
cable E	62.3	56 m at 1.112 bit/meter
grand total	511.8	

Points to Remember

- The collision constraint limits the maximum diameter of any collision domain.
- Bridges, routers, and switches can tie collision domains together into arbitrarily large networks.
- The basic topologies in Figure 3.37, and in the Simplified Constraint System, always work.
- Advanced topologies require bit budget calculations.
- Some vendors tout delay budgets better than the standard. It may not be in your interest to use these numbers. You could get boxed in.

MANAGEMENT (CLAUSE 30)

This section describes the features and options provided by Clause 30. It is not by any means an exhaustive discussion of network management.[31]

The following sections set the stage for those not familiar with network management terminology. The last section outlines management features specific to Fast Ethernet.

Purpose of Network Management

Network management systems are complex. They incorporate massive numbers of features and are difficult to compare from system to system. When studying network management systems, keep in mind the following dictum:[32]

> *The ability to remotely enable and disable ports is 90% of network management. The rest is figuring out **WHEN** to enable and disable the ports.*

The mere ability to remotely enable and disable ports (port administration) is very powerful. When something goes violently wrong, a network administrator can often turn off the offending device, freeing the remainder of the network to return to work as usual. Port administration also may be used to switch on and off bridged connections, effectively re-configuring a network by remote control. Especially in widely dispersed installations, port administration is invaluable.

Structure of Network Management Applications

A network management system consists of one or more master network management stations, called *management consoles*, and a collection of managed devices called *agents*. There may be any number of agents.

A management console is just a software application. It may be run on any computer attached to the network. A management console

---

[31] Network management is a relatively new field. The numerous network management standards available from ISO, IETF, and IEEE are, at best, confusing. A complete discussion of network management and the reasons for having it lies beyond the scope of this book. For more information about network management, see Rose, Marshall T., *The Simple Book*, Prentice Hall, Upper Saddle River, NJ: 1991.

[32] Thanks to Geoff Thompson, of Bay Networks, for this bit of wisdom.

collects and evaluates data from the agents. An agent is another piece of software that runs inside a managed device. The agent has access to information inside the device and can control certain aspects of the device's behavior. The agent responds to network management commands from any management console. Agents may reside in any of the following devices types:

- Host computer
- File server
- Workstation
- PC
- Gateway

- Bridge
- Router
- Switch
- Hub (Repeater)

In short, any network device may contain a network management agent. A management console can interact in four ways with the agents:

1. It can query an agent to determine its status.
2. It can set status registers inside the agent that control device behavior.
3. It can receive special alarm indications from the agent (power-on, power-off, link-up, link-down, and others).
4. It can issue commands to the agent, like RESET.

A management console interacts with the user (the human network manager) through a network management user interface. This interface makes available the results of queries and alarms and provides a way to control the agents. The look and feel of the management user interface is proprietary. The look and feel of the user interface strongly differentiates network management products.

Network management as used with Ethernet does not manage individual packets. Ethernet management concerns events at a higher, aggregate level. For example, a typical Ethernet management query might report an event count or a traffic statistic. A typical Ethernet control function might turn a device on or off.

Logically, a network management specification has two parts: a *management information database* (MIB) and a *management protocol* used to query and manipulate the database.

The MIB specifies how the agent should count events, report status, generate alarms, and respond to commands. There is a different MIB specification for each type of device in a network. For example, the

MIB for a MAC entity includes a *promiscuous mode* bit. The MIB for a repeater port does not. Each type of device has its own MIB.

The Fast Ethernet MIB specifications leave room for proprietary extensions to the MIB. These extensions are nonstandard. For example, a network management console from Y-Corp may not understand or interpret the MIB extensions in Z-Corp's hub. The Y-Corp system works with the standard portions of the Z-Corp MIB, but not the proprietary MIB extensions.

The management protocol communicates management queries and control commands between the management console and the agents.

Fast Ethernet Network Management Features

Clause 30 addresses only one narrow aspect of management: the MIB. It does not specify or require the use of any particular management protocol. Most manufacturers will choose to provide access to the Clause 30 MIB using SNMP (see next section).

Clause 30 defines a complete MIB for all 100BASE-T components. It also consolidates all previous Ethernet MIB specifications.[33] The result is a seamless system that manages both 10 Mb/s and 100 Mb/s agents. Existing 10 Mb/s network management stations can manage the new 100 Mb/s agents with only minor modification of their software.

Clause 30 defines MIB objects, attributes and actions for the following device types:

10 Mb/s DTE	A 10 Mb/s client, server, host, or other end station.
10 Mb/s baseband repeater unit	The core of a 10 Mb/s repeater set. A 10 Mb/s repeater set includes the 10 Mb/s repeater unit and its attached transceivers (MAUs).
10 Mb/s integrated MAU	10 Mb/s transceiver. If the MAU is attached to the DTE via an AUI interface, no management is possible. When the MAU is integrated into the DTE, some management features are possible.
100 Mb/s DTE	A 100 Mb/s client, server, host, or other end station.

---

[33] 10 Mb/s Ethernet MIB specifications were originally contained in 802.3 Clauses 5, 19, and 20. These older clauses have now been subsumed into Clause 30.

100 Mb/s baseband repeater unit	The core of a 100 Mb/s repeater set. A 100 Mb/s repeater set includes the 100 Mb/s repeater unit and its attached transceivers (MAUs and PHYs).
100 Mb/s PHY	100 Mb/s transceiver. PHY management features work the same way regardless of whether the PHY is attached to the DTE via an MII interface or integrated into the DTE.

The objects, attributes, and actions defined for these devices fall into several categories, called *capabilities*. The capabilities specify groups of logical functions that naturally go together. Manufacturers may choose to implement or not implement various combinations of capabilities.

Table 3.16 lists the names of the authorized capabilities, along with a brief description of their contents.

Protocols for Network Management

The two most popular protocol standards for network management are SNMP and CMIP. Of the two, SNMP is the runaway best seller.

The *Simple Network Management Protocol* (SNMP) is a product of the *Internet Engineering Task Force* (IETF), a technical branch of the *Internet Architecture Board* (IAB), which organizes the Internet. It was first introduced by means of a *Request for Comments* (RFC) document published by the IETF in 1988.[34]

The *Common Management Information Protocol* (CMIP) is an ISO standard first published in 1990. It is more comprehensive and powerful than SNMP. It is also so complex and overhead intensive that few manufacturers have implemented it.

The management protocols SNMP and CMIP are incompatible. A MIB developed for one is not always easily translatable into a MIB usable by the other. Yet the Fast Ethernet standard maintains strategic compatibility with both SNMP and CMIP. Figure 3.40 illustrates how Fast Ethernet achieves this feat.

The Fast Ethernet management strategy comprises three elements: a protocol-independent MIB, a CMIP MIB, and an SNMP MIB. Explaining *why* Fast Ethernet chose to support three MIBs is rather involved, but we'll do our best.

---

[34] See contact information for the IETF in Chapter 8.

Table 3.16 MIB Capabilities

		Applies To		
Capability	**Contents**	**DTE**	**RPTR**	**PHY (MAU)**
Basic	Detect equipment present. Initialize equipment. Read equipment ID numbers. (For repeaters detect port capacity.)	√	√	√
Mandatory	Count frames transmitted, received, and collided. Count received FCS errors.	√		
Recommended	Additional breakout of error conditions. Control of promiscuous receive mode.	√		
Optional	Multicast frame statistics. Frame length conditions. Control of MAC transmit and receive enable.	√		
Array	Histogram of collision activity.	√		
Excessive Deferral	Indicates severe congestion.	√		
Multiple PHY	For systems that include multiple PHY entities per MAC entity.	√		
100 Mb/s Monitor	New performance attributes detectable by 100 Mb/s devices. Symbol errors. False carrier events.	√	√	√
Performance Monitor	Count frames and octets. Errors of alignment, length, and FCS. Collisions and late collisions. Indicates repeater partitioning.		√	
Address Tracking	Tracks source address on packets.		√	
MAU Control	Reset, shutdown, standby, and operate commands.			√
Media Loss Tracking	Reports loss of media availability.			√
Broadband DTE MAU	Specific to Broadband MAU.			√
MII	Report MII type ID.			√
Auto-Negotiation	Control and configuration of Auto-Negotiation.	√	√	√

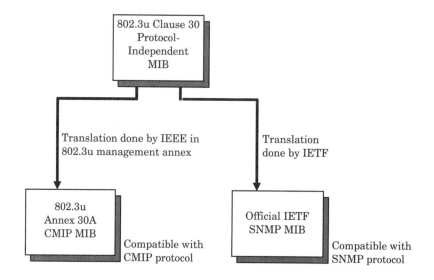

Figure 3.40 Strategy for Development of Fast Ethernet Management

First, all IEEE management documents, like Fast Ethernet Clause 30, must conform to **IEEE Std 802.1f**. This is an IEEE requirement. The 802.1f management standard was derived with CMIP conversion in mind, not SNMP, because the 802.1f committee felt that any ISO-track LAN standard, like Ethernet, should use ISO management standards, and CMIP is the *only* approved ISO management standard. It therefore follows the CMIP conventions for variable definitions, and so forth. The problem with CMIP is that a CMIP design does not always translate easily into SNMP, and customers want SNMP.

To get around this problem, the architects of Fast Ethernet management chose not to directly define a CMIP MIB. Instead, they first defined a protocol-independent MIB (defined in 802.3u Clause 30). The protocol-independent MIB was then separately translated into CMIP format (see the management annex in **IEEE Std 802.3u**). This two-step approach satisfied the IEEE requirements. It was also good for SNMP, because the Fast Ethernet protocol-independent MIB was defined with easy SNMP conversion in mind.

The final step, conversion of the protocol-independent MIB to SNMP format, was not accomplished at the IEEE at all. The IETF, which has responsibility for maintenance of SNMP, had to do that part of the work. In 1995, the IETF converted the Fast Ethernet protocol independent MIB into SNMP format. Manufacturers now base their products on the IETF SNMP MIB. This three-step management development strategy grants Fast Ethernet compatibility with both SNMP and CMIP.

Many manufacturers are now making SNMP management interfaces for Fast Ethernet. Whether anyone will ever choose to implement the CMIP format remains doubtful.

Why People Like Simple Network Management Protocol (SNMP)

SNMP is a simple request—response protocol. Requests emanating from a central management console are answered by agents in the managed devices. The network management console continually polls the agents, asking each in turn to report its status.

SNMP is easy to implement. It runs fast. Its agent does not use up much memory. These are its primary advantages.

The main disadvantages of SNMP include weak security features and a limit of 32 bits on standard counters. Emerging standards for SNMP version 2 may eventually cure both these problems.

Points to Remember

When purchasing a new piece of equipment, ask these key questions:

- Does the device support SNMP management?
- If so, which management capabilities are supported?
- What MIB extensions, if any, are available, and what do they do?

4

Generic Cabling

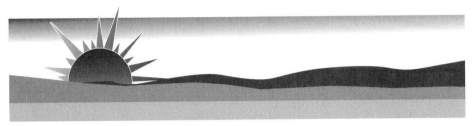

*I*nternational specifications for voice and data cabling have arrived. Customers who adhere to these cabling specifications can likely upgrade through the next few generations of LAN hardware without rewiring.

Not that long ago, each data communication standard mandated its own, unique, totally incompatible cable. As a result, conduits overflowed with different kinds of coax, twin-ax, tri-ax, multi-wire, quad, twisted-pair and fiber optic cables. Users accepted this sorry state of affairs for years. Most rationalized that the cost of new cables was small compared to the cost of the "big iron" in their computer room.

Today, that equation is reversed. LAN interface cards now sell for half the cost of wiring a new office. Installation of new wiring is no longer acceptable. Customers demand LAN systems that use existing wiring. The key term here is generic cabling. Users want systems that use generic cabling.

What is generic cabling? It is defined by two standards:

1. In North America: **EIA/TIA 568-A:1995** [1]
2. Internationally: **ISO/IEC 11801:1995** [2]

---

[1] EIA documents may be obtained from the Electronic Industries Association, 2001 Pennsylvania Avenue NW, Suite 800, Washington, D.C. 20006-1813.

[2] ANSI is the primary source and official sales agent for ISO standards in the United States: American National Standards Institute, 11 West 42nd Street, 13th Floor, New York, N.Y. 10036. Outside the United States, contact International Organization for Standardization, Case Postale 56, CH-1211, Genève 20, Switzerland. See additional contact information in Chapter 8.

These standards specify the preferred cables, preferred methods of installation, and preferred topologies for building wiring. The scope of both standards includes data and telephone wiring, but not wiring for power, HVAC, or building control systems. Building architects around the world are currently designing new structures according to these standards, which provide much needed wiring closet space within 100 m of every desktop location.

The EIA and ISO standards are related, but not identical. For example, definitions of critical terms in the two documents are, inexplicably, different. For the most part, they agree on these major points:

- Star wiring from central hubs located within 100 m of every office, is a good concept.
- Twisted-pair wiring (like phone wire) is best for desktop connections.
- For data wiring, coax is dead.

All new building wiring should be installed according to one standard, the other, or the common ground between them.

Which standard should you pick? This depends on your circumstances. The two standards emerged from different organizations, with different charters, for different purposes.

The EIA/TIA cabling standard was begun in 1985 by the Electronic Industries Association. In 1988, portions of the EIA broke away to merge with the Telecommunications Industry Association (TIA). Thereafter, this building cabling standard has been called **EIA/TIA 568**. The latest version is **EIA/TIA 568-A**, dated 1995. The EIA/TIA technical committees are dominated by U.S. and Canadian companies, and they produce standards relevant for use in North America.

The International Organization for Standardization (ISO) developed its cabling standards separately, through a joint technical relationship with the International Electrotechnical Commission (IEC). Their building cabling document is called **ISO/IEC 11801**. ISO standards take into account international considerations, such as the need for 120-Ω cabling in France. The first version of **ISO/IEC 11801** is dated 1995.

The safest choice for many users is the common ground between the two standards. The whole point of compatibility with cabling standards is to put in cabling now that future LAN products will be able to use. LAN manufacturers, when deciding what to build, look for the broadest application of their technology. For example, they may shy away from wiring practices, like 50 μm fiber, endorsed by **ISO/IEC 11801** but not by **EIA/TIA 568-A**.

For specific recommendations, see *Preferred Cable Combinations* later in this chapter.

GENERIC WIRING ARCHITECTURE

The building wiring standards, **EIA/TIA 568-A** and **ISO/IEC 11801**, define generic cabling for use in commercial buildings and between commercial buildings in a campus setting. These two standards pertain to data and telephone wiring, but not wiring for power, HVAC, or building control systems.

Generic wiring uses a star topology (Figure 4.1). In the star topology, cables fan out from a single location, called a telecommunications closet, to individual work areas. Cables running from the telecommunications closet to a work area are called *horizontal cables*. The word *horizontal* refers to the way users normally install such cables, running them along floors and ceilings. Horizontal cables are used for both computer and telephone communications.

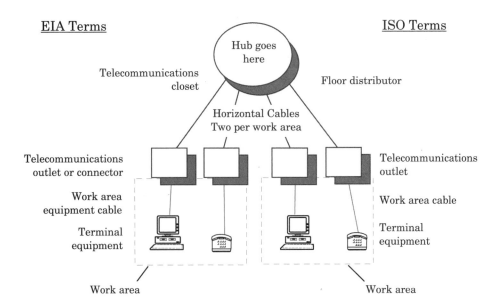

Figure 4.1 Horizontal Cabling

Early Adopters of Generic Wiring

IBM pioneered the field of integrated voice and data cabling with the IBM wiring plan introduced in 1985. It emphasized the use of star wiring, but not the reuse of existing wires. IBM defined its own, unique, incompatible wire for the task (150-Ω STP).

StarLAN, from AT&T, was the first 802.3 LAN to use *unshielded twisted-pair* (UTP) phone wiring. Like the IBM plan, it emphasized star wiring. Like the telephone system, it reused existing wires. Unfortunately, at a speed of only 1 Mb/s, this LAN was deemed too slow for widespread acceptance.

The first standard to get it all right, and as a result the most popular LAN to date, is **IEEE Std 802.3**, Clause 14 (10BASE-T). It uses star wiring and UTP and runs at a full 10 Mb/s. Users can install 10BASE-T without rewiring a building (see *10BASE-T Gets the Formula Right* in Chapter 1).

The generic wiring standards clearly define the topology for horizontal connections. A horizontal connection consists of no more than 100 m of cable, independent of cable type. The standards permit no bridges, taps, or Y connections in a horizontal cable. Each horizontal cable must be a dedicated, point-to-point connection.

The standards use different terms for some of the same horizontal cabling components. EIA terms are listed next, with their ISO equivalents in parenthesis.

Telecommunications closet (floor distributor)	A central connection point, within 100 m of the terminal equipment. Originally used (pre-1980 in the United States) exclusively for telephone equipment. Commonly called a *wiring closet*.
Horizontal cabling	Cables running from wiring closet to terminal equipment. Includes equipment cables at each end.
Telecommunications outlet	The wall jack or faceplate present in a work area.
Work area	Office, cubicle, or other place where computer equipment might be located.
Work area equipment cable (work area cable)	A flexible jumper cable or cord used to connect terminal equipment to a telecommunications outlet.
Terminal equipment	Computer, terminal, PC, server, or other computing device tied to the LAN.

Backbone cables, in the generic wiring plan, establish hierarchical connections between telecommunications closets (Figure 4.2). Backbone cables are also called *vertical cables* in reference to how they run between floors in tall buildings.

There are more choices for backbone cables than horizontal cables. For example, backbone cables often employ fiber, whereas horizontal cables usually do not. The plethora of choices makes it difficult to choose the right backbone cabling for the future.

Fortunately, most users do not have to make a permanent choice. Unlike horizontal cabling, typical installations do not have very many backbone cables. Backbone cables only run between closets, whereas horizontal cables run to every work area. Furthermore, backbone cables terminate in wiring closets, not in the work area where they have to look pretty. Both factors make backbone cables easier to replace than horizontal cables. The difference in effort required may be a factor of a hundred or more.

A user with the wrong kind of backbone cable can usually replace it. A user with the wrong kind of horizontal cable is stuck.

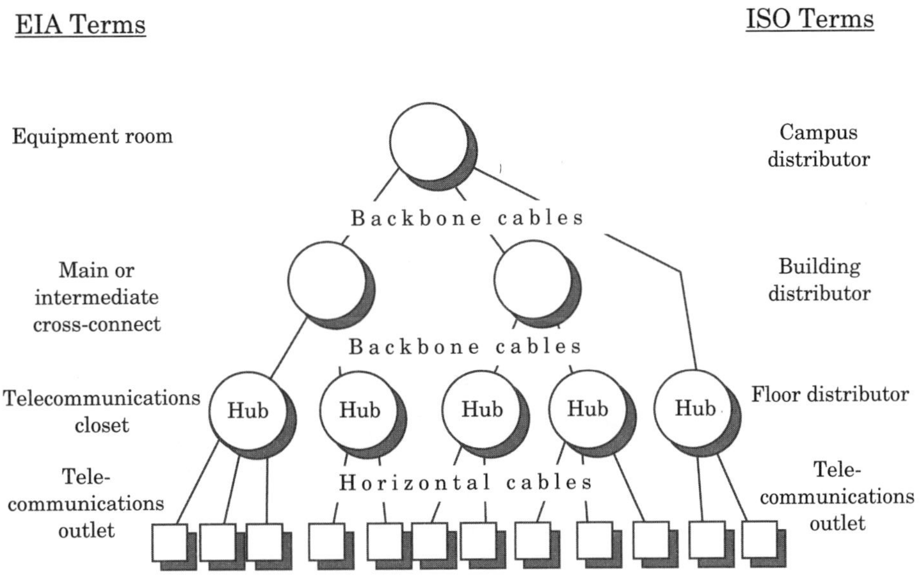

Figure 4.2 Backbone Cabling

The standards use different terms for some of the same backbone cabling components. EIA terms are listed next, with their ISO equivalents in parenthesis.

Equipment room (campus distributor)	Highest point in a cabling hierarchy. Place where a telephone switch, mainframe computer, or server pool might be located.
Main cross-connect, intermediate cross-connect (building distributor)	An intermediate wiring closet in the hierarchy.
Backbone cabling, or vertical cabling	Cables connecting floor distributors to each other and to other levels in the wiring hierarchy.

Each horizontal or backbone connection comprises a *link*. When a cable installer wires a building, there will be a lot of talk about *link performance*. Link performance is rated in terms of attenuation, crosstalk, return loss, and other factors.

Both **EIA/TIA 568-A** and **ISO/IEC 11801** contain specifications for link performance. Link specifications differ from raw cable specifications. The difference is attributed to additional components that are added to a cable in the field, that is, connectors and patch cords. Each of these additional components degrades the overall link performance. Taken as a whole, link specifications are worse than raw cable specifications. For example, in a link the attenuation is higher and there is more crosstalk than in a plain cable of equivalent length.

Definition of link specifications is an admirable goal, because it is the whole link, not just the cable in the walls, that a technician measures with field test equipment.

Unfortunately, the current ISO and EIA positions on the subject of link definition do not precisely match. Figure 4.3 illustrates the differences *as they existed in June of 1995*.[3] Apparently, there are four different kinds of links: an *ISO link*, an *EIA link*, an 802.3 *simplex link segment*, and a *basic link*.

---

[3] Beware that both ISO and EIA specifications are changing in response to pressure from the cable test equipment industry, cable manufactures, and manufacturers of LAN equipment. If these details matter to you, check the latest versions of **ISO/IEC 11801** and **EIA/TIA 568-A**. See Chapter 8 for ordering information.

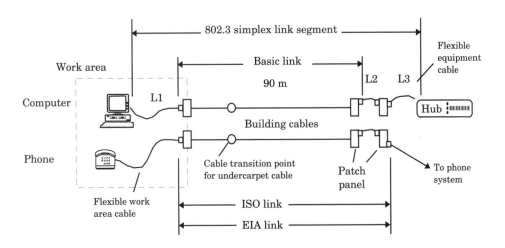

Figure 4.3 Anatomy of a Horizontal Link

ISO and EIA positions as of June, 1995

Item	ISO position	EIA position
L1 + L2 + L3	≤ 10 m	≤ 10 m
L2	≤ 5 m	≤ 6 m (recommended)
Cable transition point	Permitted, but not included in budget	Permitted, and included in budget
Flexible work area cable	50% greater attenuation than main cable	20% greater attenuation than main cable

The ISO and EIA links are very similar. They both define performance from wall jack to patch panel, with a 5-m (or 6-m) allowance for cross-connect jumpers (L2). A service technician would test to these specifications after installing the building cables and equipment patch-panels, but before attaching flexible work area or equipment cables. Minor differences between the two standards include the EIA allowance for an undercarpet transition point, the exact permitted length of patch cord L2, and the precise attenuation of the flexible work area and equipment cables.

The 802.3 simplex link segment is different. It defines performance from end to end, *including* flexible work area and equipment cables. As a consequence of their different definitions, the numerical specifications for 802.3 and ISO/EIA links differ. For example, the attenuation of an 802.3 simplex link segment[4] at 10 MHz is 11.5 dB, compared to 10.7 dB for an ISO link. The difference of 0.8 dB accounts for the last 5 m of jumper cable (L1 + L3), which is included as part of the 802.3 simplex link segment, but not the ISO link. The ISO link, plus flexible jumper cables, roughly equals an 802.3 link. Both ISO and EIA refer to the 802.3 style link definition as a *channel*. The EIA document provides advisory (that is, non-binding) values for the specification of a channel (see **EIA/TIA 568-A** Annex E).

The definition of a basic link (sometimes called a contractor's link) was created to address the need for a test specification that could be measured after installing building cabling, but before installing patch panels. In a tenant building, for example, a wiring contractor will pull cabling long before anyone knows what type of equipment, or what style of patch panels, will be installed at the ends. Specifications for testing a basic link are under development now, and may be included in future releases of the ISO and EIA building wiring standards.

Any of the four link definitions may be used. They are all roughly equivalent, but do not mix the numbers. For example, do not make the mistake of testing to the ISO link definition with the 802.3 numbers. This would be too easy a test. Defective links that should be weeded out might be inadvertently passed by such a test. When jumper cables are added to the defective links they will get worse and may fail to operate.

When discussing link compliance, specify the type of link: ISO, EIA, 802.3 (Clause 14, 23, or 25) simplex link segment or basic link.

The standards use different terms for some of the same link components. EIA, ISO and 802.3 terms are listed next.

802.3 Simplex link segment	A connection, including equipment cables, between two MDIs.
EIA link	A connection between a telecommunications outlet in the work area and a cross-connect panel in the telecommunications closet.
ISO link	A connection between a telecommunications outlet in the work area and a cross-connect panel in the floor distributor.

---

[4] See 802.3 Clause 14 (10BASE-T) simplex link segment definition.

HORIZONTAL CABLING

Let's examine the portion of generic wiring most relevant to LAN standards, the 100-m connection between a LAN equipment hub and a user desktop (Table 4.1).

EIA and ISO standards differ, but the differences regarding horizontal cabling are of little consequence. Both include support for the most popular cable type, 100-Ω UTP. Other points are explained in the following:

Cabling category rating system	The cable categories are a rating system for the data-handling capacity of twisted-pair cabling. Category 5 is the best. Category 5 cable, because of its increased data handling capacity, sells for a little more than category 3 cable. Category 4 cable fits between categories 3 and 5 both in its data-handling capacity and its cost.

Table 4.1 Cables Recognized for Use as Horizontal Cabling

EIA/TIA 568-A		ISO/IEC 11801	
Cable Type	**Pairs[a]**	**Cable Type**	**Pairs[a]**
100-Ω, category 3, 4, or 5 unshielded twisted-pair cabling (UTP)	4	100-Ω, category 3, 4, or 5 balanced cable[b]	2 or 4
150-Ω STP	2	150-Ω balanced cable	2
N/A		120-Ω, category 3, 4, or 5 balanced cable	2 or 4
62.5/125-μm multimode fiber	2	62.5/125-μm multimode fiber[b]	2
N/A		50/125-μm multimode fiber	2
50-Ω coaxial[c]	1	N/A	

[a] Or strands of fiber, or number of coaxial cables.
[b] Recommended by **ISO/IEC 11801**.
[c] Not recommended by **EIA/TIA 568-A** for new cabling installations.

Category 3

Category 3 cable corresponds roughly to the type of cable traditionally installed in North America prior to 1988 (DIW). This cable has a plastic (PVC) insulation surrounding four distinct pairs of wire. The wires in each pair gently twist around each other. The twisting reduces crosstalk between pairs.[5] The measured parameters of this generic cable have been standardized by the EIA committee and given the label *category 3 cable*. Older DIW does not necessarily meet category 3 specifications.

Category 5

The newer category 5 cable is better than category 3. It has more twists per inch (less crosstalk) and a better insulation material. The better insulation (usually a variant of Teflon™) helps reduce high-frequency signal attenuation, so signals go farther. New buildings typically install category 5 cable because it costs only a little more than category 3 and is an all-around better cable.

Number of pairs

EIA stipulates four pairs at each outlet. ISO lets users squeak by with just two. Germany is the country most adamant about using only two-pair cabling. Four is better, because it leaves the user more options. For example, T4 will not work on two-pair cabling. Also, the use of all four pairs avoids the problem of having to select which two pairs to equip at each four-pair wall outlet (FDDI TP-PMD, 10BASE-T, and Token Ring all use different combinations of two pairs).

UTP versus STP

The North American cable market draws a natural distinction between unshielded twisted-pair (UTP) and shielded twisted-pair (STP) cables. Most four-pair 100-Ω cable in North America is unshielded, while most 150-Ω cable is shielded (like IBM type-I). The terms UTP and STP, as used in this book, describe 100-Ω UTP and 150-Ω STP. This usage follows the terminology laid down in **EIA/TIA 568-A** (see Figure 4.6).

---

[5] Every half- twist, the polarity of crosstalk coupling reverses. After many twists, the alternating positive and negative crosstalk voltages tend to cancel.

ISO uses the terms shielded and unshielded differently. It reserves use of the term shielded to refer to cables having an individual shield on each twisted pair. The term *balanced cable*, in ISO terminology, encompasses both unshielded twisted-pair cables and twisted-pair cables with an overall screen (shield) over all pairs.[6]

100-Ω cable (in North America, commonly called UTP)

The most widely installed kind of twisted-pair cabling. EIA specifically calls for 100-Ω unshielded twisted-pair (UTP) cable.

The ISO standard leaves open the possibility of using 100-Ω twisted-pair cabling with an overall shield or screen (installations in Germany often use screened cable). Both T4 and TX will work with overall screens if the vendor provides a shielded RJ-45 connector.

120-Ω cable

This cable interests only a relatively small community of users (120-Ω cable is only manufactured in France). The technical argument in favor of this cable is that it has somewhat lower attenuation than 100-Ω cable. On the other hand, the majority of the installed base of cable worldwide is 100 Ω. To appease the French, ISO has standardized both. The ISO standard now leaves LAN vendors in a position of either implementing two network interfaces, for 100- and 120-Ω cable, or of compromising one basic design so that it will work on both cables.

150-Ω cable (in North America, commonly called STP)

Both standards permit use of 150-Ω cable. IBM designed this cable in the early 1980s. Physically, the cable is massive, unwieldy, and difficult to terminate.

Even though the majority of customers are not using it, 150-Ω cable is technically a very fine transmission medium. In some previous instances,

---

[6] Upcoming ISO regulations may, regrettably, require outer screens (shields) on all cables in the future, rendering systems with plastic UTP jacks incompatible. Plastic UTP jacks don't work with screened cable because, to meet proposed ISO regulations, the shield must make a continuous solid metal contact to the chassis of a product. UTP jacks made from plastic provide no such connection (they don't need it). Metal UTP jacks will soon be available to circumvent this problem.

new high-speed transmission schemes have become available on 150-Ω cable first. Customers on the bleeding edge of technology like this cable.

Mainstream LAN technology, however, uses 100-Ω UTP. The 150-Ω cable is just too bulky and expensive for practical, widespread use. Note that ISO lists 150-Ω cable on the *alternate* list, not the *preferred* list.

62.5/125-μm multimode fiber	The most popular fiber. ISO recommends this version, although many other types are available.
50/125-μm multimode fiber	A popular fiber in Europe and Japan. This fiber has better transmission properties than 62.5/125-μm fiber, but its smaller dimensions make shining light into the medium more difficult. For example, cheap surface-emitting LED's can easily spray light into a 62.5/125-μm fiber. More expensive edge-emitting LEDs with narrow beam outputs are sometimes required for use with 50/125-μm fiber.
	ISO has placed 50/125-μm fiber on the alternate list, not the preferred list. EIA does not recognize 50/125-μm fiber.
50-Ω coaxial cable	Originally used for bus-topology Ethernet. Superseded, in horizontal runs, by UTP cabling.

PREFERRED CABLE COMBINATIONS

EIA/TIA 568-A and **ISO/IEC 11801** do more than simply define acceptable types of horizontal cabling. They define in what combinations such cables should be used. According to the standards, *two horizontal links serve each work area.*

The work area in Figure 4.3 shows a pair of links in typical usage. One serves the phone and the other serves the data device.

Table 4.2 shows the cable combinations preferred by both standards. Here we have listed only the preferred arrangements, not all the compliant possibilities.

ISO specifications are more permissive than EIA. This is not good for the industry. It proliferates unnecessary cable choices. For example, ISO permits (but does not prefer) substitution of 120- or 150-Ω cable for 100 Ω, and substitution of 50/125-μm fiber for 62.5/125 μm.

The key recommendation given next is compatible with both standards. It uses high-quality preferred cables. This approach is safe and effective.

Key recommendation for a new building:

Horizontal wiring: Four-pair 100-Ω UTP, category 5, for both outlets in every work area

Backbone wiring: A mix of category 5 cables (for voice and low-bit-rate data services) and 62.5-μm multimode fiber (for data)

This recommendation retains compatibility with both standards, which provides for maximum future flexibility.

Regarding horizontal cabling, the simplicity of wiring category 5 cable to both outlets outweighs the potential cost savings of using category 3 to the telephone outlet and category 5 for the data outlet.

CROSSOVER WIRING

Many UTP star-wired LAN standards, like 10BASE-T and 100BASE-T, designate distinct pairs of wire for uni-directional transmission and reception. At the hub, and at the client, these wires occupy specific pin

Table 4.2 Preferred Horizontal Cable Combinations

EIA/TIA 568-A	ISO 11801
First outlet:	**First outlet:**
– Four-pair, 100-Ω UTP, category 3 or better	– Two- or four-pair, 100-Ω balanced cable, category 3 or better
Second outlet, any one of:	**Second outlet, any one of:**
– Four-pair, 100-Ω UTP, category 5	– Two- or four-pair, 100-Ω balanced cable, category 5
– Two-strand, 62.5/125 μm fiber	– Two-strand, 62.5/125 μm fiber
– Two-pair, 150-Ω STP	

positions on the data connectors. In the preferred arrangement, the hub and client have complementary pin assignments, so that the wiring may be accomplished straight-through, from end to end, connecting pin 1 on the client to pin 1 on the hub, pin 2 to pin 2, and so forth.

The preferred wiring arrangement is illustrated in Figure 4.4. In that figure, the client has a normal pin assignment, and the hub a complementary one. The wires run straight-through. Inside the hub, adjacent to the imaginary transmitter and receiver, there is a wiring crossover. A wiring crossover is an essential function in every link. It must reside either in the client, the hub, or the wiring.[7] The preferred location for a crossover is in the hub.

The use of straight-through wiring simplifies installation and maintenance considerably. It eliminates any concern about whether a link might have a crossover at one end, the other, or both.

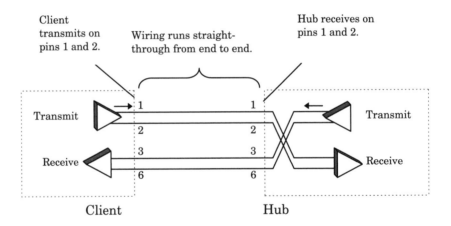

Figure 4.4 Example of Straight-Through Wiring with Internal Crossover in Hub

---

[7] Technically, the requirement is for an odd number of crossovers.

Certain exception conditions exist, like the connection between two hub ports, that require an external crossover (that is, a crossover explicitly implemented in the wiring). In these circumstances, the crossover should be implemented in a short, clearly visible section of wiring, and boldly labeled.

Wiring connections appropriate for crossover of Fast Ethernet links using 100-Ω UTP or 150-Ω STP appear in Table 4.3 and Table 4.4, respectively.

Table 4.3 Wiring Crossover for 100-Ω UTP; References are to RJ-45 Pin Numbers

	Pair		Pair		Pair[a]		Pair[a]	
From:	1	2	3	6	4	5	7	8
To:	3	6	1	2	7	8	4	5

[a] Not used by 100BASE-TX.

Table 4.4 Wiring Crossover for 150-Ω STP; References are to DB-9 Pin Numbers

	Pair		Pair		Other Pins are Not Used
From:	5	9	1	6	2,3,4,7,8
To:	1	6	5	9	

ANSWERS TO FREQUENTLY ASKED QUESTIONS

Planning an Installation

Question: What is the best way to wire a new building?

Answer: Wire at least two outlets in every work area. Use four-pair 100-Ω UTP, category 5, for all outlets. For backbone cables, put in a mix of category 5 cables (for voice and low-bit-rate data services) and 62.5-μm multimode fiber (for data).

Question: Can I mix category 3 and category 5 wiring in the same building?

Answer: Sure, if you don't care about permanently confusing your installation technicians. Without exceptional record keeping, it will be difficult to keep the two systems separate.

Question: We lost our cable records. How can I find out what cable is installed?

Answer: Ask your installer to test the cable to see if it complies with any recognized category of cabling. They should have equipment to verify compliance. If they do not, get another installer.

Question: What are the pros and cons of UTP versus STP?

Answer: First, let's straighten out what we mean by the terms unshielded twisted pair (UTP) and shielded twisted pair (STP).

In **EIA/TIA 568-A** (the North American standard) UTP refers to a 100-Ω cable with no shield, while the term STP is reserved for 150-Ω shielded cable (like IBM type I). With STP you need a shielded connector, and with UTP you do not. At one time, the LAN industry assumed that shielded cables were necessary for noise immunity. Modern, well-balanced cables have removed that obstacle. Shielding is no longer necessary.

The **ISO/IEC 11801** standard mostly avoids differentiating between UTP and STP. It uses the term *balanced cable* to refer to either type.[8]

In this author's opinion, the primary trade-off between UTP and STP has to do with cost, convenience, and the availability of equipment. UTP costs less than STP. UTP connectors are far more easily terminated. Mainstream LAN developers are making most of their equipment for UTP.

---

[8] Beware the little table buried in the back of **ISO/IEC 11801** Annex E which permits use of the term UTP to refer either to plain unshielded balanced cable *or* to a balanced cable that has an *overall screen*, but lacks individual shields on each pair. This confuses people familiar with **EIA/TIA 568-A**. ISO hints that we should call this a *shielded unshielded twisted-pair* cable (S/UTP). Connectors appropriate for this cable look like RJ-45 connectors, but have a metal shell for terminating the outer screen. Hopefully, ISO will correct this misuse of terminology in later versions of the standard.

Question: What should I use, T4 or TX?

Answer: It depends on your installed cable. Figure 4.5 shows what types of cable the two systems cover. The T4 standard covers UTP category 3 through 5, as long as you have four pairs available. The TX standard covers category 5 cable, with either two or four pairs. If you choose TX on four pairs of category 5 cable, you have two pairs left over for low-frequency services like message waiting lights, intercoms, and door buttons.

When cost is no object, rewire a building with two category 5 four-pair cables to every work area, and then install TX. This preserves maximum flexibility for the future (six open pairs for phones and low-frequency services).

Question: If my building has four-pair category 5 cable, are there any reasons to use T4 instead of TX?

Answer: You must trade off two issues.

1. **Cost.** T4 may be less expensive than TX.
2. **Saving pairs.** TX only uses two pairs, leaving two pairs free for low-frequency services.

Question: I've heard about 100BASE-T2. What is it?

Answer: T2 is a new 100 Mb/s transceiver type under development by IEEE 802.3. See *Link Transmission Technology* in Chapter 5.

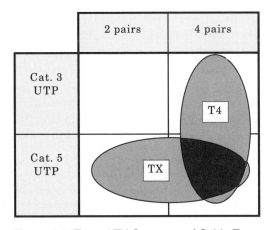

Figure 4.5 T4 and TX Coverage of Cable Types

Why Bother with Category 3?

Early in the development of Fast Ethernet, proponents of TX argued convincingly that, since many new installations were already using category 5 UTP, support for the older category 3 UTP was not required.

Other members felt that there was enough category 3 in the installed base to justify a category 3 UTP development. The problem was that practical category 3 solutions needed four pairs. TX required only two pairs. And no one wanted to burden new installations by requiring four-pair cable.

In July 1993 the 802.3 committee developed its present strategy of offering two physical layer standards. One would use four pairs of category 3 UTP (T4). The other would use two pairs of category 5 UTP (TX).

Question: Are EIA/TIA 568 B connectors OK?

Answer: This question refers to the two authorized ways of connecting twisted pairs to an RJ-45 style faceplate. These methods are designated T568A and T568B. The two methods swap the positions of the orange and green pairs on the connector. Ethernet and Fast Ethernet both work with either method as long as it is implemented the same way at every outlet in the facility.

Question: What about coax? How can I use it with Fast Ethernet?

Answer: The standard provides no way to run 100 Mb/s Ethernet over coax, but users connected to coax can still gain many of the benefits of Fast Ethernet. The trick is to use a 10 Mb/s switch with a 100 Mb/s server port. The switch will need AUI ports to connect to the old thick coax transceivers. The same approach works for thick or thin Ethernet.

First, break the coax network into a number of small collision domains. Wire each domain to a 10 Mb/s switch port. Right away, you get increased performance for peer-to-peer communications. But the server, if connected to a 10 Mb/s segment, is still the system bottleneck. Break through this bottleneck by connecting the server to the 100 Mb/s server port. Now all the coax segments funnel through a 100 Mb/s pipe to the server (see *Real Network Performance* in Chapter 2).

Question: My European branch offices have an overloaded network. They are using two-pair category 4 cable with 10BASE-T. What can we do?

Answer: Neither T4 or TX will directly address this situation, but there is a path to better performance. To avoid rewiring, keep the end stations on 10BASE-T, but use a switching hub. In the wiring closet, connect your server to a 100 Mb/s port on the switching hub. This works even better than the coax solution just mentioned, because the switch partitions the network into collision domains of one user each. Any combination of ten users can potentially drive its full bandwidth straight into the server (see Figure 2.7 in Chapter 2).

About T4

Question: Is T4 at 100 Mb/s as robust as 10BASE-T?

Answer: Inherently, raising the speed tends to make anything more susceptible to failure. The question is, how much faster is T4 and what other measures have been taken to ameliorate the problem.

First, the T4 system hardly goes any faster. 10BASE-T sends one Manchester transition (one half a bit) every 50 ns. In comparison, T4 puts out one transition, on each wire, every 40 ns. The 10BASE-T transition rate is 20 MHz. The T4 transition rate is 25 MHz, only a little faster.

T4 makes up this small difference by using a larger transmit amplitude and adaptive receiver equalization.[9]

Question: Does T4 comply with ISO cabling specifications?

Answer: 100BASE-T4 works on four-pair, 100-Ω UTP, category 3 or better, as defined in both **EIA/TIA 568-A** and **ISO/IEC 11801**. Conformance with the cable specifications is exact. Regarding installation practice, T4 goes further than ISO. T4 asks that you not leave big loops of wire hanging behind the connectors. As a result, link performance specifications for T4 differ slightly from the ISO values. See Chapter 3, *100BASE-T4: Exceptions to ISO 11801 Wiring Practice*.

Additionally, T4 assumes compliance with the ISO cable delay guideline for category 3 cable of 5.7 ns/m.

Question: I thought an ISO class C application was limited to 16 MHz. How can T4 be class C if it transmits 100 Mb/s?

---

[9] These improvements more than make up for the speed change and the change from binary (Manchester) to ternary (8B6T) coding.

Answer: The limitation for ISO class C is 16 megahertz, not 16 megabits per second. Hertz are different from bits per second. The highest fundamental frequency transmitted by 8B6T coding is 12.5 MHz, formed from a strictly alternating ternary pattern [1, -1, 1, -1, ...]. This frequency falls below 16 MHz, so T4 complies with class C. The aggregate data rate for all four pairs using 8B6T coding is 100 Mb/s.

Question: Do I have to use category 5 connectors with T4?

Answer: No. The T4 specification provides guidelines for the use of category 3 connectors (see Chapter 3, 100BASE-T4: *Exceptions to ISO 11801 Wiring Practice*). It asks that you not leave big loops of wire hanging behind the connectors.

The T4 spec does *recommend* category 5 connectors, but does not require them. Category 5 connectors exhibit less crosstalk and better noise immunity than category 3 connectors and should be used whenever possible.

Question: What about older cables, like categories 1, 2 and DIW? Can I use them?

Answer: These cables are not sanctioned by Fast Ethernet. You should be aware that DIW (classic 24 AWG twisted phone wire manufactured prior to the specification of category 3 cable) was the original basis for category 3 specifications. It should, in theory, meet category 3 specifications, but there are *no guarantees*. If you are not sure, have each link professionally tested for compliance with category 3.

Question: We have two-pair category 3 UTP in our building. Can I put T4 on two separate two-pair cables?

Answer: Not a good idea unless you can qualify the differential delay between cables. T4 tolerates up to 50 ns of differential delay, but no more. In a single jacket, differential delay never exceeds this figure. Between two jackets, routed over possibly different paths, a large delay difference could accumulate. Symptoms of excessive differential delay include flaky performance, FCS errors, and *rxerror* events in the transceiver. The rxerror events might or might not be counted by your management system.

Question: Can I use 25-pair cable with T4?

Answer: In the wiring closet, jumper cables made from 25-pair cable are allowed *only if category 5*. Limit jumper cables to 10 m. This permits use of high-density 25-pair connectors on a hub, which may then be wired to cross-connect blocks using a 25-pair jumper. Other uses of 25-pair cables with T4 are precluded.

Question: What does EIA say about 25-pair cables?

Answer: EIA/TIA 568-A, Annex G, states regarding the use of 25-pair horizontal cabling: "Although such an arrangement may provide installation efficiencies, it is not recommended for the general case ... the use of 25-pair cables for horizontal distribution should be undertaken only as a special case considering system engineering guidelines." The standard then goes on to stipulate how, *if they must be used*, 25-pair cables should be installed and labeled. Also see information in **EIA/TIA 586-A** Annex D about operating different services in the same cable. ISO remains mute on this issue.

Question: Can I use PVC cable in an exposed attic?

Answer: It depends on the type of air-conditioning system in your building, and the temperature of the attic. All air-conditioning systems pump cold air out through enclosed ducts. The conditioned air flows through the building and then returns to the main blower. At the main blower, part of the air is recirculated back through the fans. This saves a lot of energy compared to continually cooling fresh outside air. Building architects have the option of letting air return to the main blower through the open spaces in the attic (the *plenum*) or through separate return ducts. If the attic is used for returning air, you have a plenum-return system. When a fire happens in the attic of a plenum-return building, smoke from flammable materials in the attic pours directly into the main blower. This distributes deadly smoke instantly throughout the building. As a safety measure, plenum-return systems must use nonflammable materials in the attic. Polyvinyl-chloride (PVC), which emits dangerous gases when burned, is not permitted in plenum-return air systems. Plenum-rated cables are required.

Assuming that your attic does not constitute a plenum-return system, the other issue with PVC is excessive signal attenuation at elevated temperatures. PVC-insulated cable exhibits significant temperature dependence. Do not use PVC cable at temperatures greater than 40 degrees Celsius, or 104 degrees Fahrenheit, a temperature easily attained in an enclosed attic. Instead, use a less temperature-dependent cable, such as many FEP, PTFE, or PFA plenum-rated cables.

About TX

Question: Is TX at 100 Mb/s as robust as 10BASE-T?

Answer: Inherently, raising the speed tends to make anything more susceptible to failure. The question is what other measures have been taken to ameliorate this problem.

In the TX system, the improved quality of category 5 cable more than makes up for the increased speed. For example, category 5 cable, compared to the category 3 cable used in 10BASE-T, picks up far less noise. Category 5 cable also has less attenuation. These properties combine to make TX a very robust system.

Question: Does TX comply with ISO cabling specifications?

Answer: 100BASE-TX works on either two-pair, 100-Ω UTP, category 5, or on two-pair 150-Ω STP, as defined in both **EIA/TIA 568-A** and **ISO/IEC 11801**. It conforms to all EIA and ISO link specifications.

Additionally, TX assumes compliance with the ISO cable delay guideline for category 5 cable of 5.56 ns/m.

Question: We are planning a new building and will use category 5 UTP. Why do you recommend four pairs of category 5 cable instead of just two pairs?

Answer: The two extra pairs are almost free and may be used for low-frequency services like message waiting lights, intercoms, and door buttons. Also, if one pair breaks, you have backups.

Question: Can a four-pair category 5 cable support two TX devices?

Answer: This feature is not guaranteed by the specification. Ask your vendor (most say no).

Question: Will TX run on category 3 cable?

Answer: No, TX will not work on category 3 cable. Category 3 cable, even in short lengths, generates too much near-end crosstalk for TX.

Question: Why is category 5 cable better?

Answer: Compared to category 3 cable, category 5 cable has tighter twists and a better-quality plastic insulation. The resulting cable picks up less noise and has less attenuation.

Question: Can I use 25-pair cable with TX?

Answer: No. The TX specifications do not accommodate additional crosstalk that would result from other TX transmitters (or transmitters of another type) present in a 25-pair cable bundle.

Question: What is the difference between two-pair UTP and quad cable?

Answer: The difference is in the twist. Two-pair UTP has two pairs of wire, each of which twists round and round its mate, but not around the other pair. Low crosstalk in this wire derives from the way alternating positive and negative crosstalk effects cancel as the wires twist.

High-quality quad cable, or star quad, is often found in Europe. It

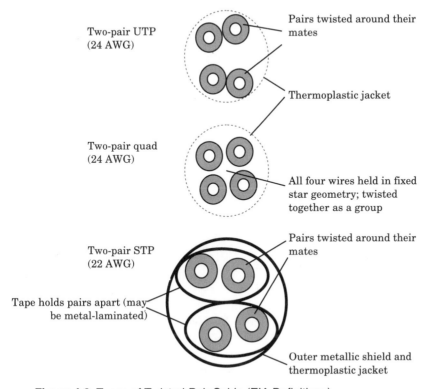

Figure 4.6 Types of Twisted-Pair Cable (EIA Definitions)

holds all four wires in a square configuration and then twists the whole bunch. The wires of each pair stay on opposite corners of the square (Figure 4.6). Low crosstalk in this wire derives from its exact geometrical symmetry.

Persons familiar with telephone cable might remember the old telephone-grade quad cable, which also had four wires, but no controlled symmetry. In the old telephone-grade quad cable, the wires of each pair could flop into any position. With no controlled symmetry, it had terrible crosstalk. Do not use it for data. Newer, data-grade quad cable carries a category rating of 3, 4, or 5, just like UTP.

About FX

Question: What are the grades of fiber? Which one does FX need?

Answer: Fiber is segmented into multimode and single-mode grades. Most short-haul LAN systems use multimode fiber. Among the multimode grades, the most important parameters are the core diameter (50, 62.5, 85, 100, or 140 μm), the attenuation in dB/km, and the modal bandwidth in MHz-km. Attenuation and bandwidth are specified separately at two operating wavelengths: 850 and 1300 nm. Multimode fibers are also classified according to their index profile. Ratings include step index and graded index. Graded-index fibers have higher performance.

FX is designed for 1300-nm operation over two strands of 62.5/125-μm graded-index multimode fiber. Both EIA and ISO provide fiber specifications suitable for use with FX.

In North America, use **EIA/TIA 568-A** *horizontal 62.5/125-μm optical fiber cable* (**ANSI/EIA/TIA 492AAAA**). The same grade of fiber is also authorized by EIA for backbone applications.

Internationally, use **ISO/IEC 11801** *62.5/125-μm multimode optical fibre* (IEC 793-2 type A1b, with 1.0 dB/km attenuation and 500 MHz/km bandwidth). For FX applications, the slight differences between this and the EIA fiber may safely be ignored.

If your fiber does not meet either of these standards, **ISO/IEC 9314-3**, the FDDI fiber-PMD document cited by FX, recommends at least meeting the detailed parameters in Table 4.5. Adherence to these parameters will guarantee operation up to 2 km. Operation at lesser distances is possible with poorer fiber. Finally, **ISO/IEC 9314-3**

Table 4.5 FX Fiber Parameters (Recommended)

Parameter	Value[a]
Core diameter	62.5/125 μm
Numerical aperture	0.275
Total attenuation	11 dB
Modal bandwidth	500 MHz-km
Zero dispersion wavelength	1295 to 1365 nm
Dispersion slope	Less than 0.093 ps/nm^2-km

[a] Values specified for operation at 1300 nm.

Annex C provides useful information about the use of FDDI optics with other multimode fiber sizes.

Question: Can I use FOIRL fiber for FX?

Answer: The **EIA/TIA 568-A** and **ISO/IEC 11801** recommended fibers listed above will work with either the Fast Ethernet 100BASE-FX standard or the older, 10 Mb/s FOIRL (and 10BASE-F) standards.

The existence of cables that satisfy both sets of standards does not, however, guarantee that *any* cable good for FOIRL is also good for FX. The two systems operate at different wavelengths (850 versus 1300 nm, respectively), and specify distinct sets of parameters. For example, FX includes important limits on chromatic dispersion that do not apply to FOIRL. In general, FOIRL will accommodate a lower grade of fiber.

Question: Will 50-μm fiber work with FX?

Answer: FX is designed for use with 62.5-μm multimode fiber. Just like the single-mode fiber problem, the smaller core diameter of 50-μm fiber reduces the amount of effective transmitted power, but only by about 5 dB. By shaving the fiber attenuation budget, the system can still be made to work. Informative Annex C of **ISO/IEC 9314-3** computes the expected coupling loss for various types of fiber. The fiber loss budget for a complete FX system is about 11 dB, of which at least 3 dB should be allocated to margin and aging. This leaves 8 dB to divide between coupling losses and fiber attenuation.

Question: Can I use single mode fiber with FX?

Answer: An FX transmitter produces a divergent light beam, much like a flashlight. When the FX transmitter illuminates the end of a multimode fiber core, most of the light hits the core and enters the fiber. Some light spills out the side of the fiber and is lost, but not enough to cause concern.

Single-mode fiber is different. Compared to a multimode fiber core, the cross section of single-mode fiber is much smaller (about 50 times smaller). Consequently, only one-fiftieth of the transmitted light from an FX source hits the core. This causes a reduction in the effective transmitted power of 17 dB. No receiver will pick up such a small signal. FX transmitters can not drive single-mode fiber.

Outboard optical converters, however, can solve this problem. An outboard conversion device can accept the FX multimode optical signal, convert it to electrical format, and then re-transmit the same signal with a narrow-beam single-mode laser transmitter. The resulting signal will propagate about 20 km on high-quality fiber. Full-duplex mode is required to achieve these distances (see Chapter 3, *100BASE-FX: Distances*).

Question: Which FX connector should I use?

Answer: In practical terms, this will be dictated by the style of adapters you purchase. If you want to use a particular connector, you will have to find adapters that support it. At present, FX authorizes use of three different fiber optic connectors (see *100BASE-FX: Cables and Connectors* in Chapter 3):

1. **ST** (also called BFOC/2.5) FX authorizes only the *simplex* ST, having separate connectors for the transmit and receive fibers. See also **EIA/TIA 604-2.**
2. **FDDI fiber-MIC** (ISO/IEC 9314-3) This duplex connector was originally developed for FDDI.
3. **Duplex SC** (also called duplex SCFOC/2.5) FX authorizes only the *duplex* SC, which houses both fiber connectors in a single plastic molded shell. See also **EIA/TIA 604-3**, and **IEC 874-14.**

At this time, ST is the most widely deployed. ISO has designated SC as the connector of choice for future facilities designs, but Fast Ethernet vendors will likely stick with ST, because ST is used for fiber in 10 Mb/s Ethernet.

Points to Remember

- Customers who adhere to international cabling specifications can likely upgrade through the next few generations of LAN hardware without rewiring.
- In a new building, install two outlets in every work area. Use four-pair, 100-Ω UTP, category 5, for both outlets.
- For backbone cables put in a mix of category 5 cables (for voice and low-bit-rate data services) and 62.5-μm multimode fiber.
- Building cabling standards are evolving rapidly. If you want the latest information, order the latest standards (see Chapter 8).

5

The Future of Fast Ethernet

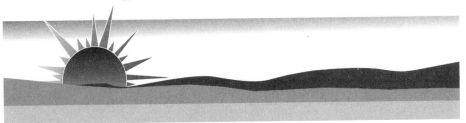

*F*ast Ethernet is a standard in motion. Like 10 Mb/s Ethernet, it will be maintained, enhanced and upgraded along with general improvements in technology. If you set company strategy or plan network growth, the following sections will show you where Fast Ethernet is going:

- Switching
- Full-Duplex Ethernet
- Multimedia
- Flow Control
- Link Transmission Technology
- ISO-Ethernet
- Wide Area Networking

SWITCHING

Switching, in most networks, will be deployed from the top down. It will start at central locations in the network, at critical junctures, and near the servers. Over time, it will push its way down toward end user desktops. Switching costs more, but boosts performance substantially (see *Switch Architecture* in Chapter 2).

The two most popular forms of switching today are *collapsed backbones* and *high-speed server connections*. Both are top-level applications of switching.

The collapsed backbone architecture uses a switch in place of an FDDI backbone. Figure 5.1 illustrates the idea. The users in this architecture all connect via 10BASE-T to local repeaters. Each 10BASE-T repeater has a long link leading to the central switch.

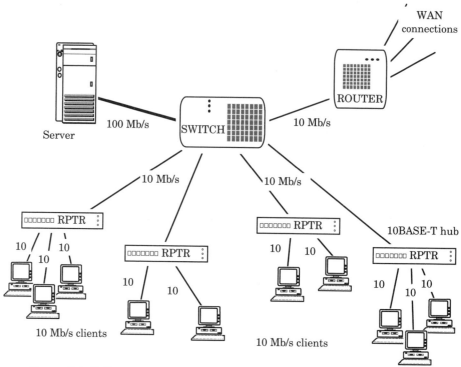

Figure 5.1 Collapsed Backbone Architecture

Remember that 10 Mb/s configuration rules permit such connections to span up to several kilometers.

The central switch can easily provide a total switching bandwidth far in excess of 100 Mb/s (FDDI speed). The aggregate bandwidth of a typical switch is already running close to 1 gigabit per second, with faster products just around the corner. That's at least two orders of magnitude faster than existing shared-media 10 Mb/s LANs.

The server in Figure 5.1 connects to the switch over a high speed 100 Mb/s link. The high speed link allows the server to run at its maximum potential, fanning data out to multiple 10 Mb/s clients simultaneously.

As individual users outgrow their 10 Mb/s shared-media segments and begin demanding more bandwidth, the repeaters in the collapsed backbone scenario will be replaced. There will be two choices for the early replacements: a 100 Mb/s repeater or a 10 Mb/s switch. In either case, the links from wiring closet to central switch will be upgraded from 10 to 100 Mb/s (Figure 5.2).

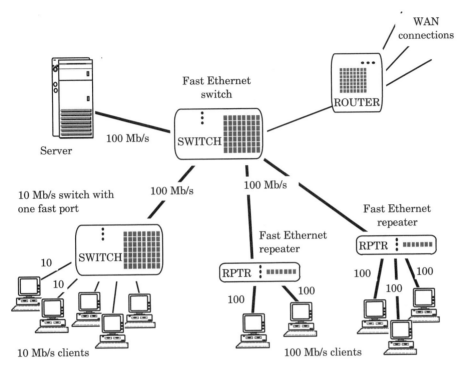

Figure 5.2 Upgrading Hierarchical Links to 100 Mb/s

The 100 Mb/s repeater provides a single 100 Mb/s collision domain that is shared by all its clients. The 10 Mb/s switch provides a dedicated 10 Mb/s link to each client. The repeater supports a higher instantaneous burst rate from each client, while the switch may provide greater overall throughput (especially if configured with a local workgroup server).

Eventually, as the price of switching comes down, and the demand for bandwidth goes up, all components of the network will migrate to switching technology (Figure 5.3). We will finally enter the era of high-speed switching to every desktop.

To handle increased bandwidth at the backbone level, there will undoubtedly emerge gigabit class full-duplex links between Fast Ethernet switches. These are depicted in Figure 5.3 as double-bold lines. Operating in full-duplex mode, these links will easily span campus-sized networks.

A full switching configuration will provide an aggregate system bandwidth in the multiple-gigabit range, plenty to support even the most demanding full-motion video applications.

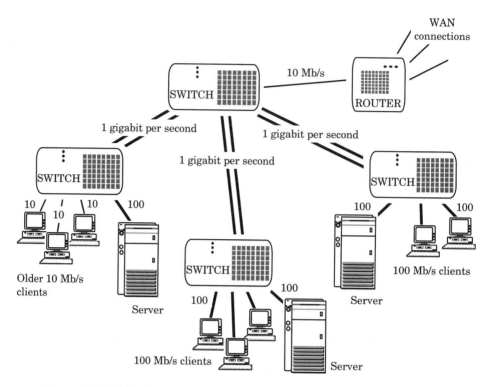

Figure 5.3 Full Deployment of Switching

To support the downward migration of switching, Fast Ethernet vendors will develop the following features for their products:

More ports	Today's backbone switches support Fast Ethernet ports only for server connections. Future switches will support every user. The addition of more ports will allow direct deployment of switching technology in very large networks.
Faster switching fabric	Inside a switch, the *switching fabric* routes packets to their destinations.
	Both the growth in number of ports and the increase in proportion of 100 Mb/s ports compared to 10 Mb/s ports will drive the development of faster switching fabrics. Switching fabrics with aggregate switching bandwidths as high as 10 or 20 gigabits per second are not unreasonable for near-term development.

More buffering	In response to the continuing fall in memory prices, switches will inherit larger internal packet buffers. Larger buffers will reduce the occurrence of switch buffer overflow, allowing use of switches at higher average traffic capacities. Overall network throughput will rise.
Better address filtering	Fast Ethernet ports used solely for fast server connections do not require sophisticated address filtering. With only one device attached to each port, recognition of a single MAC address per port is sufficient. Switch ports intended to support a hierarchy of other devices need more complex address recognition circuits.
	Full support for the spanning tree algorithm and other sophisticated address filtering features currently found on 10 Mb/s bridges will find their way into future switches. As users begin to demand multitiered hierarchies of switches, these features will become increasingly important.
Management tools	Expect to see a number of new management tools designed to help users deal with the complexity of hybrid repeater/switch networks. They will assist network planners with modeling network performance, selecting the right network components, order entry, and revision control.

Switching will fuel an explosion of available bandwidth at the desktop. This bandwidth will be used to expand the number of users connected to the corporate network, and to move files of increasingly large size. For example, the average size for a word processor file is growing at the alarming rate of 30% annually. At that rate, files double in size every three years. People are not writing longer documents. The documents they write just contain more formatting and images. This trend appears unstoppable. As sound, image processing, and full-motion video penetrate popular corporate applications the requirements for bandwidth will skyrocket. Only switching has the potential to satisfy this demand.

FULL-DUPLEX ETHERNET

Full-duplex operation will become prevalent between switches and between switches and servers. Major manufacturers are already implementing chips that will support full-duplex operation wherever possible, in switches, in adapters, and in bridges.[1] As switching technology trickles down to the desktop level, full duplex will follow.

Full duplex is a link feature that works with switching. This feature, when enabled, permits the simultaneous flow of data in both directions across a link. Not all Ethernet transceivers support full duplex. (see *Advanced Capabilities*, Chapter 2).

The effectiveness of full duplex hinges on local traffic patterns. If the traffic is evenly balanced between transmit and receive, then full duplex should, theoretically, deliver a 100% increase in throughput. If the traffic is less evenly balanced, the improvement diminishes.

There are technical circumstances in which full duplex can deliver more than a 100% increase in performance. Because full-duplex links experience no collisions, their efficiency in *each direction* is higher than the efficiency of shared-media links. Proponents of full duplex use this idea to concoct situations where full duplex provides more than a 100% increase in throughput. Be aware that these claims may involve unrealistic assumptions about the size of packets (they will be very small), and the balance of transmit to receive traffic (it will be unusually well-balanced).[2] When planning a system upgrade, do not rely on projections of anywhere near 100% improvement.

Most of the full-duplex argument will revolve around comparisons between two alternative architectures: 10 Mb/s full-duplex switches and 100 Mb/s repeaters. Figure 5.4 depicts the relation between these alternatives and an even higher performance alternative: 100 Mb/s switching. The arrows in this figure represent steps to higher performance alternatives.

---

[1] Full-duplex technology is not applicable to repeaters.

[2] Note that the balance of traffic over the short term, not the long-term average, determines the effectiveness of full duplex. At the client level, applications that store one chunk of data, then read another chunk, will derive almost no benefit from full duplex. Full-duplex benefits accrue only with *simultaneous* transmission and reception. Over time, operating systems and applications may begin to take advantage of this peculiar property of full duplex.

The arrows in Figure 5.4 depict the following seven rules of thumb:

1. Switching beats sharing at the same speed. It's never worse.
2. Full-duplex switching beats regular switching. The improvement may be as much as 100%, depending on the assumed traffic patterns.
3. 100 Mb/s switching beats any form of 10 Mb/s switching
4. At 100 Mb/s, full-duplex switching beats regular switching. The improvement may be as much as 100%, depending on the assumed traffic patterns (same as rule 2).
5. 100 Mb/s sharing is 10 times better than 10 Mb/s sharing
6. Switching beats sharing at the same speed. It's never worse (same as rule 1).
7. The relative performance of 10 Mb/s switching versus 100 Mb/s sharing varies widely. Parameters affecting performance in individual installations include the patterns of traffic, the number of switched ports, the size of the switch buffer, and the effectiveness of full duplex for the applications in use.

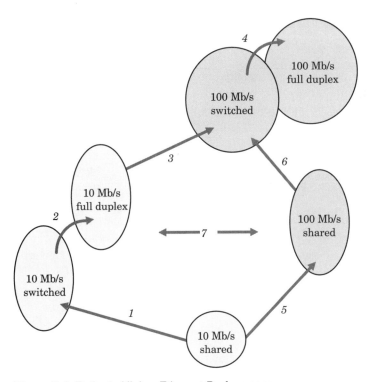

Figure 5.4 Paths to Higher Ethernet Performance

Full duplex is most useful in the following three circumstances:

Between server and switch	This is the most popular configuration for full duplex right now. In this configuration, expect a measurable, but not overwhelming, increase in throughput when full-duplex mode is enabled.
Between two switches	As switching pushes its way down through the network hierarchy, users will develop large, distributed networks in which each switch manages its own local server farm. In these applications, full-duplex links will provide close to a 100% increase in throughput. This increase will extend the life of 100 Mb/s backbone connections.
Between widely separated switches	For links greater than 412 m, full-duplex mode is essential. The CSMA/CD protocol cannot tolerate the delays associated with fibers longer than 412 m. Full duplex bypasses this part of the protocol, allowing communication at greater distances. Ordinary 100BASE-FX transceivers in full-duplex mode will communicate at 2 km. With single-mode fiber converters, longer lengths are possible (see *100BASE-FX: Use of Single-Mode Fiber*, in Chapter 3).

MULTIMEDIA

Significant multimedia applications will evolve for Fast Ethernet networks. These applications will bring interoffice communications, teleconferencing, broadcast TV, and video-based corporate training to the desktop.

This section describes how Fast Ethernet, as specified today, works with these new applications. There are good points and bad ones. The next section, *Flow Control*, points the way toward new features and capabilities that will hasten the arrival of true video-based multimedia applications for Fast Ethernet.

Already, people are building multimedia applications based on MPEG, JPEG, H.261, and the older DVI video compression algorithms. Several of these algorithms were originally developed to support CD-ROM-based video applications on stand-alone PC workstations. A typical example of a stand-alone video architecture appears in Figure 5.5. From a CD-ROM, the system reads compressed video files at a rate

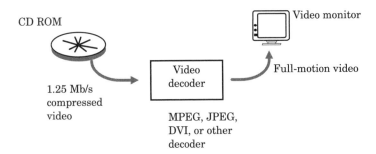

Figure 5.5 Standalone Video Architecture

of 1.25 Mb/s (or less). These feed into a video decoder, which converts them to full-motion video signals in NTSC, RGB, or some other monitor-compatible format. The decoder hardware also performs the task of mixing decoded video with other locally generated computer images, like the operating system window.

These applications work well with existing 10 Mb/s Ethernet.[3] As shown in Figure 5.6, the data link between CD-ROM and the decoder hardware can be replaced by a network connection. Large, high-speed buffers at each end of the network connection filter the jerky, sporadic flow of network data, so motion on the screen looks smooth and uninterrupted. This strategy easily transports video across even the busiest of networks.

The biggest drawback to such a scheme is the delay imposed by network buffering. Delay affects some video applications more than others, but is always undesirable. The acceptable video delay for various applications ranges from a low of twenty to a high of a few hundred milliseconds.

The challenge is to insert enough buffering to smooth out the jerky packet flow, but not so much as to introduce unacceptable video delay. The jerkier the flow, the more buffering is required.

---

[3] Starlight Networks of Mountain View, California, manufactures a 100-user video server. It delivers 100 simultaneous, completely independent, full-motion video channels through a 10 Mb/s Ethernet switch to 100 clients.

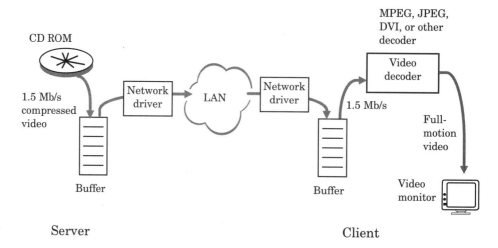

Figure 5.6 Networked Video Application

One recent study details the number of continuous video channels that can safely traverse an Ethernet network.[4] It takes into account factors such as the video compression bit rate, the network bandwidth, amount of other traffic present, and tolerance for video delay. The number of channels is a strong function of delay tolerance. That is, if you are willing to accept more buffering, or delay, from end to end, then more channels can be packed onto the Ethernet.

Video training applications, for example, can tolerate quite a bit of delay. A 100-ms delay between pressing the start key and the reaction of the video server is hardly noticeable. In video conferencing or other live interactions, a 20-ms delay is more appropriate. Given these delay assumptions, the video traffic-handling capacity of Ethernet is detailed in Table 5.1. This table is broken into two section, for 10 Mb/s Ethernet, and Fast Ethernet. In the 10 Mb/s Ethernet section, the table assumes that each video channel consumes 384 kb/s of bandwidth. Various combinations of network bandwidth and background traffic appear in the leftmost column. The two right-hand columns list how many video channels can safely traverse the network for either video training or video conferencing applications. As illustrated in this table, 10 Mb/s

---

[4] Ismail Dalgiç, William Chien, and Fouad A. Tobagi, "Evaluation of 10BASE-T and 100BASE-T Ethernets Carrying Video, Audio and Data Traffic," Proceedings of IEEE INFOCOM, Toronto, Canada, June 1994.

Table 5.1 Video Channel Capacity of Ethernet

Configuration	Channels[a] (Training Application)	Channels[b] (Video Conferencing)
10 Mb/s Ethernet[c]		
— background traffic 5% (low)[d]	18	1
— background traffic 15% (high)[d]	12	0
100 Mb/s Ethernet[e]		
— background traffic 5% (low)[d]	>>37[f]	37
— background traffic 15% (high)[d]	>>25[f]	25

[a] 100 ms maximum delay required, 0.001 probability of packet loss.
[b] 20 ms maximum delay required, 0.001 probability of packet loss.
[c] Assumes 384 kb/s fixed bit rate per video channel.
[d] Random bursts of 10 kilobyte packet transmissions.
[e] Assumes higher, better quality fixed bit rate of 1536 kb/s per video channel.
[f] Exact data unavailable.

Ethernet will support a few channels of video training type applications, but can't reliably handle the ultra-low delay requirements of video conferencing.

The Fast Ethernet portion of the table assumes the use of 1.5 Mb/s video streams, four times the rate used with regular Ethernet. The quality of these higher-rate video streams is much better than the 384 kb/s streams. The finished image looks smoother, and has better resolution. Even at the higher coding rate, Fast Ethernet supports more than twice as many video training applications as regular Ethernet. Even more impressive, Fast Ethernet, because its network delays are cut to one-tenth the size, can easily handle the 20-ms video conferencing delay requirement. Keep in mind that these numbers are *per link*. In a switching architecture, a video conferencing system could handle this many video channel *per link*.

Until now, two factors have limited the widespread deployment of video applications over shared-media 10 Mb/s Ethernet.

1. Insufficient network bandwidth. A shared-media 10 Mb/s LAN does not support very many video channels.

2. Uncontrolled contention from other sources. Massive transmissions from unknown sources may wipe out video traffic.

Fast Ethernet fixes the insufficient bandwidth problem.

Contention and the resulting variation in network delay must be attacked by other means, discussed in the next section, *Flow Control.*

In the absence of severe latency requirements, here are two rules of thumb for predicting how much traffic an Ethernet can handle:

1. For a random mixture of small packets, Ethernet tops out between 15% and 30% utilization.
2. For heavy traffic mixtures, containing mostly giant packets, with no limit on delay, Ethernet can handle up to an 80% load.[5]

For video applications that demand low latency, customers may deal with the contention problem in four ways:

Move to 10 Mb/s switching	Switching decouples traffic between stations, preventing contention at the hub. Each client gets a clear 10 Mb/s channel to the switch. From the switch, use 100 Mb/s connections to video servers.
Install a 100 Mb/s repeater	This increases the network bandwidth by a factor of 10, and at the same time shrinks the duration of each packet. The shrinkage in packet duration bestows an immediate tenfold improvement in the packet flow jerkiness problem. In addition, the same video traffic now represents a much smaller proportion of overall system capacity. A lower proportion of capacity smoothes the packet flow considerably. Between these two effects, the jerkiness problem vanishes.
Install a 100 Mb/s switch	The ultimate in bandwidth and privacy for each client. Such a system can support oodles of video conferencing channels together with bursty data on every link in the system. This is the future of multimedia.

---

[5] In a Fast Ethernet demonstration at the 1995 Interop in Las Vegas one network sustained a continuous throughput of more than 80 Mb/s, with a mix of video traffic (17 Mb/s) and bursty data traffic (70 Mb/s).

Adopt flow control   Several alternatives are emerging for flow control (see next section). All these measures significantly improve packet flow jerkiness, allowing more video channels at a given level of background traffic.

FLOW CONTROL

Video training and other playback applications less sensitive to network delay will develop first on Fast Ethernet, because it already supports viable numbers of those types of video channels. Other more time sensitive applications may not emerge until something happens to smooth the flow of traffic. Fortunately, five flow-control solutions to this problem are on the way. They all address the jerkiness of Ethernet packet flow.

The jerkiness of packet flow, and therefore the amount of buffering and delay required in video applications to smooth the video image, all react strongly to the offered load. As you approach the maximum throughput for a particular network, jerkiness increases sharply. Beyond this point, network delays become unpredictable. Conversely, if the background traffic remains just below the limit, network performance smoothes out considerably.

This principle defines two classes of flow-control approaches: those that limit the flow data onto a network, and those that increase the capacity of a network to handle bursty data (Table 5.2).

Table 5.2 Flow Control Solutions

Approach	Limits Flow	Increases Capacity
Full duplex		√
Link level flow control	√	
Bandwidth allocation	√	
BLAM		√
PACE	√	√

Full Duplex

Full duplex is a capacity-enhancing technique. To be effective, it must be applied in conjuction with switching. Both DTEs and switch ports must support full-duplex capability (for details, see *Advanced Capabilities* in Chapter 2).

Full duplex greatly reduces the jerkiness associated with Ethernet packet flow. It does this by eliminating collisions, the root source of the problem. Without collisions, devices can transmit as they please, and packets flow much more smoothly. No device ever has to back off and retransmit. To accomplish this feat, full-duplex links (like FX, TX and 10BASE-T) provide separate paths for transmitted and received data.

Of course, even with full duplex the packet flow is not completely tamed. Other mechanisms, like contention inside a PC for the network driver and contention inside a switch for outgoing links, still disrupt the smooth flow of packets. But these effects may be ameliorated by more intelligent drivers and switches. The use of full-duplex mode, in conjunction with switching, will open the door to many new video services.

Full-duplex switched systems are not perfect. They occasionally suffer from buffer overflow. For example, if too many devices pour packets into a central switch, all destined for the same output port, the buffer on that output port quickly overflows (the same effect happens in ATM networks). Manufacturers size their buffers so that, statistically, overflow occurs rarely. When an overflow does happen, packets are lost. Higher layers of software must come to the rescue. Nevertheless, full-duplex switches will play a major role in future video applications.

Many types of full-duplex switches and adapters are available today (see *Advanced Capabilities*, Chapter 2).

Link-Level Flow Control

Link-level flow control is a flow-limiting technique. It applies to links between switches, and to links between end devices and switches. To be effective, both ends of each link must support link-level flow control.

The 802.3 committee is presently debating several general-purpose schemes for flow control. These schemes all involve *back pressure*. These back-pressure schemes provide means for a switch to inform its neighbors when its internal buffers are approaching full capacity. The type of back-pressure scheme likely to be approved by 802.3 will be a *link-level flow control* algorithm. Link-level flow control provides a back pressure indication across a link, without indicating which substreams carried by that link are causing the problem.

For example, in Figure 5.7 two data paths, *A* and *B*, both share use of a common link between switches *Y* and *Z*. At point *X*, congestion has occurred. This backs up packets into switch *Z*. Switch *Z* responds by sending a back pressure signal to switch *Y* telling it to slow down. Because both paths *A* and *B* traverse link *Y-Z*, this back-pressure signal affects both of them. Traffic path *A*, which logically has nothing to do with congestion in path *B*, is affected by the blockage at point *X*. This is a prime disadvantage of link level flow control. On the other hand, link-level flow control does a good job of limiting buffer overflow. It is therefore a useful, if somewhat blunt, tool.

An 802.3 project has been authorized for the development of flow control proposals. The existence and enabling of link-level flow control features, once standardized, will be accomplished using Auto-Negotiation. Bits have already been allocated in the Auto-Negotiation data structure for this purpose.

Bandwidth Allocation

Bandwidth allocation is another flow-limiting technique. It applies to high-level software in the end stations, and in switches. To be effective, most devices in a network must support bandwidth allocation.

Bandwidth allocation software offers the most attractive long-term solution to all types of congestion problems. Bandwidth allocation algorithms are designed to keep the network running at or below some rated maximum capacity. By setting the rated maximum somewhat lower than the absolute maximum throughput, network administrators can substantially smooth the flow of packets.

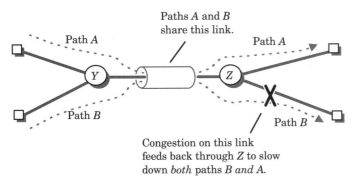

Figure 5.7 Link-Level Flow Control

Bandwidth allocation software requires that client devices register their intentions before using the network. For example, if a client wishes to engage an application that uses a 1.25 Mb/s video stream, it first must request permission. The bandwidth allocation algorithm uses its knowledge of other applications running on the network to decide to either grant the new request, or send the digital equivalent of a network *busy* signal. The busy signal prevents too many applications from engaging at once. This is the primary advantage of bandwidth allocation.

There are two main disadvantages. First, bandwidth allocation requires new driver software in every client attached to the network. Nobody wants that. Second, it requires that applications have some knowledge of their own network bandwidth requirements. Most do not. These two disadvantages have prevented the widespread deployment of bandwidth allocation software. As future applications begin to make heavy use of video transmission, drivers will likely change anyway to accommodate massive smoothing buffers. At the same time, applications will develop a much better grasp of their own network requirements. Eventually, the leap to bandwidth allocation will appear more reasonable, and some form of it will probably be adopted. At that point, video traffic will be so massive that ordinary data transfers will probably constitute only a tiny percentage of the total network load. Ordinary data traffic may then be left unmanaged for compatibility with older applications. There will not be enough of it to matter.

With the current generation of bit-mapped graphic applications, when too many people log on, the network slows to a crawl. In the coming era of video-based applications, the network will police itself to prevent oversubscription. Everyone who *has* a connection will have a *good* connection.[6]

Proposed ATM wide area network standards, when complete, will include bandwidth allocation services. In ATM, these services go by the names *Connection Admission Control* (CAC) and *Usage Parameter Control* (UPC). Bandwidth allocation is a good general principle that will overcome many congestion and flow control issues.

Bandwidth allocation will become more important as users develop heavily interconnected networks of switches and routers.

---

[6] This is the same mechanism used in the phone system. On Mother's Day, the busiest phone calling day of the year, many people cannot get through. Those who do obtain a perfectly clear connection.

One proprietary transport protocol that incorporates bandwidth allocation from Starlight Networks. This protocol, called MTP, shapes the traffic flow with specialized rate control algorithms to achieve a smooth, congestion-free flow of Ethernet packets.

A project may be authorized soon in the 802.1 committee for the development of bandwidth allocation proposals. In addition, the *Internet Engineering Task Force* (IETF),[7] which specifies the TCP/IP protocol suite, is reportedly working on a proposal called RSVP to address related flow control issues.

Binary Logarithmic Arbitration Method

Another new technique for smoothing packet flow is called *Binary Logarithmic Arbitration Method* (BLAM).[8] BLAM is a capacity-enhancing technique. To be effective, it must be installed on every DTE in a collision domain.

The BLAM technique attacks a rarely discussed characteristic of all Ethernet systems called the *capture effect*. The capture effect is a consequence of Ethernet's backoff rules, which govern the behavior of the network after a collision. The capture effect sometimes grants one device, for a very short period, a virtual monopoly on transmission. While the capture effect lasts, a fast device can pump out a long stream of packets virtually uninterrupted. This streaming effect is fine for the transmitter. The problem is that while one device is streaming, everyone else is waiting. Delayed packets build up at the other devices, making their traffic flow jerky and sporadic.

The BLAM technique eliminates the capture effect by changing the backoff rules to permit more fair access to the network. These changes smooth the flow of packets on a busy network. A smoother flow is better for time-sensitive traffic like video. If fully deployed, BLAM would increase the number of video channels that may safely traverse an Ethernet collision domain.

Fortunately, BLAM is backward compatible with existing Ethernet devices. Mixed networks with some new BLAM-capable devices and some older non-BLAM devices can coexist and interoperate. As long as

---

[7] See contact information in Chapter 8.

[8] "A New Binary Logarithmic Arbitration Method for Ethernet," Mart L. Molle, Technical Report CSRI-298, April 1994, Computer Systems Research Institute, University of Toronto, Toronto, Canada, M5S 1A1.

BLAM is installed on the fastest devices, the ones most likely to stream, it will smooth the flow.

BLAM applies equally well to switches and repeaters, as long as there is contention. It does not apply to full-duplex links. They are already immune from collisions, so BLAM has no effect. Full-duplex links do not suffer from the capture effect.

An 802.3 project has been authorized for standardizing the BLAM technique.

Priority Access Control Enabled

The final new technique we will discuss for smoothing packet flow is called *Priority Access Control Enabled* (PACE). It is a capacity-enhancing technology, applicable to switched networks. To be effective, PACE need only be installed on switch ports that carry multimedia traffic.

PACE is inherently compatible with existing Ethernet adapters and end-user software. In this sense, it is unique among the flow control alternatives. It only affects the switch, not the end devices.

PACE was designed to speed the flow of packets across congested networks.[9] It accomplishes this goal using two separate technologies: *interactive access* and *implicit class of service*.

The *interactive access* technology applies to the link between a switch port and its associated client device. It minimizes collisions on the link, and ensures fair utilization of the link. This is done by clever manipulation of the CSMA/CD *backoff algorithm* in the switch. No modifications are required in the client. An important feature of PACE is that it does not generate artificial traffic, or artificial jam sequences, as part of its operation.

The *implicit class of service* technology applies to both switch and client. The class of service logic uses clues in each packet header to determine which packets are bound for video or other high-priority services. These packets may then be routed to the head of the queue for outbound transmission. This class-based approach is basically a priority scheme. It prevents ordinary data traffic from getting in the way of high-priority video transmissions.

A switch equipped with PACE technology is well suited for video applications. PACE is backed by an consortium of industry leaders.

---

[9] Perhaps it should be called *Packets Across Congested Ethernets* (PACE).

LINK TRANSMISSION TECHNOLOGY

New Fast Ethernet transceiver types will emerge. They will expand the number of cable types available to Fast Ethernet users. They will also increase the maximum data rate.

In 1995, the 802.3 working group opened a new project to study transmission at 100 Mb/s on *two pairs* of category 3 UTP. Table 5.3 compares the properties of this new proposed transceiver to the existing T4 and TX transceivers. The new transceiver, called 100BASE-T2, would potentially work in all UTP applications now satisfied by T4 and TX products, plus the relatively rare cases of two-pair category 3 and 4 cables. That's the good news.

The bad news is that this new UTP transceiver type requires sophisticated near-end crosstalk cancellation and adaptive digital equalization to perform its function. These features, at the speeds

Table 5.3 Present and Potential New Transceiver Types

	Transceiver Type	Cable Type	Number of Pairs	Notes
	100BASE-T4	Cat. 3 UTP[a]	4	Workhorse design for category 3 cabling
		Cat. 4 UTP	4	
		Cat. 5 UTP	4	
	100BASE-TX	Cat. 5 UTP	2	Only needs two pairs, but requires category 5 cable
		150-Ω STP[b]	2	
NEW	100BASE-T2	Cat. 3 UTP[a]	2	Only needs two pairs, but likely to be more expensive than T4 in the near term
		Cat. 4 UTP	2	
		Cat. 5 UTP	2	
	100BASE-FX	62.5/125 mm multimode fiber	2	Same optics as FDDI
NEW	*(no project authorized at this time)*	single-mode fiber	2	Gigabit class backbone link

[a] Unshielded twisted pair (UTP), for example, phone wire.
[b] Shielded twisted pair (STP), for example, IBM type-I cable.

required, will likely increase its silicon chip area substantially, leading to higher costs, and a long development cycle. We will probably have to wait for faster, smaller chips before this technology becomes cost effective.

If the 802.3 working group finishes its work on time, look for T2 transceivers in 1998. If the working group slows down, some of the vendors involved may go ahead with their plans anyway. In either case, the market window for this new UTP transceiver type is rapidly closing. On one hand, T4 sales are ramping up. On the other, as customers replace older cabling with newer category 5 UTP, the installed base of category 3 cable will begin to shrink.

The other new transceiver listed in Table 5.3 is a fiber transceiver. Many vendors feel that a standard gigabit class fiber link would perform well as an interswitch link. After all, Fast Ethernet switch backplane bandwidths are already in the gigabit range and will continue doubling every few years.

The new fiber transceiver type is envisioned as a fiber backbone for Fast Ethernet. It will operate in full-duplex mode across single-mode fiber at great distances. Single-mode fiber provides a bandwidth growth path for Fast Ethernet. Look for this transceiver to emerge as 100 Mb/s switching becomes widespread.

If standardized, a Fast Ethernet gigabit fiber link would probably supplant many backbone applications now being slated for service by ATM switches.

ISO-ETHERNET

ISO-Ethernet is a standard adopted by the IEEE 802.9 working group, a sister working group to the 802.3 committee. ISO-Ethernet integrates Ethernet with wide area switched digital services. It is appropriate for users that anticipate heavy amounts of public switched data communications (like ISDN, T1 switched lines, or T1 leased lines). The official name of this standard is **IEEE Std 802.9a**.

The ISO-Ethernet plan provides three components:

1. A new ISO-Ethernet signaling standard that mixes 10 Mb/s Ethernet and the equivalent of 48 bi-directional ISDN B-channels onto a single cable.
2. New client devices that combine Ethernet-style data with ISDN isochronous voice, video and data communications.

3. New hubs that perform the combined functions of an Ethernet hub and a digital PBX (digital telephone system).

As illustrated in Figure 5.8, the ISO-Ethernet signaling standard simultaneously conveys two types of data. First, it provides a 10 Mb/s channel with collision detection that is completely analogous to 10BASE-T. Second, it provides the equivalent of 48 isochronous 64 kb/s ISDN B-channels in each direction. Both data types are mixed onto a common signaling interface. ISO-Ethernet signaling works over category 3, 4, or 5 UTP at distances up to 100 m.

An 802.9a link set is required at both ends of the link to handle both Ethernet and ISDN traffic. The 802.9a standard supports Auto-Negotiation, which can be used to connect an 802.9a device to a pure 10BASE-T interface when necessary.

At the hub end, manufacturers have a choice of how to handle the Ethernet data. This is where ISO-Ethernet and Fast Ethernet fit

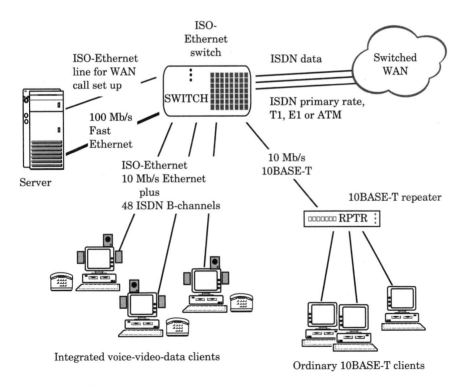

Figure 5.8 ISO-Ethernet Architecture

together. The hub can do one of three things:

1. Emulate a 10BASE-T style repeater
2. Emulate a 10BASE-T switch
3. Emulate a 10BASE-T switch with some Fast Ethernet switched ports for server connections (see Figure 5.8)

At the client end, manufacturers may use the 10 Mb/s Ethernet and ISDN data for any purpose, either separately or in integrated applications.

The goal for 802.9a is to promote the development of products and applications that integrate voice, video, and data services. If successful, 802.9a would integrate these services into common desktop platforms and into common switch room hardware.

A drawback to this approach is the rapid pace of development for voice, video, and data services. Manufacturers that take the time to integrate all three services into common platforms may find their products are obsolete before they hit the street. In addition, improvements in the multimedia capabilities of Fast Ethernet and the approach of pure ATM services squeeze 802.9 from both sides.

The best applications for 802.9a have a clear and immediate need for integrated computer/telephony platforms. These applications include specialized call-centers, automatic call distribution (ACD) applications, and customer service centers.

WIDE AREA NETWORKING

Ethernet users will continue to deploy *routers* as the agents of exchange between LAN and WAN networks. Ethernet will remain prevalent in the campus arena. Over time, ATM will emerge as the preferred WAN interconnection medium. Fast, effective routers will be developed to tie Fast Ethernet into the ATM WAN.

Local Area Networking (LAN) and Wide Area Networking (WAN) protocols, hardware, and standards will remain separate for years to come. No single technology (not even ATM) will emerge as the best solution to all LAN and WAN problems. The LAN and WAN situations are too different. That's why routers will continue to be present at the LAN/WAN boundary.

The differences between LAN and WAN networks have traditionally been enforced by long-standing market forces. In the LAN market, customers demand three things: *low cost, ease of installation,* and *excess bandwidth.*

Users emphasize low cost because LAN hardware connects to *every desk* in some office environments. Intense pricing pressure has driven the cost of LAN hardware below the cost of wiring.

Installation has to be simple because of the broad distribution of LAN technology. Estimates place the number of current Ethernet users at around 60 million worldwide.[10] If installation were difficult, the industry could not train sufficient numbers of technicians to install and maintain the product. At present, installation *is* simple. Ordinary office personnel without specialized technical training can install Ethernet.[11]

Excess bandwidth buys peace of mind for network administrators. Users can upgrade their applications or add more clients without fear of saturating the network. Excess capacity simplifies the process of network planning. Bandwidth at the local level is very cheap, so this is a good trade.

Issues in the WAN market are different. WAN customers demand *low-cost long-distance transmission services, optimization of transmission facilities,* and *reliability.* The specialized device that has evolved to service these needs is called a *router.*

For WAN customers, it is the cost of transmission lines, not the cost of hardware at each end, that dominates their thinking. The cost of a long-distance high-speed link, while it has come down considerably in recent years, continues to overwhelm the cost of router hardware. The router hardware exists to make the most efficient possible use of the communications pathways.

Typical LAN products lack the capability to optimize use of long-distance connections. For example, the *spanning tree* algorithm used by LAN switches and bridges would never satisfy WAN users (see box entitled *Spanning Tree*). The spanning tree algorithm identifies a transmission path between every pair of users. It is a simple-minded strategy. When presented with multiple alternative paths, it sometimes makes a poor choice. The WAN approach, on the other hand, takes into account the different speeds, bandwidths, costs, and other characteristics of each link, and sets about minimizing total operating

---

[10] This number is growing *very* rapidly. Industry shipments for 1995 are projected to total more than 20 million Ethernet nodes.

[11] Last summer, a neighbor borrowed my RJ-45 crimp tool to install Ethernet in his house. He's a swim instructor.

Spanning Tree

Spanning tree refers to a learning process that takes place inside a switch or bridge. It comes into play when there are multiple paths to a given client. In simple tree-structured hierarchies (Figure 5.9), where only one path exists between any two clients, route optimization serves no purpose. In more complex configurations, where redundant links (or forgotten or accidental links) exist between collision domains, there may be multiple paths between clients (Figure 5.10). If there are multiple paths, then at some point the paths may touch and make a loop. If there is a loop, the possibility exists that packets may travel around and around the loop in infinite distress.

In switches designed for complex hierarchies, the spanning tree algorithm prevents loop situations. It discovers loops and seals them off, so no packets ever take the looping branches. This fixes the recirculation problem.

Sometimes, the sealing-off process does not look very smart. For example, if a link becomes congested, none of the sealed-off loops are able to help carry the load.

costs. For WAN applications, the spanning tree approach is insufficient. For LAN applications, least-cost path routing is overkill.

Reliability is another issue of prime concern to WAN network administrators. WAN links typically concentrate traffic from many users. Installation of multiple redundant paths and designation of routing priorities in the event of failure typify WAN concerns. This is an OSI network-layer issue. Routers can support sophisticated redundant path configurations. Data-link layer LAN protocols can't.

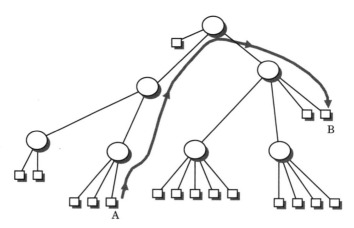

Figure 5.9 Simple Tree Hierarchy with No Loops

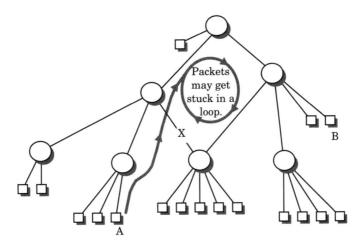

Figure 5.10 Complex Configuration with Loops

In the LAN world, bandwidth is the *cheapest* of all commodities. It is available to trade for easier installation and network simplicity. The cost of service technicians and pulling wires, not hardware, dominates LAN design.

In the WAN world, bandwidth is the most *precious* of all resources. It must be preserved, protected, and optimized. To achieve this goal, no amount of installation or configuration effort is spared.

These conflicting objectives will not be reconciled by any single network technology. In the foreseeable future, routers will continue to stand between the LAN and WAN worlds. They will translate LAN standards into WAN standards.

The existence of a router is not, in itself, a bad thing. Even if there were a consistent, seamless LAN/WAN network,[12] a router would still be desirable for several reasons. First, it severs a network into distinct parts, limiting the flow of unnecessary traffic (for example, local broadcast messages do not need to go everywhere). Second, it serves as a security firewall, preventing unauthorized access from outside parties. Third, it is responsible for managing parallel and redundant pathways between sites. For all these reasons, the use of routers at the LAN/WAN boundary will not diminish.

---

[12] In case you are wondering, ATM at the present time is neither seamless nor consistent. ATM as proposed for local area usage is discussed in Chapter 6.

In any network where a router divides the LAN and WAN worlds, users are free to separately choose the best LAN for their situation, and the best WAN. This principle will dictate the structure of LAN and WAN markets for years to come.

In the local area environment, for cost reasons, users will likely pick the most prevalent network, the one shipping in the highest volumes. This will be Ethernet, fast or regular.

In the wide area environment, users will likely gravitate toward the interexchange carriers' long-term connectivity solution of choice, *Asynchronous Transfer Mode* (ATM).[13] This network, because of anticipated wide deployment in the 21st century, will eventually deliver the lowest-cost long-distance data communications service. As ATM rolls out, very high-speed routers specifically designed to mediate between the Ethernet LAN and the ATM WAN will emerge.

Look for a convergence of switching and routing functions. Users with wide area connectivity requirements today must separately buy switching and routing components and then hook them together. For example, today routers are often connected to a collapsed backbone switch in the center of a campus network (Figure 5.1). Future developments will consolidate the switch and router products into a single box. Relentless downward pressure on per-port switching and routing costs will force this consolidation. The electronic guts of products today cost so little that the chassis and power supply represent a significant fraction of the customer's total investment. Consolidating the boxes reduces the chassis and power cost. It also saves parts because external ports will no longer be required to interconnect the two boxes.

Regarding multimedia, improvements in Ethernet technology like switching, higher speed links, BLAM, PACE and full duplex have already enabled transmission of full-motion video across campus-wide networks. When coupled with wide area ATM services, end-to-end video, sound and graphic communications will soon become a world-wide reality.

---

[13] ATM as proposed for local area usage is discussed in Chapter 6.

Points to Remember

- Switching, in most networks, will be deployed from the top down.
- Full-duplex operation will become prevalent between switches, and between switches and servers.
- Significant multimedia applications will evolve for Fast Ethernet networks.
- Various schemes for flow control will hasten the arrival of multimedia applications.
- New Fast Ethernet transceiver types will emerge.
- ISO-Ethernet is appropriate for users that anticipate heavy amounts of public switched data communications.
- Wide Area Networking (WAN) and Local Area Networking (LAN) protocols, hardware, and standards will remain separate for years to come.
- Routers will continue to pose as the agents of exchange between LAN and WAN networks.

6

Competing Networks

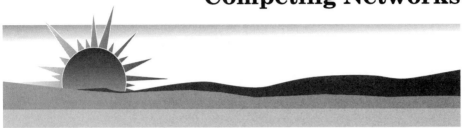

*F*ast Ethernet thrives in a very competitive market. The success of Fast Ethernet derives from its unique position as a simple, easily understood upgrade for the enormously popular 10BASE-T system. Other competing standards for high-speed local area networking are listed in Table 6.1.

Each of these standards has its place. Depending on the application at hand, one or the other may be superior. If you are deciding which network to implement, the following comparative snapshots may help. Please keep in mind that standards change, and products evolve. Although your author has made every reasonable effort to ensure the accuracy of information at time of writing, the absolute latest details on competing products are best obtained directly from their vendors.

Table 6.1 100 Mb/s Local Area Network Standards

Nickname(s)	Full Name	Origin
FDDI	*Fiber Distributed Data Interface*	ANSI X3.T12 [a] ISO/IEC
ATM	*Asynchronous Transfer Mode*	ITU [b], ATM Forum
DPAM, 100BASE-VG, AnyLAN	*Demand Priority Access Method.*	Hewlett-Packard
Fiber Channel	Fiber Channel	ANSI X3.T11 [c]
Fast Ethernet	100BASE-T	IEEE 802.3

[a] Formerly X3T9.5.
[b] Formerly CCITT.
[c] Formerly X3T9.3.

FDDI

FDDI was written by the ANSI X3T9.5 committee. The main bulk of the FDDI fiber standard attained ISO/IEC approval in 1990. The UTP physical link layer was adopted by ANSI in 1995.

The primary documents defining FDDI at this time are:

ISO/IEC 9314-1	Main body of the standard, including fiber
ISO/IEC 9314-2	interface
ISO/IEC 9314-3	
ANSI X3.263	Category 5 UTP transceiver (TP-PMD)
ANSI X3.237	Low-cost, reduced distance fiber transceiver

FDDI Overview

FDDI is a token-passing ring system. It operates on 62/125-µm multimode fiber. FDDI is a *shared media* network, providing a total 100 Mb/s system bandwidth that is shared among all users.

When used as a backbone network, FDDI is often configured in the *counter rotating ring* configuration depicted in Figure 6.1. This configuration provides redundancy in the event that a fiber link breaks or a station malfunctions. FDDI incorporates elaborate measures, including automatic optical bypass switches, to prevent failure in the event that stations are unplugged or powered off.

At inception, the high initial cost of FDDI adapters disenchanted many users. Over the years this cost has dropped dramatically, but has still not fallen below the cost of Ethernet adapters. The combination of perceived high cost and the difficulty of installing fiber has prevented FDDI from achieving its goal of providing fiber to every desktop.

Even though the desktop strategy did not work, FDDI has been very successful as a backbone for 10 Mb/s networks. In this capacity its long distance features and high bandwidth, relative to 10 Mb/s Ethernet, are a distinct advantage. The best application for FDDI is as a backbone for 10 Mb/s networking.

Recently, the ANSI X3T12 committee has been hard at work on FDDI-II, also called FDDI HRC. It may someday extend the capability of FDDI to handle isochronous data streams. At present, support for this new proposed standard is lagging.

The discussion below pertains to use of FDDI as a 100 Mb/s desktop LAN.

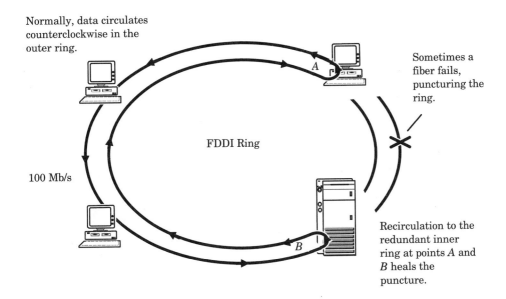

Normally, data circulates counterclockwise in the outer ring.

Sometimes a fiber fails, puncturing the ring.

FDDI Ring

100 Mb/s

Recirculation to the redundant inner ring at points A and B heals the puncture.

Figure 6.1 FDDI Counter Rotating Ring Configuration

FDDI Strong Points

FDDI can span great distances. It is therefore an ideal backbone for connecting Ethernet repeaters in a campus setting.

FDDI uses fiber, which is immune to electromagnetic interference,. again, an ideal property for a backbone.

FDDI incorporates redundant features (the counterrotating ring). This advantage is tempered by the fact that all data must traverse active electronics in all stations as it circulates around the ring, a substantial reliability disadvantage, in comparison to hub-oriented networks. The redundant ring configuration brings FDDI back to parity on the reliability index.

FDDI runs 10 times faster than 10 Mb/s, a true advantage in the heyday of 10 Mb/s networking. As Fast Ethernet gains prevalence, and particularly when gigabit class links are available for connecting Fast Ethernet switches, FDDI will look pedestrian by comparison.

FDDI has recently implemented a UTP configuration, illustrated in Figure 6.2. The physical layer interface in this configuration is called *TP-PMD*. It runs over category 5 UTP, and 150-Ω STP. This is the same TP-PMD sublayer that was adopted by reference for use with Fast Ethernet in 100BASE-TX.

FDDI has deterministic delay performance, as is characteristic for token-based networks. It can be loaded to a high percentage of its maximum capacity without clogging.

FDDI Weak Points

Highly complex *station management* (SMT) protocols are required to manage and track FDDI tokens. These SMT requirements increase the size of FDDI chips and software, making them more complex and expensive than their Ethernet counterparts. Another factor that raises the cost of FDDI components is their relatively low volumes, compared to Ethernet parts.

FDDI has not yet announced plans for higher-speed capabilities. Fast Ethernet, ATM, and DPAM will all soon support links faster than 100 Mb/s.

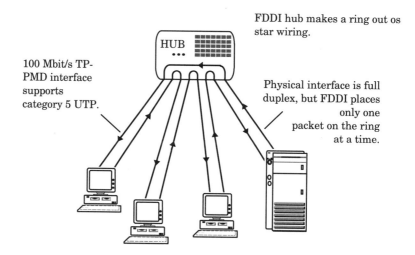

FDDI hub makes a ring out os star wiring.

100 Mbit/s TP-PMD interface supports category 5 UTP.

HUB

Physical interface is full duplex, but FDDI places only one packet on the ring at a time.

Figure 6.2 FDDI Over UTP

ATM

The *Asynchronous Transfer Mode* (ATM) standards have been stitched together from two different sources: the ITU and the ATM Forum. ATM is intended to cover both wide area and local area network applications.

The *International Telecommunications Union* (ITU)[1] is an advisory committee established under the United Nations. Since the early 1980s, it has standardized many aspects of Broadband ISDN for long-term wide area applications. Wide area aspects of ATM are controlled by the ITU.

The ATM Forum is an international non-profit organization formed with the objective of accelerating the use of ATM products and services. It works with sanctioned standards bodies, such as ANSI and the ITU, to promote existing standards, resolve differences between standards, and recommend new standards where necessary.

In 1991, the ATM Forum Technical Committee took the ITU specifications for wide area ATM and began modifying them for use as a local area network standard. Portions of the ATM local area network standards are complete now, with more to follow.

In addition to the ITU series of documents defining SDH, SONET, and the basic ATM cell format, the primary documents defining local area ATM usage at this time are listed below. The ATM Forum may soon provide additional specifications for traffic management, signaling, physical interfaces, network management, LAN emulation, and other issues.

UNI (User Network Interface)	Provides for interoperation of customer premise ATM equipment with carrier networks.
DXI (Data Exchange specification)	Specifies use of existing bridges, routers and hubs as front-end processors to an ATM network.
B-ICI (Broadband Inter-carrier Interface)	Defines inter-carrier services.

---

[1] Formerly the Comité Consultif Internationale Télégraphique et Téléphone, or International Consultative Committee for Telephone and Telegraph, (CCITT).

ATM Overview

ATM is like the metric system. It's a good idea, but it isn't going to happen overnight.[2]

ATM is a switching network. It uses tiny, fixed-sized packets to convey massive amounts of information in a simple way through relatively dumb switches. Use of a small, fixed-sized cells (each packet, or cell, contains 53 octets) is helpful for voice applications and other applications that require very low switching delay.

ATM will make an excellent national backbone network. It can carry voice, data, and video traffic over a common wiring and switching infrastructure. The wide area network version of ATM (ITU version) can carry data across vast distances at 155 Mb/s, 622 Mb/s, 1.2 gigabits per second, or 2.4 gigabits per second using single-mode fiber. As a wide area network, ATM is unparalleled. Unfortunately, the ITU standards, while ideal for large-scale telephony, are viewed as too complex and expensive for a LAN.

The ATM Forum was created in 1991 to adapt the ITU standards for local area usage. The ATM Forum proposed to remap the ITU ATM standards from single mode fiber onto *unshielded twisted-pair* wiring (UTP). It then planned to provide additional functions needed for LAN operation, like *Simple Network Management Protocol* (SNMP) support. Unencumbered by big standards politics, its originators believed they could finish the job quickly.

Unfortunately, by 1994 a swell of new members overwhelmed the ATM Forum. About the same time, the technical issues surrounding congestion control for bursty local traffic were recognized as more difficult than originally believed. Progress in early 1995 ground almost to a halt.

In the meantime, Fast Ethernet narrowed the gap between the future promises of ATM and today's available performance. As a result, widespread deployment of ATM *to the desktop* has probably been pushed out to the year 2000 or beyond. That doesn't mean ATM is dead. Far from it. It just means that ATM may not reach the desktop any time soon. ATM as a *wide area* network still has very bright prospects.

The local area network version of ATM uses centralized hubs connected to clients with star wiring. The client links may run at 155 Mb/s, 51 Mb/s, or 25 Mb/s, depending on the link technology

---

[2] Thanks to Jim Long of Starlight Networks for this pithy statement.

employed (Figure 6.3). The same links are used as backbone connections between hubs. Historically, the first link approved was a 155 Mb/s SDH link, technically called OC-3. The 155 Mb/s link is specified for fiber only (although several groups are working on proposals for UTP versions). The other links, at 51 and 25 Mb/s, both run on UTP.

ATM at the local level is an attractive option primarily because of its perceived capability to provide wide area ATM connectivity once wide area ATM networks are deployed. During the next several years, before the ATM WAN becomes a reality, users will face a choice between ATM, for its perceived future WAN compatibility, and other 100 Mb/s networks, with their greater availability, greater range of options and configurations, and greater software support. For now, ATM is best applied only when long-term compatibility with future ATM WAN services is the utmost priority.

At the local level, ATM was the first network to offer both high-speed links and switching features. ATM switches are now beginning to appear in collapsed backbone configurations, where they can easily interchange data between the local LAN (of any type) and the future ATM WAN. Today, they can communicate over T1-type long distance lines.

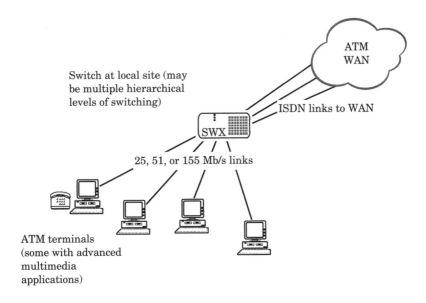

Figure 6.3 ATM Local Area Network

Over time, if pure end-to-end ATM applications emerge, ATM switching may penetrate down in pockets to the desktop, on an as-needed basis. On the other hand, if multimedia applications emerge in a form suitable for use over existing 100 Mb/s LANs, with an ATM WAN backbone, then ATM may never penetrate to the desktop. There would be no reason for it.

As a wide area network, ATM makes a lot of sense. Users will certainly connect existing LANs to the ATM WAN when it becomes available (see *Wide Area Networking* in Chapter 5). It's just a question of when. The success of ATM as a local area network is still very much in question.

The points below discuss ATM as a local area network.

ATM Strong Points

ATM should integrate smoothly with future wide area ATM services when those become available. It is difficult to predict what those services may be or when they will materialize.

The small ATM cell size provides very low delay. This feature is not needed strictly for local area usage, but could become important when coupled with future wide area multimedia services.

In the wide area environment, ATM will become the interexchange carriers' long-term connectivity solution of choice. When widely deployed in the 21st century, it will eventually deliver the lowest-cost long-distance data communications service.

ATM links can operate at a range of speeds spanning upward of several gigabits per second. In addition to high link speeds, ATM uses a switched architecture. The switched architecture, in conjunction with high link speeds, provides almost unlimited bandwidth capability for future expansion.

ATM links operate over a wide range of cables, covering almost all types currently in use. Supported cables include single-mode and multimode fiber, 150-Ω STP, and category 3, 4, and 5 UTP.

The ATM Forum and the ITU have both worked long and hard toward defining means to guarantee delay properties across interconnected networks of switches. When complete, this body of work will benefit not only ATM, but probably other standards as well.

ATM Weak Points

ATM is an emerging system. The specifications are not yet complete. For example, critical mechanisms for monitoring and policing traffic to prevent buffer overflow internal to the public network are missing. When standardized, these functions may prove incompatible with some equipment already in the field. Only a true pioneer would deploy a network before all the standards are complete.

Once ATM standards are completed, their benefits at the local level will have been seriously eroded by advances in other 100 Mb/s networks. For example, Fast Ethernet offers both high speed links and switching features, just like ATM. Fast Ethernet is also developing PACE, BLAM, and flow control to enhance the transport of multimedia data. These developments may precede the completion of ATM.

ATM also must face some tough traffic issues. When used to transport ordinary LAN data, the basic ATM traffic assumptions may be invalidated. For example, the original ATM traffic models assumed that most devices, like phones and video codecs, would generate fine, continuous streams of tiny packets. When aggregated, thousands of these fine streams were supposed to merge into large, smooth rivers of data. The smoothness is crucial to the economics of ATM. The smoothness helps minimize ATM switch buffer requirements, making an ATM network cheaper than competing architectures.

In a local area network two things go wrong with the ATM traffic model. First, the flow of data on a typical LAN is inherently jerky. Servers disgorge data in huge bursts, not fine, continuous streams. Second, there are not enough devices present in a typical LAN to average out the inherently jerky flow of data. As a result, the traffic calculations for typical LAN applications do not necessarily favor ATM switch designs.

DPAM

DPAM (the official name is *Demand Priority Access Method*, but many people call it 100BASE-VG AnyLAN, or just VG, or just AnyLAN) was adopted by the IEEE 802.12 committee as a new standard in 1995. The primary document defining DPAM at this time is:

IEEE Std 802.12a	Complete specification of new MAC, new hub, and all physical layer interfaces

DPAM Overview

DPAM combines the hub-and-spoke architecture of 10BASE-T with the token-passing attributes of 802.5 Token Ring. The result is a shared-media LAN with deterministic delay features. It operates on category 3, 4 or 5 UTP, 150-Ω STP, and fiber.

DPAM incorporates round-robin arbitration and two classes of priority in its *Media Access Control* (MAC) algorithm, called *Demand Priority*. The MAC extends to serve several hubs cascaded in a hierarchical configuration. The entire cascade forms one large, shared bandwidth network.

The round-robin arbitration method controls access to the transmission medium. The round-robin method scans each client, looking for high-priority packets, in a tree-sorted order (see Figure 6.4). If no high-priority packets are waiting, it scans for regular-priority packets. DPAM accomplishes its scanning by having each DTE maintain a token in the hub, as opposes to Token Ring, which circulates a token among the end stations. The DPAM token stays in the box, so it scans more quickly.[3]

When a packet is selected for transmission, all other nodes are

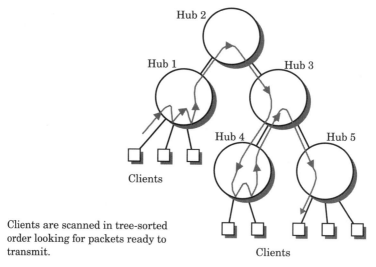

Clients are scanned in tree-sorted order looking for packets ready to transmit.

Figure 6.4 DPAM Round-Robin Arbitration Sequence

---

[3] DPAM might have more aptly been named *Token Box*.

notified that a transmission is imminent. The network makes sure all other devices are inactivated, and then engages the transmitter. While the designated device talks, all other devices remain inactive. After transmission, the system reverts to scanning where it left off, in true round-robin fashion.

DPAM products may operate with either the 802.3 (Ethernet) packet format or the 802.5 (Token Ring) packet format, but not both at the same time.

The original goal of DPAM was to create a new, expandable, 100 Mb/s LAN with special features for multimedia applications (determinism and priority). Had Ethernet switching and Fast Ethernet not evolved as quickly as they did, there might have been a vacuum between 10BASE-T and the coming ATM deployment large enough to support the deployment of yet another new network. As it is, switching and Fast Ethernet have filled much of the anticipated void. The ultimate success of DPAM remains questionable.

As of 1995, the majority of networking manufacturers have adopted Fast Ethernet as the high-speed network of choice. Few companies remain committed exclusively to DPAM. Vendors of routing products and other devices that interoperate between networks will probably supply interfaces for both Fast Ethernet and DPAM.

The best applications for DPAM are in systems that do not require more than 100 Mb/s total system bandwidth and where determinism is of substantial benefit.

DPAM Strong Points

DPAM is at heart a token-passing system. No tokens actually circulate in the DPAM network, but the effect is the same. The token-like qualities are built into its central hub, which permits transmissions on a round-robin priority basis. This scheme behaves a lot like Token Ring. If deterministic performance is important to your application, then the token-passing qualities of this system will be of interest.

DPAM permits the use of either the 802.3 Ethernet or 802.5 Token Ring packet format (but not both at the same time). Whichever format is selected, the DPAM hub uses the same round-robin arbitration method. This feature is the genesis of the nomenclature *AnyLAN*. When IBM, the originator of Token Ring, first decided to work with the IEEE 802.12 committee on support for Token Ring it seemed like a great idea. Later, when IBM withdrew most of its support, some of the 802.12 members felt they had spent too much time working on Token Ring compatibility for too little gain.

DPAM incorporates a two-level priority scheme. Some members of the 802.12 committee asked for eight levels in order to maintain compatibility with the eight priority levels present in Token Ring, but the standard ended up with only two. The DPAM priority concept assumes that video-based applications will use high priority and others will use low priority. The two classes are therefore somewhat non-interacting. That is a useful feature. There are, however, no safeguards to prevent video-based users from interfering with each other. For example, if too many video users log onto the network they will crash, blocking video service for everyone. This points out the need for some form of bandwidth allocation system for video applications. It is bandwidth allocation software, not priority features, that will enable the wide deployment of video-based applications.

DPAM operates at 100 Mb/s. It is a shared-bandwidth network. As a result, performance is roughly 10 times the performance of a shared-bandwidth 10 Mb/s Ethernet configuration. In comparison with a shared bandwidth 100 Mb/s Fast Ethernet configuration, the DPAM system's maximum usable bandwidth is probably higher, owing to the advantages of its deterministic token-passing like operation. In comparison with switched 100 Mb/s Ethernet, the DPAM bandwidth is markedly lower.

DPAM operates over a wide range of cables, covering almost all types currently in use. Supported cables include multimode fiber, 150-Ω STP, and four-pair category 3, 4, and 5 UTP.

DPAM Weak Points

The DPAM system, much like Token Ring, suffers from overcomplexity. For example, DPAM supports priority modes, round-robin arbitration, and two different packet frame formats (802.3 and 802.5). As a result, specification of the DPAM repeater state machine (the RMAC) occupies 127 pages in the standard. The corresponding function in Fast Ethernet is only 34 pages. Significant amounts of training may be required for network administrators to understand and use these new features.

When evaluating performance, keep in mind that the DPAM MAC does not support full-duplex connections. The hub architecture is inherently half duplex.

Although DPAM hubs may be cascaded over great distances, it may not be to the customer's advantage to do so, because large cascaded networks perform sluggishly. In addition, the shared bandwidth of a large cascaded network is quickly spread too thin.

The determinism and priority mechanisms of DPAM do not extend through most bridges, switches, or routers. For example, in a typical switch buffer, there is no circulating token to assure guaranteed latency performance. If your application depends on determinism and priorities, then it may be difficult to expand it beyond a single shared-media DPAM domain. That's OK if 100 Mb/s is all the bandwidth you will ever need. If you need more total bandwidth (most video conferencing systems will), then a single shared-media DPAM domain will prove insufficient.

The point here is that determinism and priorities at the shared-media LAN level do not by themselves make a good multimedia transmission system. The characteristics of switches and wide area links between LANs have far more to do with multimedia performance than the details of operation at the individual end-point LANs. Old concerns about LAN link performance are rapidly being replaced with more global concerns about traffic control, buffer overflow, and regulation of high-bandwidth switched services. Networks designed to accommodate high-performance switching will dominate in the multimedia marketplace. In the switched environment, DPAM's deterministic performance loses much of its appeal.

Other factors affect DPAM's viability as well, particularly its perception as a single-vendor network. While it is true that more vendors than just Hewlett-Packard do support the DPAM system, attendance at some IEEE 802.12 interim working group meetings, where the standardization process takes place, have dwindled to little more than a dozen attendees. That's simply not enough to advance the standard in a timely manner.

In contrast, the Ethernet standards effort, supported by over a hundred members is simultaneously moving forward with BLAM, Full Duplex, and 100BASE-T2. New efforts may soon be underway on PACE and higher-speed fiber links. The BLAM and PACE techniques are rapidly closing the gap between Ethernet's historically uncertain packet latency and the guaranteed response time of a token-passing style of network, eliminating one of the key selling points of the DPAM system.

FIBER CHANNEL

Fiber Channel is an ANSI data communications standard. It was written by the ANSI X3T11 committee, the same committee that wrote the HIPPI and SCSI peripheral interface specifications.

The primary document defining Fiber Channel is:

ANSI X3.230:1994	Complete specification of physical layer signaling interface

Fiber Channel is not widely deployed as a local area network, although in theory it could be used as one. The primary application for Fiber Channel is as a peripheral interconnect bus for fast disk arrays and other high-speed devices inside a computer room.

Fiber Channel has designated five link speeds, running at 133 Mb/s (not much used), 266 Mb/s, 1 gigabits per second, 2 gigabits per second and 4 gigabits per second. Specifications for the 133 and 266 Mb/s links are complete. These links will operate over single-mode or multimode fiber at 800 nm, or over coaxial cable.

Fiber Channel may come under consideration as one alternative means to link Fast Ethernet switches in very fast backbone configurations.

FAST ETHERNET

Fast Ethernet is an IEEE local area network standard. The official IEEE name for the Fast Ethernet standard is *100BASE-T*. It was written by the IEEE 802.3 committee, the same committee that wrote the original Ethernet specifications. Fast Ethernet is a supplement for the existing Ethernet standard.

The primary documents defining Fast Ethernet at this time are:

IEEE Std 802.3u	Complete specification of Fast Ethernet hub, all physical layer interfaces, Auto-Negotiation, and management
ISO/IEC 8802-3:1993	MAC specification, and legacy components of 10 Mb/s Ethernet

Fast Ethernet Overview

Fast Ethernet is a 100 Mb/s local area network. It uses the same *Collision Sense Multiple Access with Collision Detection* (CSMA/CD) *Media Access Control* (MAC) that is at the core of 10 Mb/s Ethernet. All the MAC timing parameters are sped up by a factor of 10, but the remainder of the MAC algorithm remains unchanged.

Fast Ethernet uses the same types of hub-and-spoke topologies used by 10BASE-T Ethernet, the dominant form of 10 Mb/s networking in use today. It uses the same types of wiring and the same software protocols. It is supported by a large number of the same vendors. In short, 100BASE-T provides a nondisruptive, smooth evolution from current 10BASE-T Ethernet to high-speed 100 Mb/s performance.

As shown in Figure 6.5, the basic architecture is a hub-and-spoke configuration. From a central hub, point-to-point links radiate out to the client stations. This basic architecture may be extended both in distance and aggregate bandwidth through the use of switching (see *Switch Architecture*, Chapter 2).

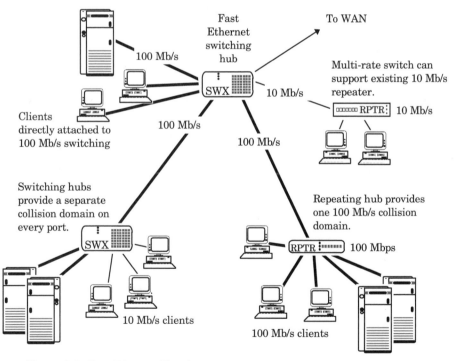

Figure 6.5 Fast Ethernet Topology

Fast Ethernet is the natural upgrade path for existing Ethernet users. When configured as a shared-media network, it provides a ten-fold increase in performance for less than twice the price. In switching configurations, its performance skyrockets *another* order of magnitude.

Fast Ethernet is best known for its clear migration path from 10 Mb/s shared networking to the ultimate in performance, pure 100 Mb/s full-duplex switching. As explained in *Application of Fast Ethernet*, Chapter 2, customers can easily tailor the performance of their network to fit a wide range of situations.

Fast Ethernet Strong Points

Support for Fast Ethernet is phenomenal. At last count, over 85 vendors are working together to guarantee interoperation among Fast Ethernet products. Compatible devices are widely available. Where openness is important, this is a primary strength.

As a shared-media LAN, Fast Ethernet provide 10 times the performance of 10BASE-T.

As a switched LAN, Fast Ethernet provides a growth path to system bandwidths in the multigigabit range (see Chapter 5, *Switching*).

Collapsed backbone hubs provide a perfect point of attachment for future wide area ATM services (see Figures 5.1 through 5.3). Eventually, the separate switching and routing functions will merge into one unit (see *Wide Area Networking*, Chapter 5).

Dual-speed 10/100 Mb/s hubs preserve investment in 10 Mb/s devices, while providing a clear upgrade path to higher performance (see *Adapter Architecture* and *Implementing a Mixed 10/100 Mb/s Network*, in Chapter 2).

Fast Ethernet supports a wide variety of cable types, covering almost all types currently in use, including most 10BASE-T configurations. This preserves the customers' investment in cable (see Chapter 2, *Cables Supported*).

Migration strategies for Fast Ethernet are particularly well thought out. Auto-Negotiation (Chapter 3) significantly eases the burden of upgrading when the time comes.

Fast Ethernet is compatible with the *Simple Network Management Protocol* (SNMP). The SNMP *Management Information Database* (MIB) for Fast Ethernet perfectly overlays the 10BASE-T MIB, with a few

---

Determinism

Networks designed to provide determinism (Token Ring, FDDI, DPAM) only do so in shared-media configurations. In a shared-media configuration all the nodes in the system share the same bandwidth, and all participate together in intricate packet-sequencing decisions. Once such a network is connected through a bridge, switch, or router, the determinism evaporates.

For example, in wide area multimedia applications, given that the WAN itself will likely provide nondeterministic performance, what is the point of insisting on a deterministic LAN? There is none. All that matters is bounding the delay through each network segment at some reasonable probability of packet loss (say, 0.1%). Such bounds may be attained with Fast Ethernet (see Chapter 5, *Flow Control*).

---

extra capabilities to support advanced Fast Ethernet features (see *Management*, Chapter 3).

Network administrators already familiar with CSMA/CD traffic considerations and management will find little has changed in the transition to Fast Ethernet. Administrators can draw on their own direct, hands-on experience with 10 Mb/s Ethernet.

Fast Ethernet Weak Points

Ethernet is a nondeterministic system. There are no deterministic guarantees of performance for individual packets. This complaint is often lodged against Ethernet, but to little effect.

The fact is, *switches and bridges fall prey to precisely the same effect*. They, too, are susceptible to statistical variations in packet delay and even packet loss in the event of buffer overflow. Even ATM switches suffer from this effect. As a general principle, any modern system built around the switching concept has to take statistical factors into account. The nondeterminism of Ethernet, then, is merely a matter of degree, not of quality. Many elements in a large network contribute to variations in packet delay, and they must all be combined to determine the overall statistics of packet delay. Nondeterminism in Ethernet is only a small part of a much larger picture.

Ethernet collision domain constraints are another potential weakness. With fiber, each Fast Ethernet collision domain is limited in diameter to 412 m. With UTP cabling, the limits shrinks further to 205 m. Proponents of other networks would like to argue that these limitations are too restrictive, but in practice they have almost no measurable effect. That is because the collision domain limitations do

not apply across switching devices. With switches, bridges, or routers,
Fast Ethernet networks may be extended to arbitrary dimensions (see
Chapter 2, *Switch Architecture* and Chapter 3, *100BASE-FX: Distances*).

SUMMARY OF HIGH-SPEED LANs

Table 6.2 Summary of High-Speed LANs

	FDDI	**ATM**	**DPAM**	**Fast Ethernet**
Link data rate	100 Mb/s	25, 51 or 155 Mb/s[b]	100 Mb/s	100 Mb/s
Media	Cat 5 UTP STP 62/125 fiber	Cat 3,4,5 UTP 150-Ω STP 62/125 fiber	Cat 3,4,5 UTP 150-Ω STP 62/125 fiber	Cat 3,4,5 UTP 150-Ω STP 62/125 fiber
MAC protocol	Token passing with SMT	Full duplex using 53 byte cells	Demand priority (token circulates inside hub)	CSMA/CD or full duplex
Switching	Optional (but sacrifices determinism)	Required	Optional (but sacrifices determinism)	Optional
Maximum diameter	200 km[a]	Unlimited	12 km[a]	412 m[a]
Topology	Logical ring, typically wired as a physical star	Tree	Tree	Tree

[a] With switches, bridges or routers, the network diameter is unlimited.
[b] Link rates for desktop usage.

Points to Remember

- FDDI is best used as a backbone for 10 Mb/s networking.
- ATM will make an excellent national backbone WAN.
- Widespread deployment of ATM as a LAN has probably been pushed out to the year 2000 or beyond.
- The best applications for DPAM are in systems that do not require more than 100 Mb/s total system bandwidth and where determinism is a substantial benefit.
- Fiber Channel is under consideration as one alternative means to link Fast Ethernet switches in very fast backbone configurations.
- The success of Fast Ethernet derives from its unique position as a simple, easily understood upgrade for the enormously popular 10BASE-T system.
- When configured as a shared-media network, Fast Ethernet provides a tenfold increase in performance for less than twice the price.
- In switching configurations, Fast Ethernet performance skyrockets *another* order of magnitude.

7

Collision Domains: Extra for Experts

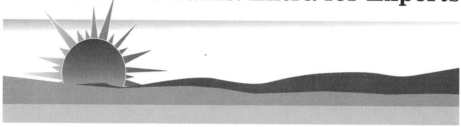

As explained in *Topology*, Chapter 3, and Clause 29 of the standard, Fast Ethernet repeaters must obey certain timing rules. The timing rules limit the way networks may be connected. This chapter explains what those rules are, and why they exist.

If network timing doesn't excite you, this might be a good time to step out for a cup of tea. Plenty of people use the configuration rules in Clause 29 without every questioning *why* they take effect. On the other hand, if you *want* to know why timing matters, keep reading.

This discussion will involve properties of the MAC protocol and Ethernet collision domains. Let's start with a few definitions.

WHAT IS A COLLISION DOMAIN?

A *collision domain* is a collection of Ethernet devices (nodes) connected by any number of repeaters. Only one node at a time may successfully transmit inside a collision domain. When any node in the domain talks, all the other nodes listen. For a discussion of repeater architecture and operation, see *Repeater Architecture*, Chapter 2.

The term *Media Access Control* (MAC) *protocol* refers to any protocol used to control access to a shared transmission system. In Ethernet, the MAC protocol is CSMA/CD. A general overview of the CSMA/CD MAC is presented in Chapter 1, *The Ethernet Control System*. The CSMA/CD MAC resides in every Ethernet client, be it a PC, workstation, server, bridge, or router. Any device containing a MAC is termed a piece of *data terminal equipment* (DTE).

Repeaters are different from DTEs. The MAC is not present in a repeater. The repeater uses different (simpler) rules to control packet forwarding. For a discussion of repeater architecture and operation, see *Repeater Architecture*, Chapter 2.

Collisions happen when two DTEs in a collision domain try to transmit at the same time. Their packets clobber each other during the collision, both transmitting DTEs must back off, and the colliding packets must be re-transmitted.

The *diameter* of a collision domain is defined as the cable distance (that is, length of cable) between the two maximally separated nodes in the domain. Diameter is expressed in meters. Cable distance is always greater than the straight line distance between nodes. For example, two adjacent nodes may each have 75-m cables running back to a central hub. The cable distance between those nodes is 150 m.

The *collision domain timing constraint*, or *collision constraint*, is the primary timing rule limiting the topology of individual collision domains in Fast Ethernet. It limits the maximum round-trip delay in a collision domain. Because data signals travel at finite speed, the round trip delay through a network depends on its physical extent. As a network grows, the round-trip delay lengthens. By this logic, the collision constraint also limits the maximum physical extent, or diameter, of a collision domain.

Collision domains do not penetrate *switch*, *bridge*, or *router* ports. Such devices provide an independent collision domain at every port (see *Switch Architecture* in Chapter 2). As a consequence, the collision constraint does not apply across a switch, bridge, or router boundary. *This feature permits construction of Ethernet networks of arbitrary size, using switches, bridges, and routers to interconnect collision domains.*

HOW MAC TIMING WORKS

Figure 7.1 illustrates the MAC packet transmission cycle. The three protocol entities apparent in this figure are the *Logical Link Control* (LLC) sublayer, the *Media Access Control* (MAC) protocol, and the *Physical Layer Device* (PHY).

The packet transmission cycle begins when the *Logical Link Control* (LLC) sublayer hands the MAC a packet.[1] The MAC waits for a good opportunity and then tries to send the packet. Usually, the packet

---

[1] Many MAC implementations begin transmissions when LLC hands over the *beginning* of a packet, without waiting for the remainder of the packet to arrive.

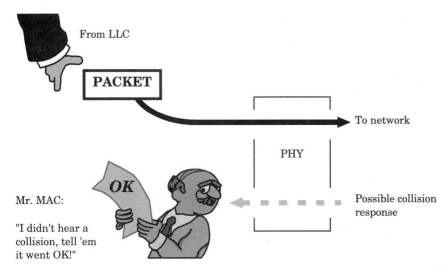

From LLC

PACKET

To network

PHY

OK

Mr. MAC:

"I didn't hear a
collision, tell 'em
it went OK!"

Possible collision
response

Figure 7.1 MAC Protocol

goes through without collision. In that case, the MAC tells the LLC that
transmission is complete and promptly forgets about it. The LLC then
prepares the next packet.

The MAC to LLC timing is crucial. As *soon as the packet goes
through*, the MAC tells the LLC it is complete, and ready for the next
packet (Figure 7.1).

So far, so good. When a collision happens, things go differently.
The nature of collision processing depends on precisely *when* the MAC
recognizes the collision.

If a collision happens *while* the MAC is still transmitting, the MAC
immediately stops sending. It then schedules the packet for
retransmission. The MAC tells the LLC nothing. Higher layers of
software are not even aware that a collision took place. The low-level
MAC protocol just reschedules the transmission and keeps working.

If a collision indication appears *after* the MAC has finished sending
the packet, it is too late. The MAC has already told the LLC it is done,
discarded the packet, and *is no longer able to re-transmit it*.[2] The
colliding packet is lost.

---

[2] The MAC is considerably more complex than this simple caricature, but the basic
conclusions remain unchanged.

Such an event is called a *late collision*. The loss of a packet is not fatal, but it does affect system performance. The system eventually recovers from this loss when the upper protocol layers recognize that the packet is missing. The problem is that it takes a long time for the software in the upper protocol layers to react. If the MAC hardware had known about the collision in time, re-transmission would have occurred more quickly, and cheaply in terms of system resources. This is a classic performance issue. Re-transmission from the MAC hardware is faster than re-transmission from the upper protocol layer software.[3]

Fundamental, then, to efficient network operations is this concept:

Collisions must be reported to the MAC during transmission of any packet in which they occur.

We call this the *collision domain timing constraint*, or just the *collision constraint*.

The worst case for the collision constraint occurs on the shortest possible packets. The shortest packets are 512 data bits long.[4] The constraint can thus be restated:

Collisions must be reported to the MAC before the 512th bit of any transmission.

WHY THE DIAMETER OF A COLLISION DOMAIN MATTERS

It takes time for packets to traverse a network. It takes even more time for a packet to traverse a network and collide with another packet and for news of the collision to return to the original source. If this time exceeds 512 bit times (one *slot time*), the originating MAC will not find out about the collision before it has transmitted its 512th bit. The collision constraint will not be satisfied. Late collisions will result.

The collision constraint thus affects the maximal topology of the system in a very direct way. It implies that the round trip propagation time of the network must be less than 512 bit times. Limiting the round trip time to 512 bit times ensures that collisions occur within 512 bit

---

[3] Late collisions also cause big network management headaches. Late collisions are never supposed to occur, and some network management systems set off alarms when they do.

[4] A period of 512 bits is called, in Ethernet, a *slot time*.

times, and thus the MAC will maintain its normal, efficient operation. This brief analysis ignores complicating factors such as collision detection time and transmission deferral time and other delays internal to end nodes and repeaters. When those factors are added to the round-trip time, the total result must still fall below 512 bit times. The raw cable round-trip time must then be somewhat less than 512 bit times. Nevertheless, we have settled on the final form of our collision domain timing constraint:

> *In any Fast Ethernet collision domain, the round-trip propagation delay must not exceed 512 bit times (one slot time).*

From the collision constraint, we may compute the maximum allowed network diameter. The computation proceeds in four steps:

1. Add up the delays of the DTEs and repeaters in the network.
2. Subtract them from 512 bits.
3. The remainder is available for the total cable delay.
4. Divide the total cable delay by the cable speed in ns/m to get the permitted length of cable.

Table 7.1 summarizes typical network delays for near-maximal configurations of 10 Mb/s Ethernet and Fast Ethernet, showing the proportions of cable delay and repeater or DTE delay (see configurations shown in Figure 7.2 and Figure 7.3). Compared to regular Ethernet, Fast Ethernet reserves a similar proportion of its budget for the repeaters and DTEs, but it supports fewer repeaters. On a per-repeater basis, Fast Ethernet repeaters use more bits. That effect is due to the large number of bit times of delay associated with the parallel clocking of bits across the nibble-wide MII interface, and other nibble-wide paths internal to the MAC and repeater state machines.

Finally, note that there exist other timing constraints besides just the collision constraint. For example, the duration of the largest possible collision fragment must be less than a slot time. Within 100BASE-T, the limiting constraint is always the collision constraint, which can be directly related to the round-trip propagation delay. In other Ethernet systems this simple relationship does not always hold true.

Near-Maximal 10 Mb/s Thick Coax Ethernet Configuration

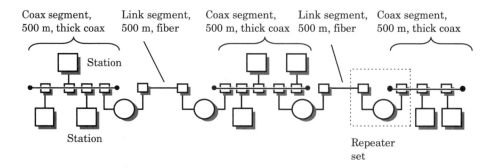

Bit Budget Worksheet

Total of all coax segments		
length (m)	1,500	
round trip bits/m ×	4.3	
=	coax cable delay:	6,450
Total of all fiber segments		
length (m)	2,000	
round trip bits/m ×	5.0	
=	fiber cable delay:	10,000
Total cable delay		
	total delay (ns)	16,540
	double for round trip	× 2
Round-trip cable delay		
=		32,900

Figure 7.2 Example 10 Mb/s Ethernet Configuration

Near-Maximal Fast Ethernet UTP Configuration

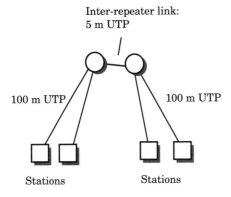

Bit Budget Worksheet

Total of all UTP segments		
length (m)	205	
round trip bits/m ×	5.7	
=	UTP cable delay:	1,168
Total cable delay		
	total delay (ns):	1,168
	double for round trip	× 2
Round-trip cable delay		
=		2337

Figure 7.3 Example Fast Ethernet Configuration

Table 7.1 Collision Domain Facts and Figures

Item	10 Mb/s Ethernet[a] Timing Budget		Fast Ethernet[b] Timing Budget	
	(seconds)	(bit times)	(seconds)	(bit times)
Bit time	100 ns		10 ns	
Collision constraint	51,200 ns	512	5,120 ns	512
Less cable delay (round trip)	27,900 ns	279	2,337 ns	234
Remaining budget for other factors, including multiple repeaters and DTE circuitry	23,300 ns	233	2,783 ns	278
Number of repeaters	4		2	

[a] Configurations are shown in Figure 7.2. Timing numbers are approximate. At 10 Mb/s, diameters up to 4 km are possible using fiber links and fewer repeaters. See **IEEE Std 802.3j** (supplement **j**) for more details.

[b] Configurations are shown in Figure 7.3. Timing numbers are approximate. At 100 Mb/s, a single collision domain as large as 412 m is possible using fiber links and no repeaters (a point-to-point link). A 100 Mb/s full-duplex switched link may span more than 20 km. See *Topology* in Chapter 3 for more details.

Points to Remember

- Collisions must be reported to the MAC during transmission of any packet in which they occur.
- Late collisions affect performance.
- In any Fast Ethernet collision domain, the round-trip propagation delay must not exceed 512 bit times.
- Repeater timing constraints do not apply across bridge, switch, or router boundaries.
- With bridges, routers and switches, Fast Ethernet networks can grow to arbitrary size.

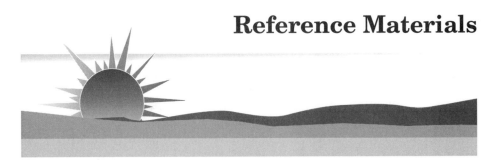

8

Reference Materials

BOOKS ABOUT ETHERNET

HEGERING, HEINZ-GERD AND LAPPLE, ALFRED, *Ethernet - Building a Communications Infrastructure.* Wokingham, England: Addison-Wesley, 1993. ISBN: 0-201-62405-2.

Full coverage of 10 Mb/s Ethernet networking. Includes discussion of higher protocols, applications, and management.

NEMZOW, MARTIN A. W., *The Ethernet Management Guide* (2nd ed.), New York, NY: McGraw-Hill, 1992. ISBN: 0-07-046320-4.

An excellent treatise on the planning and installation of large 10 Mb/s Ethernet sites. It includes discussion of network management as a general human management problem, as well as from a hardware and software perspective.

PEATFIELD, TONY, Editor, *Network Systems Tutorial for IEEE Std 802.3: Repeater Functions and System Design Topology Considerations for Carrier Sense Multiple Access with Collision Detection (CSMA/CD) Local Area Networks (LANs).* New York, NY: IEEE Standards Press, 1995.

SMITH, DOUGLAS K. AND ALEXANDER, ROBERT C., *Fumbling the Future, How Xerox Invented, Then Ignored, the First Personal Computer.* New York, NY: William Morrow and Company, Inc., 1988. ISBN: 0-688-06959-2.

An entertaining and informative historical narrative about the early days of personal computer development at Xerox. It touches peripherally on Ethernet and its relation to the Alto and other early Xerox computers.

BOOKS ABOUT OTHER HIGH-SPEED LANS

COSTA, JANIS FURTEK, *Planning and Designing High Speed Networks, Using 100VG-AnyLAN*. Englewood Cliffs, NJ: Prentice Hall, 1994. ISBN: 0-13-168685-2.

A handbook from the Hewlett Packard Professional Series.

DE PRYCKER, MARTIN, *Asynchronous Transfer Mode, Solution for Broadband ISDN* (2nd ed.), Hertfordshire, England: Ellis Horwood, 1993. ISBN: 0-13-178542-7.

In-depth coverage of ATM. A good book, but watch out, ATM is changing very rapidly.

JAIN, RAJ, *FDDI Handbook: High-Speed Networking Using Fiber and Other Media*. Reading, MA: Addison-Wesley Pub. Co., 1994. ISBN: 0-201-56376-2.

SHAH, AMIT, AND RAMAKRISHNAN, G., *FDDI, A High Speed Network*. Englewood Cliffs, NJ: Prentice Hall, 1994. ISBN: 0-13-308388-8.

In-depth coverage of FDDI.

GENERAL BOOKS ABOUT LAN TECHNOLOGY

BLACK, UYLESS, *TCP/IP and Related Protocols*. New York, NY: McGraw-Hill, 1992. ISBN: 0-07-005553-X.

A first-class, practical overview of the TCP/IP protocol suite. Includes discussion of SNMP and the base OSI standards used to define an SNMP MIB.

COMER, DOUGLAS, *Internetworking with TCP/IP*. Englewood Cliffs, NJ: Prentice Hall, 1988. ISBN: 0-13-470154-2.

The forward to the first book of this three-volume set summarizes the series very well: "This book brings together information about the various parts of the TCP/IP architecture and protocols and makes it accessible."

FORTIER, PAUL J., Editor, *Handbook of LAN Technology* (2nd ed.), New York, NY: McGraw Hill, 1992. ISBN: 0-07-021625-8.

A wide-ranging collection of essays on popular LAN issues including network planning, topology, security, modeling, and management.

GASMAN, LAWRENCE, *Broadband Networking*. New York, NY: Van Nostrand Reinhold, 1994. ISBN: 0-442-01168-7.

Broad survey of high-speed networking issues, including high-level comparisons of ATM, T1, Frame Relay, SMDS, HIPPI, Fiber

Channel, FDDI, FDDI-II, Fast Ethernet, and other networking standards.

MARTIN, JAMES, *Local Area Networks* (2nd ed.), Englewood Cliffs, NJ: Prentice Hall, 1994. ISBN: 0-13-533035-1.

A general work about local area networking. It includes discussion of Ethernet, Token Ring, Token Bus, FDDI, Apple™ LocalTalk® and, at the higher layers, NetBios, Novell NetWare®, TCP/IP and AppleTalk®.

NAUGLE, MATTHEW G., *Local Area Networking*. New York, NY: McGraw-Hill, 1991. ISBN: 0-07-046455-3.

A general work about local area networking, with an emphasis on Ethernet, Token Ring and, at the higher layers, NetBios.

ROSE, MARSHALL T., *The Simple Book* (2nd ed.), Englewood Cliffs, NJ: Prentice-Hall, 1994. ISBN: 0-13-177254-6.

A detailed examination of the Simple Network Management Protocol (SNMP).

TANENBAUM, ANDREW S., *Computer Networks* (2nd ed.), Englewood Cliffs, NJ: Prentice Hall, 1988. ISBN: 0-13-162959-X.

Excellent technical presentation of the layered structure of computer networks. This book graces the shelves of almost every computer network designer I know.

WHITTAKER, SIR EDMUND, *The History of Modern Physics, 1800-1950, Volume 7, A History of the Theories of Aether and Electricity*. New York, NY: American Institute of Physics, 1987. ISBN: 0-88318-523-7.

Just what the title says. Not much to do with LANs, but it includes a really good description of lumineferous ether.

TERMS AND ACRONYMS USED IN THIS BOOK

Here is a collection of useful definitions from throughout the book.

100-Ω cable (commonly called UTP)	The most widely installed kind of twisted-pair cabling.
120-Ω cable	A twisted-pair cable used primarily in France.
150-Ω cable (commonly called STP)	A shielded, twisted-pair cable originally designed by IBM. Physically, the cable is massive, unwieldy, and difficult to terminate.
50-Ω coaxial cable	Originally used for bus-topology Ethernet. Superseded, in horizontal runs, by UTP cabling.
50/125 μm multimode	A popular fiber in Europe and Japan. This fiber has better transmission properties than 62.5/125 μm fiber, but its smaller dimensions make shining light into the medium more difficult.
62.5/125 μm multimode	The most popular fiber. ISO recommends this version, although many other types are available.
802.3 simplex link segment	A connection, including equipment cables, between two MDIs.
ALOHA	An early local area network developed at the University of Hawaii.
ANSI	American National Standards Institute. Accepts IEEE standards and forwards them to ISO. Also publishes its own standards, such as FDDI, HIPPI, SCSI, and Fiber Channel.
Asynchronous Transfer Mode (ATM)	A method of packet communication using fixed-sized cells of 53 octets.
ATM Forum	Asynchronous Transfer Mode Forum. An industry group working on specifications for LAN applications of ATM.
Attachment Unit Interface (AUI)	The standard 10 Mb/s Ethernet transceiver interface.

Auto-Negotiation (AUTONEG)	A sublayer of Fast Ethernet. It provides extensive support for determination of link options and optimal settings. With Auto-Negotiation enabled, an adapter card may determine for itself what the capabilities are at the far end of the link and select the best operational mode as needed.
Backbone cabling, or vertical cabling	Cables connecting floor distributors to each other and to other levels in the wiring hierarchy.
Binary Logarithmic Arbitration Method (BLAM)	An emerging technique for smoothing the flow of packets on an Ethernet network.
Carrier Sense Multiple Access with Collision Detection (CSMA/CD)	MAC algorithm used in Ethernet. See Chapter 1, *The Ethernet Control System*. Fast Ethernet uses the same CSMA/CD MAC protocol used in regular Ethernet, except for a 10 times faster bit rate. It connects to higher layer protocols (that is, your computer I/O bus and NDIS driver) in precisely the same way as regular Ethernet.
Cascading	Many repeater architectures provide a 100 Mb/s switched port. Such ports permit many interesting configurations including multi-tiered hierarchies.
Category 3,4,5	These categories are a rating system for the data-handling capacity of twisted-pair cabling. Category 5 is the best. Category 5 cable, because of its increased data handling capacity, sells for a little more than category 3 cable. Category 4 cable fits between categories 3 and 5 both in its data handling capacity and its cost.
CCITT	International Consultative Committee for Telephone and Telegraph. An advisory committee established under the United Nations. Publishes standards for ISDN and wide area applications of ATM.
Class I repeater	A type of Fast Ethernet repeater. One is permitted per collision domain. This repeater has a relaxed timing budget, which makes possible translation, stacking, and other features.

Class II repeater	A type of Fast Ethernet repeater. With maximal length links, up to two are permitted per collision domain (more with shorter links). This repeater has a tight timing budget. Translation between T4 and the X family is probably precluded. Stacking is not as flexible as in Class I.
Common Management Information Protocol (CMIP)	An ISO standard for the exchange of management information.
Collision Domain	A collection of Ethernet devices (nodes) connected by any number of repeaters. Only one node at a time may successfully transmit inside a collision domain. When any node in the domain talks, all the other nodes listen.
Crossover correction	Some repeaters in the 10 Mb/s market can detect cross-wiring of the transmit and receive pairs, and fix the problem themselves.
Data Terminal Equipment (DTE)	A hoary old term that harks back to the early days of punch-card computing. Today, generally, it refers to the computer on your desk. In Ethernet systems, specifically, it refers to any host system that contains a MAC.
DTE-to-DTE communication	A point-to-point connection of two Ethernet devices.
EIA link	A connection, including equipment cables, between terminal equipment in the work area and equipment in the telecommunications closet.
Equipment room (campus distributor)	Highest point in a cabling hierarchy. Place where telephone switch, or mainframe computer, or both is usually located.
Exposed MII	The standard MII connection for an external transceiver. Vendors may place a Fast Ethernet transceiver on an adapter card, or a system motherboard, omitting the exposed MII interface.
Far End Fault	An optional feature helpful for debugging cabling problems with fiber.

Fiber Distributed Data Interface (FDDI)	An ANSI standard 100 Mb/s local area network.
Full duplex	Simultaneous use of both transmit and receive paths in a Fast Ethernet link.
	All TX and FX interfaces naturally have full-duplex capability. If connected to a full-duplex MAC, they can be placed in a full-duplex operating mode. For switch-to-switch links, this mode is highly desirable.
Half-repeater	An early Ethernet term, referring to either end of a repeater system that has been split down the middle and stretched across the landscape through the use of some non-Ethernet transmission technology. A half-repeater connected two Ethernet segments in remote locations. This term is no longer in current usage.
Horizontal cabling	Cables running from wiring closet to terminal equipment. Includes equipment cables at each end.
IEC	International Electrotechnical Commission. In the field of information technology, the IEC and ISO jointly publish standards.
IEEE	Institute of Electrical and Electronic Engineers. Published Ethernet, Token Ring, Token Bus, and many other LAN standards.
IETF	Internet Engineering Task Force. Publishes standards for Internet operation, including TCP/IP and SNMP.
Internal crossover	Complementary RJ-45 pin assignment used on hubs to permit straight-through wiring between client and hub.
ISO	International Standards Organization. Ultimate international approval source for all types of standards.
ISO link	A connection between a telecommunications outlet in the work area and a cross-connect panel in the floor distributor.

ISO Model for Open Systems Interconnection (OSI)	A famous seven-layer representation of network systems.
Local Area Network (LAN)	A private network used for data communication among data stations located on a customer's premises.
Logical Link Control (LLC)	A protocol sublayer defined in **IEEE Std 802.2**.
Main cross-connect, intermediate cross-connect (building distributor)	An intermediate level in a building cabling hierarchy.
Management Information Database (MIB)	A specification of how a management agent should count events, report status, generate alarms, and respond to commands.
Media Access Control (MAC)	A general term for the protocol sublayer used to control access to a shared communication medium. It determines who transmits and when.
Media Independent Interface (MII)	The standard Fast Ethernet transceiver interface. It supports all the standard 802.3 Fast Ethernet transceivers.
Medium	The 802.3 standard uses the word *medium* to refer to the wire (or fiber) that links nodes.
Medium Attachment Unit (MAU)	Official term for a 10 Mb/s Ethernet *transceiver*. The MAU contains the analog circuitry necessary to communicate with the physical medium.
Medium Dependent Interface (MDI)	A fancy name for *connector*. Connectors for T4, TX and FX are specified along with the PMD or PMA sublayer of each transceiver type.
Next page feature	Part of the Auto-Negotiation specification, this feature provides a general mechanism for exchanging additional optional information, including a unique identifier code, as well as other vendor-specific information.

Priority Access Control Enabled (PACE)	An emerging technique for smoothing the flow of packets between a switch port and its associated client.
Physical Coding Sublayer (PCS)	A sublayer of the PHY. Responsible for coding transmitted data into a form suitable for the physical medium, and decoding it at the receiver.
Physical Layer Device (PHY)	Official term for a Fast Ethernet *transceiver*. The PHY contains the analog circuitry necessary to communicate with the physical medium.
	The PHY is a combination of the PCS, PMA, PMD, and AUTONEG sublayers. The PHY may be located either external to a host computer (external transceiver) or embedded onto an adapter.
Physical Medium Attachment Sublayer (PMA)	A sublayer of the PHY. In conjunction with the PMD, it is responsible for analog functions like transmit wave-shaping and receive data discrimination.
Physical Medium Dependent Sublayer (PMD)	A sublayer of the PHY. In TX and FX transceivers, this sublayer is borrowed from FDDI. In T4 transceivers, the PMD functionality resides within the PMA sublayer.
Polarity reversal	Polarity reversal refers to the swapping of the two wires within a given pair. It is different from a wiring crossover, which, for example, swaps pair 2 with pair 3.
Protocol Implementation Conformance Statement (PICS)	A document listing what exact features and options from the 802.3 standard have been implemented in a particular piece of equipment.
Reconciliation sublayer	A "weenie" sublayer. It translates the terminology used in the MAC into the terminology appropriate for the MII sublayer.
Remote fault indication	Auto-Negotiation allows signaling of any local fault condition to the other end.

Repeater Set	An entire functional repeater, including the repeater unit (the core) and its associated transceivers. A repeater set couples together DTEs into a single collision domain.
Repeater Unit	This term is used in Clause 27 to refer to the logical inner workings of a repeater (the *core*). A repeater unit connects to the physical medium through many of the same sublayers used in the DTE.
Shielded twisted pair (STP)	Common term for 150-Ω twisted-pair cable with shielding (like IBM type-I). This usage follows the terminology laid down in **EIA/TIA 568-A**.
Simple Network Management Protocol (SNMP)	An IETF standard for the exchange of management information.
System Network Architecture (SNA)	An IBM architecture originally designed for the networking of mainframe computer products.
Telecommunication closet (floor distributor)	A central connection point, within 100 m of the terminal equipment. Originally used (pre-1980 in the U.S.) exclusively for telephone equipment.
Telecommunication outlet	The wall jack, or faceplate, present in a work area.
Terminal equipment	Computer, terminal, PC, server, or other computing device tied to the LAN.
Unshielded twisted pair (UTP)	Common term for 100-Ω twisted-pair cable, with no overall shield, and no shield around any of its pairs. This usage follows the terminology laid down in **EIA/TIA 568-A**.
Wide Area Network (WAN)	A network generally using public data communication facilities for data communication among widely separated data stations.
Work area	Office, cubicle, or other place where computer equipment might be located.
Work area equipment cable (work area cable)	A flexible jumper cable, or cord, used to connect terminal equipment to a telecommunications outlet.

ORDERING ETHERNET DOCUMENTS

As explained in Chapter 1, *Who Published the Ethernet Standard*, the official name for what most people call *Ethernet* is:

IEEE Std 802.3 Carrier Sense Multiple Access with Collision Detection (CSMA/CD) Access Method and Physical Layer Specifications

It is a complex standard, composed of many parts, which can make ordering the standard rather difficult. This section explains how the parts of the Ethernet standard are organized, and where to get them.

At present, the complete Ethernet standard contains thirty clauses. They have been assigned clause numbers 1 to 30. In the back of this chapter, Table 8.2 lists the contents of each clause approved as of the time of writing. Unfortunately, even though all the pieces are available through the IEEE, *there is no way to order all of the clauses bound together into one document*. They are available only in the form of a *base document* plus a number of *supplements* and *revisions*.

The IEEE 802.3 working group periodically releases supplements and revisions. These documents have been designated **a** to **y**. Following the list of clauses, Table 8.3 lists the most recent supplements and revisions, and their contents. As listed in Table 8.3, supplements usually create whole new clauses, while revisions modify existing clauses. Fast Ethernet is one of the supplements. Its supplement designation letter is **u**. It created new Clauses 21 to 30. The exact title of the Fast Ethernet supplement is:

IEEE Std 802.3u:1995 MAC Parameters, Physical Layer, Medium Attachment Units and Repeater for 100 Mb/s Operation.

Periodically, the IEEE combines all the latest supplements and revisions together into a new base document. That new base document is then submitted to ISO for international approval (see Chapter 1, *How the IEEE Works with Other Standards Bodies*), and jointly released as an ISO/IEC/ANSI/IEEE standard. The latest base document (as of the time of writing) was released in 1993. Here is the exact title:

ISO/IEC 8802-3 Carrier Sense Multiple Access with Collision Detection (CSMA/CD) Access Method & Physical Layer Specifications.

The 1993 version of **ISO/IEC 8802-3** includes all the Ethernet standards up through supplement **i**. A new version of **ISO/IEC 8802-3** is planned for release in late 1995. It will likely include everything up through supplement **p** (Table 8.1).

Table 8.1 Contents of ISO Base Documents

ISO/IEC 8802-3:1993	All Ethernet standards through supplement *i*
ISO/IEC 8802-3:1995	All Ethernet standards through supplement *p*

To get the latest information, you must obtain both the main ISO standard, plus the latest supplements. Here's how to do it:

1. Order the latest version of **ISO/IEC 8802-3**. This document is a joint ISO/IEC/ANSI/IEEE standard. It is best ordered directly from the IEEE (see *Sources*, following this section).
2. Find out which supplements are in the latest ISO version (see Table 8.1, or ask the IEEE).
3. Order the remaining IEEE supplements (see *Sources*).

SOURCES

Points of contact, as of June 1995, for various standards organizations appear below.

Global Engineering and Standard Sales are commercial distributors that keep many popular standards in stock. They offer convenient, one-stop shopping for standards. They accept major credit cards.

Joint IEEE/ANSI standards, and the Ethernet series of ISO/IEC standards, are best obtained directly from their publisher, the IEEE.

With any of these organizations, ask for a catalog. Also ask to be included on their update service to keep informed of new standards and supplements as they are approved. Some offer discounts with the update service.

ANSI	Sales Department
	American National Standards Institute
	11 West 42nd Street, 13th Floor
	New York, NY 10036
	tel: 212 642 4900
	fax: 212 302 1286
ATM Forum	ATM Forum
	303 Vintage Park Drive
	Foster City, CA 94404
	tel: 415 578 6860
	fax: 415 525 0182
	faxback service: 415 688 4318
	WWW http://www.atmforum.com
	EMAIL info@atmforum.com
EIA	Electronic Industries Association
	2500 Wilson Blvd.
	Arlington, VA 22201
	tel: 703 907 7500
	fax: 703 907 7501
	Standards are available through the EIA, but they like to refer people to Global Engineering.
Global Engineering	15 Inverness Way East
	Englewood, CO 80112-5704
	tel: 800 624 3974
	tel: 303 792 2181
	fax: 303 790 0730
IEEE	IEEE Customer Service
	445 Hoes Lane, P.O. Box 1331
	Piscataway, NJ 08855-1331 USA
	tel: 800 678 4333 (US and Canada only)
	tel: 908 562 1393 (outside US and Canada)
	fax: 908 981 9667
	Gopher stdsbbs.ieee.org
	FTP stdsbbs.ieee.org /pub/catalog

IETF	Internet Engineering Task Force
	Standards for the Internet, TCP/IP, and SNMP are described in Request for Comments (RFC) documents, which are stored on-line in the Internet. RFC1780, among others, lists additional contact information for IETF officers and staff.
	WWW http://ds.internic.net GOPHER internic.net FTP ds.internic.net
	Or, for information about obtaining RFCs:
	Send EMAIL to: rfc-info@isi.edu, with the single text line: help: ways_to_get_rfcs
	Or, send EMAIL to: mailserv@ds.internic.net, with the single text line: help
ISO	ANSI is the official sales agent for ISO standards in the United States (but most people call Global or Standard). Outside of the United States, contact: International Organization for Standardization Case Postale 56 1 rue de Varembé CH-1211 Genève 20 Switzerland/Suisse tel: 41 1254 5454 fax: 41 1254 5474
ITU *(formerly CCITT)*	International Telecommunication Union (Formerly Comité Consultif Internationale Télégraphique et Téléphone, or International Consultative Committee for Telephone and Telegraph)
	Place des Nations 1211 Geneve 20, Switzerland tel: 41 22 730 61 41 fax: 41 22 730 51 94 int'l fax: 41 22 733 72 56
Standard Sales	2801 E 12th Street Los Angeles, CA 90023 tel: 800 421 6131 tel: 619 946 0500 fax: 213 269 2761

STANDARDS CLOSELY RELATED TO FAST ETHERNET

ANSI X3.263 **Rev. 2.2, 1 March 1995**	FDDI twisted-pair transceiver as referenced by 100BASE-TX. Specifies cabling appropriate for use with TX. Also note that the X3T9.5 committee has been renamed X3T12.
IEEE Std 802.1 (and supplements)	MAC bridging standards applicable to switching hubs. Spanning tree algorithm.
EIA/TIA 568-A	Building cabling standards for North America. Revised in 1995.
ISO 11801: 1995	International building cabling standards. Similar to **EIA/TIA 568-A**, but different.
ISO 9314-3: 1990	FDDI fiber transceiver as used by 100BASE-FX. Specifies cabling appropriate for use with TX.

CLAUSES OF IEEE STD 802.3

Table 8.2 Clauses of **IEEE Std 802.3**

Clause	Nickname	Contents
1	*Introduction*	Nomenclature, list of references to international standards, and (with revisions per supplement **u**) consolidated definitions of special terms for all clauses.
2	*MAC interface*	Formal interface between Logical Link Control (LLC) and Media Access Control (MAC) sublayers.
3	*MAC frame structure*	Definition of packet format: preamble, start of frame delimiter, destination address, source address, length field, data, pad (for short packets), and CRC-32.
4	*MAC protocol*	The inner workings of the CSMA/CD access protocol.
5	*DTE Management*	Management functions for 10 Mb/s DTEs; *Superseded by Clause 30.*

Table 8.2 Clauses of **IEEE Std 802.3**

Clause	Nickname	Contents
6	*PLS Interface*	Formal interface between MAC and Physical Signaling (PLS) sublayer.
7	*PLS, AUI*	Electrical signaling and physical cabling specifications for the Attachment Unit Interface (AUI).
8	*10BASE5*	10 Mb/s thick coax transceiver (500 m span).
9	*10 Mb/s Repeater*	10 Mb/s baseband repeater and fiber optic inter-repeater link (FOIRL).
10	*10BASE2*	10 Mb/s thin coax transceiver (a.k.a. Cheapernet, Thin Ethernet, 185 m span).
11	*10BROAD36*	10 Mb/s broadband transceiver (multiple Ethernet channels and CATV can co-exist on the same 75-Ω coax).
12	*1BASE5*	1 Mb/s UTP transceiver (StarLAN, 250 m link span).
13	*Topology*	Timing constraints; specifies allowed topologies for 10 Mb/s networks.
14	*10BASE-T*	10 Mb/s UTP transceiver (100 m link span).
15	*10BASE-F*	Common elements of 10 Mb/s fiber optic transceivers (850 nm, multimode).
16	*10BASE-FP*	10 Mb/s fiber optic passive-star type transmission system (500 m radius).
17	*10BASE-FB*	10 Mb/s fiber optic inter-repeater link (same cable as FOIRL, but incompatible signaling, 2 km link span).
18	*10BASE-FL*	10 Mb/s fiber optic link DTE to repeater (supersedes FOIRL previously defined in Clause 9.9, 2 km link span).
19	*Repeater Management*	Management functions for 10 Mb/s repeaters; *Superseded by Clause 30.*
20	*MAU Management*	Management functions for 10 Mb/s integrated transceivers; *Superseded by Clause 30.*
21	*Introduction*	100BASE-T: Overview, list of abbreviations, defines terms used in PICS and state machine descriptions.

Table 8.2 Clauses of **IEEE Std 802.3**

Clause	Nickname	Contents
22	*MII*	100BASE-T: Reconciliation sublayer and Media Independent Interface.
23	*100BASE-T4*	100 Mb/s four-pair category 3 UTP transceiver (100 m link span).
24	*100BASE-X*	Common portions of TX and FX specifications.
25	*100BASE-TX*	100 Mb/s two-pair category 5 UTP transceiver (100 m link span).
26	*100BASE-FX*	100 Mb/s multimode fiber transceiver (2 km link span).
27	*100 Mb/s Repeater*	100 Mb/s repeater, defines both Class I and II.
28	*Auto-Negotiation*	Automatic signaling to select link operating modes.
29	*Topology*	Timing constraints; specifies allowed topologies for 100 Mb/s networks.
30	*Management*	Consolidated 10 Mb/s & 100 Mb/s management definitions (MIBS); supersedes Clauses 5, 19 and 20.

RECENT SUPPLEMENTS TO IEEE STD 802.3

Table 8.3 Recent Supplements and Revisions to **IEEE Std 802.3**

Supplement	Nickname	Contents
j	*10BASE-F*	Clauses 15 through 18, plus major revision and expansion of 10 Mb/s topology rules in Clause 13.
k	*10 Mb/s Repeater Management*	Clause 19. *Superseded by supplement* **u**.
l	*10BASE-T PICS*	Formal list of requirements for 10BASE-T MAU conformance.
m	*Maint. #2*	Revisions to Clauses 1, 7, 8, 9 and 10.

Table 8.3 Recent Supplements and Revisions to **IEEE Std 802.3**

Supple- ment	Nickname	Contents
n	*Maint. #3*	Revisions to Clauses 4, 6, 7, 8 and 10.
o	*N/A*	*There is no supplement o*
p	*10 Mb/s MAU Management*	Clause 20. *Superseded by supplement* **u**.
q	*10 Mb/s DTE Management*	Reformatting of Clause 5 in GDMO format. *Superseded by supplement* **u**.
r	*10BASE5 PICS*	Formal list of requirements for 10BASE5 MAU conformance.
s	*Maint. #4*	Revisions to Clauses 7 and 8.
t	*120 Ω*	Guidelines for use of 10BASE-T with 120-Ω UTP cabling.
u	*100BASE-T Fast Ethernet*	Clauses 21 through 30 plus amendments to Clauses 1, 2, 4, and 14; Supplement **u** supersedes Clauses 5, 19 and 20.
v	*150 Ω*	Guidelines for use of 10BASE-T with 150-Ω STP cabling.
*	*BLAM*	Revision of CSMA/CD to improve performance (*not yet approved, see Chapter 5*).
*	*Full Duplex*	Permit simultaneous transmission and reception (*not yet approved, see Chapter 5*).
*	*100BASE-T2*	New physical layer specification (*not yet approved, see Chapter 5*).

* Supplement designations not yet assigned.

Index

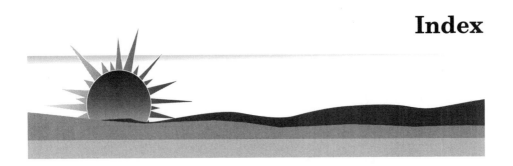

—E—

—F—

—J—

—L—

—T—

—U—

—V—